The Autobiographies of the Haymarket Martyrs

The Autobiographies of the HAYMARKET MARTYRS

Edited with an introduction
by Philip S. Foner

PATHFINDER
New York London Montreal Sydney

ISBN 978-0-87348-879-2
Library of Congress Catalog Card Number 77-85125
Manufactured in Canada

First paperback edition, 1977
Thirteenth printing, 2026

Cover design by William O. Neebe, grandson of Oscar Neebe
The Haymarket defendants clockwise from top left: Albert Parsons, August Spies, George Engel, Samuel Fielden, Michael Schwab, Oscar Neebe, Adolph Fischer, Louis Lingg

Pathfinder
pathfinderpress.com
Email: pathfinder@pathfinderpress.com

Attention Workingmen!

GREAT

MASS-MEETING

TO-NIGHT, at 7.30 o'clock,

AT THE

HAYMARKET, Randolph St., Bet. Desplaines and Halsted.

Good Speakers will be present to denounce the latest atrocious act of the police, the shooting of our fellow-workmen yesterday afternoon.

Workingmen Arm Yourselves and Appear in Full Force!

THE EXECUTIVE COMMITTEE

Achtung, Arbeiter!

Große

Massen-Versammlung

Heute Abend, ½8 Uhr, auf dem

Heumarkt, Randolph-Straße, zwischen Desplaines- u. Halsted-Str.

☞ Gute Redner werden den neuesten Schurkenstreich der Polizei, indem sie gestern Nachmittag unsere Brüder erschoß, geißeln.

☞ Arbeiter, bewaffnet Euch und erscheint massenhaft!

Das Executiv-Comite.

REVENGE!

Workingmen, to Arms!!!

Your masters sent out their bloodhounds — the police —; they killed six of your brothers at McCormicks this afternoon. They killed the poor wretches, because they, like you, had the courage to disobey the supreme will of your bosses. They killed them, because they dared ask for the shortenin of the hours of toil. They killed them to show you, 'Free American Citizens' that you must be satisfied and contended with whatever your bosses condescend to allow you, or you will get killed!

You have for years endured the most abject humiliations; you have for years suffered unmeasurable iniquities; you have worked yourself to death; you have endured the pangs of want and hunger; your Children you have sacrificed to the factory-lords — in short: You have been miserable and obedient slave all these years: Why? To satisfy the insatiable greed, to fill the coffers of your lazy thieving master? When you ask them now to lessen your burden, he sends his bloodhounds out to shoot you, kill you!

If you ar men, if you are the sons of your grand sires, who have shed their blood to free you, then you will rise i your might, Hercules, and destroy the hideous monster that seeks to destroy you. To arms we call you, to arms!

Your Brothers.

Rache! Rache!

Arbeiter, zu den Waffen!

CONTENTS

I

Editor's Introduction

On the night of May 4, 1886, a dynamite bomb was thrown into a group of policemen who had just begun to disperse a small crowd of workingmen still milling about in the Haymarket in Chicago's West Side. One policeman was killed instantly by the bomb, several others were wounded so severely that they died later. The police immediately opened fire, and before the Haymarket riot ended, several workers were killed (how many is unknown) and at least 200 were wounded.

A wave of hysteria swept Chicago and the rest of the nation. During it a number of anarchists were indicted. Though no sound evidence proved their connection with the actual bomb-throwing, they were tried freely for their opinions. Seven men—Albert R. Parsons, August Spies, Samuel J. Fielden, Michael Schwab, Adolph Fischer, George Engel, Louis Lingg—were condemned to death, and one—Oscar Neebe—to fifteen years' imprisonment.

The Haymarket Affair is linked to two important developments in the post-Civil War period: the battle for the eight-hour day and the rise of the Social Revolutionary or anarchist movement. The eight-hour day was a major slogan of the labor movement. The struggle for the eight-hour day began in the 1860s and produced some early results. Six states adopted eight-hour laws by 1867. A number of city councils enacted ordinances extending the eight-hour day to their public employees. In June, 1868, Congress enacted the first federal eight-hour law in American history, granting the eight-hour day to government employees.

These laws, however, were ineffectual. The state laws did not provide any means of enforcement, and the federal law was subject to such varied interpretations that it did not secure the eight-hour day for all workers who were supposed to be covered. In 1876, the United States Supreme Court completely nullified the law by declaring that the federal government could make separate agreements with its employees.

In the early 1880s emphasis in the struggle for the eight-hour day was still on legislative action. But it soon became obvious that if labor was to secure the shorter working day it would have to achieve it by its own power, by its ability to stop work at plants whose employers refused to grant the eight-hour day. At its 1884 convention, the Federation of Organized Trades and Labor Unions of the United States and Canada (organized in 1881 and changing its name in 1886 to American Federation of Labor) adopted an historic resolution which asserted that "eight hours shall constitute a legal day's labor from and after May 1, 1886, and that we recommend to labor organizations throughout this district that they so direct their laws as to conform to this resolution." The following year the Federation repeated the declaration that an eight-hour system was to go into effect on May 1, 1886.

In the months prior to May 1, 1886, thousands of workers, skilled and unskilled, men and women, Negro and white, native and immigrant, organized and unorganized, members of the Knights of Labor and of the Federation, were drawn into the struggle for the shorter working day. "There is an eight-hour agitation everywhere," *John Swinton's Paper,* a leading labor weekly, reported in mid-April, 1886. By that time almost a quarter of a million industrial workers were involved in the movement, and so powerful was the upsurge that about 30,000 workers had already been granted a nine-or-eight-hour day.

In Chicago alone, 400,000 workers went out, and more than 45,000 were granted a shorter working day without striking. A Chicago paper reported that "no smoke curled up from the tall chimneys of the factories and mills and things had assumed a Sabbath-like appearance."

Chicago was the main center of the agitation for a shorter day, and in Chicago the anarchists were in the forefront of the movement. It was to no small extent due to their activities that Chicago became the outstanding labor center in the country and made the greatest contribution to the eight-hour movement. An examination of this group is essential to a correct understanding of the events that were taking place in May, 1886.

As far back as 1875, a small group of Chicago socialists, the vast majority German immigrants, had formed an armed club to protect workers against police and military assaults. This club came to be known as the *Lehr und Wehr Vereine* (Study and Resistance Association). The attacks on workers during the Railroad strikes of 1877 by the police, the militia, and the United States Army resulted in the movement's growth. Although most of the members of the armed groups belonged to the Socialist Labor Party, the national executive committee denounced such organizations on the grounds that they gave a false picture of the objectives and policies of the socialist movement. In 1878 all members of the S.L.P. were ordered to leave the clubs, but this order was resented by the Chicago socialists, and, together with other issues, led to a split in the party in 1880.

That same year, a group that had seceded from the S.L.P. in New York formed an organization known as the Social Revolutionary Club. Soon Social Revolutionary clubs sprang up in other cities—Boston, Philadelphia, Milwaukee and Chicago—where there were large populations and immigrants whose new and bitter experience in labor struggles in the United States made them particularly receptive to anarchist ideas with their emphasis on the abandonment of political action in favor of physical force as the mechanism of social revolution.

The Chicago club, the most important in the movement, was led by Albert R. Parsons and August Spies. Both were militant trade unionists who had run for office on the socialist ticket in Chicago. But both had lost faith in political action, and were searching for a new method to meet the attacks by the police upon the working class and their organizations, the most brutal of which had occurred in Chicago.

A national conference of Social Revolutionary clubs was held in Chicago in 1881. But it was not until the arrival of Johann Most from England in 1882 that the Social Revolutionary movement united its ranks and became an active force. A powerful orator, a caustic and brilliant writer, temperamental and egotistical, he rapidly became the acknowledged leader of the American anarchists. Following a tour of the country, Most paved the way for a congress of American anarchists at Pittsburgh in October, 1883.

Twenty-six cities were represented at the convention where the International Working People's Association (the "Black International") was formed. Most dominated the convention. An ardent advocate of terroristic tactics, he opposed the struggle for immediate demands—shorter hours, higher wages, better working conditions—as mere sops thrown to the workers which only served to tie them closer to the capitalist system. The manifesto of the I.W.P.A., written in the main by Most, ended with an appeal to one remedy for the evils of capitalism—*force*!

Two distinct elements were present at the Pittsburgh congress—united primarily by their opposition to political action. The delegates from New York and the other eastern cities, led by Most, favored individualistic acts of terrorism. The western delegates, led by Parsons and Spies, agreed with Most on the futility of political action and the value of force, but they believed firmly in trade-union work. Basing itself upon the direct action of the rank-and-file, the trade union would not concern itself with immediate demands. Instead, it would serve as the instrument of the working class for the complete destruction of capitalism and the nucleus for the formation of a new society. Its chief weapon as a fighting unit against capitalism would be force and violence.

This mixture of anarchism and syndicalism came to be known as the "Chicago Idea," and was adopted by the Pittsburgh congress. Although the trade union was not to contend for immediate demands, in practice the followers of the I.W.P.A. were often compelled, in order to win a hearing from workers, to support immediate demands. Consequently, the I.W.P.A. made headway among trade unions, especially in the mid-west, where the Chicago section, led by colorful and militant personalities like Parsons, Spies, Schwab, Fielden, and others, penetrated deeply into the trade-union movement. Chicago had five to six thousand members of the I.W.P.A., and the Social

Revolutionaries published five papers including the *Alarm* in English, a fortnightly and monthly edited by Parsons with an edition of 2,000–3,000; the daily *Arbeiter-Zeitung*, edited by Spies, with an edition of about 5,000. There was also the short-lived paper, *Der Anarchist,* a monthly published by George Engel and other extremist members of the I.W.P.A.

By staging impressive mass demonstrations and parades, conducting speaking tours all over the mid-west, the Chicago Social Revolutionaries were able to exert much greater influence than their numbers would indicate. They dominated the Central Labor Union of Chicago which consisted of 22 unions in 1886, among them the seven largest in the city. The Social Revolutionaries threw themselves wholeheartedly into the movement for the eight-hour day, and were largely responsible for the tremendous upsurge in Chicago for the shorter working day. At the outset, the anarchists had not looked with favor on the eight-hour demand, first, because its acceptance was "a virtual concession that the wage system is right," and, secondly, because even if successful, the shorter working day was trivial compared to the struggle to abolish the wage-system and might even divert the energies of the workers from activity to overthrow wage slavery. But when the Chicago anarchists saw how deeply the working class was stirred and how bitterly the industrialists opposed the movement, they understood that they would have to join in the common front. As Parsons explained later, the Social Revolutionaries endorsed the eight-hour movement, "first, because it was a class movement against domination, therefore historical, and evolutionary and necessary; and secondly, because we did not choose to stand aloof and be misunderstood by our fellow workers."

Despite their work for the eight-hour day, the Social Revolutionaries repeatedly made it clear that direct action—force, violence—was the cure-all for the problems facing the workers. As the following resolution of the Chicago Central Labor Union, introduced by Spies in October, 1885, put it: "We urgently call upon the wage-earning class to arm itself in order to be able to put forth against their exploiters such an argument which alone can be effective: Violence. . . ."

Since February 16, 1886, a strike had been in progress at the McCormick Harvester Machine Company. When on May 1 the eight-hour strikes convulsed Chicago, one-half of the McCormick work force joined the eight-hour strike movement. On Monday afternoon, May 3, an eight-hour mass meeting was held by 6,000 members of the lumber shovers' union of Chicago. The meeting was held on Black Road, a block from the McCormick plant, and was joined by 500 McCormick strikers. The workers listened to a speech by August Spies, who had been asked to address the workers by the Central Labor Union. While Spies was speaking, urging the workers to stand together and not retreat before their employers, the strikebreakers were beginning to leave the nearby McCormick factory. The McCormick strikers, aided by several hundred lumber shovers, demonstrated against the scabs, trying to drive them back into the plant. Suddenly a special detail of 200 police arrived, and, without warning, attacked the strikers with clubs and revolvers, killing at least one striker, seriously wounding five or six others and injuring an undetermined number.

Outraged by the brutal assaults he had witnessed, Spies returned to the office of the *Arbeiter-Zeitung* and composed a circular in which he called upon the workers of Chicago to "rise in your might. . . . To Arms! We call you to arms." This came to be called, because of its heading, the "Revenge Circular." Spies originally had headed it

"Workingmen! To Arms!" A compositor of the *Arbeiter-Zeitung* added the word "Revenge" without Spies' knowledge. It appeared in both English and German.

About half of the 2,500 copies of the circular were distributed, and a protest meeting was later called at Haymarket Square, Randolph Street between Desplaines and Halsted, for the night of May 4. In the announcement of the meeting was inserted the lines, "Workingmen Arm Yourselves and Appear in Full Force." Spies insisted that these be stricken from the announcement or he would not speak at the meeting. Although the line was cut out of the circular, some two to three hundred of the 20,000 handbills distributed did contain the words to which Spies had objected.

The Haymarket Square could accommodate over twenty thousand people, and it was chosen for the gathering because the promoters of the meeting expected close to that number of workingmen to turn out. They were disappointed. When the meeting began about twelve to thirteen hundred were on hand, many having left because the gathering was an hour late in getting started. Because of the small crowd, it was decided to change the site from Haymarket proper to the mouth of Crane's alley, a half block away. A truck wagon was used for a speaking stand.

Spies opened the meeting at 8:30 P.M., and spoke for half an hour. He was followed by Parsons. Throughout their speeches, the crowd was orderly. Mayor Carter H. Harrison was present from the beginning of the meeting, and after listening to the speeches of Spies and Parsons, concluded that "nothing had occurred yet, or looked likely to occur to require interference." He advised Police Captain John Bonfield at the near-by Desplaines station house that all was orderly at the meeting, and suggested that the large force of police reserves concentrated at the station house be sent home.

It was close to ten in the evening when Parsons introduced Samuel Fielden for the final talk. Fielden spoke about ten minutes when a threatening storm caused many of the people in the gathering to seek shelter. Not more than two hundred persons were now on hand. Fielden was finishing his talk. Suddenly a police column of 180 men, headed by Captains Bonfield and William Ward, moved toward the speaker, halting about three or four paces from the end of the wagon. Captain Ward turned to the people present and commanded the meeting immediately and peaceably to disperse. He waited a moment and repeated the order, this time calling upon individuals in the small audience to assist. Fielden protested, "We are peaceable." At the same time, he, Spies, and others on the wagon began to descend.

At this moment a bomb was thrown among the police. It killed Policeman Mathias J. Degan instantly; six others died later. About seventy police officers were wounded. The police opened fire upon the spectators. How many civilians were wounded or killed from police bullets never was ascertained exactly.

A reign of terror swept over Chicago. The press and pulpit called for revenge, insisting that the bomb was the work of socialists, anarchists and communists. Staging "raids" in the working-class districts, the police rounded up all known anarchists and socialists. Meeting halls, printing offices, and even private homes were broken into and searched in the round-up. "Homes were invaded without warrant," writes Professor Harvey Wish, "and ransacked for evidence; suspects were beaten and subjected to the 'third degree'; individuals ignorant of the meaning of socialism and anarchism were tortured by the police, sometimes bribed as well, to act as witnesses for the state." "Make the raids first and look up the law afterward!" publicly counseled Julius S. Grinnell, the state's attorney, when a question was raised about search warrants.

On May 27 thirty-one persons were indicted. They were charged with being accessories to the murder of Policeman Mathias J. Degan and with a general conspiracy to murder. Of those indicted, only eight actually stood trial: Spies, Parsons, Schwab, Fielden, Fischer, Engel, Lingg, and Neebe. Several purchased immunity by turning state's evidence. One, Rudolph Schnaubelt, was arrested and released but never found again. The others were to wait until the trial of the eight was completed.

The trial opened on June 21, 1886, at the criminal court of Cook County, with Joseph E. Gary as trial judge, State's Attorney Grinnell as chief prosecutor, and William P. Black, a successful corporation lawyer with liberal beliefs, heading the defense. The candidates for the jury were not chosen in the usual way by drawing names from a box. In this case, a special bailiff, nominated by the State's Attorney, was appointed by the court to select the candidates. The defense was denied an opportunity to present evidence that the special bailiff had publicly stated: "I am managing this case and I know what I am about. These fellows are going to be hanged as certain as death. I am calling such men as the defendants will have to challenge peremptorily and waste their time and challenges. Then they will have to take such men as the prosecution wants."

Exactly what the bailiff predicted happened. After the defense had exhausted all its peremptory challenges, a jury, openly prejudiced against the defendants, was selected. The defense accused Judge Gary of having made trial by an impartial jury impossible, by allowing jurors to serve "who had *formed and expressed* an opinion of the guilt and innocence of the accused, based upon newspaper articles and rumors." The judge, the defense charged, even allowed jurors to sit when they acknowledged that they had formed an opinion in reference to the guilt or innocence of the defendants, based upon what they had read, heard or believed to be true.

Seven of the defendants were present when the trial got under way. Missing was Albert R. Parsons, who had baffled a police search for six weeks, and, thoroughly disguised, was perfectly safe in Wisconsin. Just as the preliminary examination of candidates for the jury began, Parsons walked into the courthouse and informed Judge Gary: "I present myself for trial with my comrades, your Honor."

No proof was offered by the State that any of the indicted men had thrown or planted the bomb, and at no time during the trial was the State able to connect the defendants directly with the throwing of the bomb, or even to establish that they had in any way approved or abetted this act. In fact, only three of the defendants had been present—Spies, Parsons, and Fielden—and only Spies and Fielden were at the scene when the bomb exploded. No proof was offered that the speakers had incited violence; indeed, Mayor Harrison described the speeches as "tame." No proof was offered that violence had been contemplated. Parsons, in fact, had brought his wife and his two small children to the meeting.

That the eight men were being tried for their ideas and not for any deeds was made clear from the outset. The trial closed as it had opened on this note, as witness the final words of State's Attorney Grinnell's summation speech to the jury: "Law is on trial. Anarchy is on trial. These men have been selected, picked out by the grand jury and indicted because they were leaders. They are no more guilty than the thousands who follow them. Gentlemen of the jury; convict these men, make examples of them, hang them and you save our institutions, our society."

In his instructions to the jury, Judge Gary made it clear that it was not necessary for the State to identify the bomb-thrower or even to prove that he came under the advice or influence of the accused. The judge held that it was entirely competent for the State to prove that "these several defendants have advocated the use of deadly missiles against the police on occasions which they anticipated might arise in the future. . . ."

On August 19 the case was given to the jury, which returned a verdict of guilty against all eight defendants, condemning seven to death and Neebe to fifteen years in prison.

After a motion by the defense for a new trial was denied by Judge Gary, the convicted men were called upon to speak before sentence was pronounced. Their speeches lasted three days.

"Your Honor," began Spies who spoke first. "In addressing this court I speak as the representative of one class to the representative of another. . . ." He spoke for hours, refuting the charge of murder and conspiracy, charging the State with deliberately plotting to use the Haymarket tragedy as an excuse to assassinate the leaders of the working class, accusing the employers of using the same episode to destroy the eight-hour movement by murdering those whom the workers looked up to as their leaders. But he was confident that this conspiracy would not succeed:

"If you think that by hanging us you can stamp out the labor movement . . . the movement from which the downtrodden millions, the millions who toil in want and misery expect salvation—if this is your opinion, then hang us! Here you will tread upon a spark, but there and there, behind you—and in front of you, and everywhere, flames blaze up. It is a subterranean fire. You cannot put it out."

The case was appealed to the Illinois Supreme Court and argued by Leonard Swett, the old law associate of Abraham Lincoln, and Captain Black and Sigismund Zeisler in the March 1887 term. Judgement was affirmed on September 14, with the entire court sustaining both the rulings and verdict of the lower court. An appeal to the United States Supreme Court was denied on November 2.

Immediately after the Supreme Court had denied the defendants writ of error, a movement for a pardon was launched. The A.F. of L. at its convention passed a resolution pleading for clemency. "In the interests of the cause of labor and the peaceful methods of improving the condition and achieving the final emancipation of labor," wrote Samuel Gompers, A.F. of L. president, "I am opposed to the execution. It would be a blot on the escutcheon of our country." While the leadership of the Knights of Labor refused to join the defense efforts, many K. of L. locals did. Many prominent Americans also protested against the verdict and petitioned for a commutation of the sentences. Among them were William Dean Howells, Robert G. Ingersoll, Lyman Trumbull, who had been a judge of the Illinois Supreme Court and 18 years a U.S. Senator, Henry Demarest Lloyd, Stephen S. Gregory, later president of the American Bar Association, Murray F. Tuley, then chief justice of the Illinois Circuit Court, and Lyman Gage, later Secretary of the Treasury. Howells, a distinguished novelist and editor and dean of American letters, called the verdict "the greatest wrong that ever threatened our fame as a nation."

The defense movement transcended national boundaries. William Morris and George Bernard Shaw addressed a protest meeting in London. A group in the French Chamber of Deputies telegraphed protests to the Governor of Illinois, as did the Municipal Council of Paris and the

Council of the Department of the Seine. The petition called the impending executions a "political crime" which would be an "everlasting mark of infamy upon republicanism." Meetings of workers urging a pardon were held in France, Holland, Russia, Italy, and Spain, and many contributed out of their scanty wages for the Haymarket defense fund.

As the execution date, November 11, 1887, drew near, a petition signed by thousands pleaded for amnesty, and a flood of resolutions, letters, and memorials, in which leaders in the professions and business joined heads of labor unions, poured in upon Governor Richard J. Oglesby asking for a pardon. The defense chartered a train which left Chicago on November 8, 1887 for Springfield. Another delegation came on the next day and a large delegation from New York City. Of the three hundred persons who came to plead with the Governor, probably a third came from outside the state.

Two of the defendants, Fielden and Schwab, petitioned the governor to spare their lives, and Spies asked Oglesby to release the other defendants and execute him to satisfy the demand for vengeance. The letter which Spies, Fielden and Schwab addressed to Governor Oglesby stated that "we never advocated the use of force excepting in the case of self-defense. . . . Whatever we said or did, or said or did publicly, we have never supported, or plotted to commit, an unlawful act, and while we attack the present social arrangements, in writing and speech, and exposed their iniquities, we have never conspicuously broken any laws. . . ."

Judge Gary and prosecutor Grinnell joined in asking mercy for Fielden and Schwab, and Governor Oglesby commuted their sentence to life imprisonment. Lingg committed suicide by exploding a bomb in his mouth a day before the execution. Parsons, Spies, Engel, and Fischer were hanged on November 11, 1887.

The authorities turned over the four bodies to friends for burial, and one of the largest funeral processions in Chicago history was held. It was estimated that between 150,000 to 500,000 lined the route taken by the funeral cortege. The five caskets—Lingg was buried with the other four—were buried in a temporary vault at Waldheim Cemetery. Estimates of the number who observed the burial exercises varied from 10,000 to 25,000. On December 18, 1887, the caskets were placed in a permanent grave. A monument to the executed men was unveiled June 25, 1893 at Waldheim Cemetery.

The struggle for amnesty for Fielden, Schwab, and Neebe continued, and more and more thousands, convinced of the injustice of the convictions, urged clemency upon Oglesby, and upon his successor, Governor Joseph Fifer. But it was not until the election of John Peter Altgeld as governor of Illinois in 1892 that a victory was at last won.

On June 26, 1893, Altgeld issued his famous pardon message in which he made it clear that he was not granting the pardons because he believed that the men had suffered enough, but because they were innocent of the crime for which they had been tried, and that they and the hanged men had been the victims of hysteria, packed juries and a biased judge. He noted that the defendants were not proven guilty because the state "has never discovered who it was that threw the bomb which killed the policeman, and the evidence does not show any connection whatsoever between the defendants and the man who threw it." Altgeld attacked Judge Gary's ruling that it was not necessary for the State to identify the bomb-thrower or even prove that he came under the advice or influence of the accused, pointing out that "in all the centuries during which government has been maintained among men, and crime has been punished, no judge in a civilized country has ever laid down such a rule."

The fearless governor was subjected to a torrent of abuse and invective. But the A.F. of L. convention in December, 1893 praised the pardon as "an act of justice," and the trade unions distributed 50,000 copies of the message.

In his definitive study of the Haymarket Affair, published in 1936, Henry David concludes: "On the basis of the reliable evidence, they (the eight individuals convicted of the murder of Degan) must be considered innocent."

To bring matters more closely down to the present: On May 14, 1968, Chicago's administration again commemorated the seven policeman who were slain in the Haymarket Affair. Once again there was a memorial parade. But in the year 1968, for the first time in eighty-two years, a leading Chicago paper dissented; since this itself is historic, it is worth lengthy quotation. On April 25, 1968, the Chicago *Daily News* editorialized:

> Surely Chicago can find a better way to honor her policemen than by maintaining the fiction that the so-called Haymarket Riot was a glorious chapter in anyone's history. . . .
>
> For the police were attempting to break up a peaceful meeting, and doing so against the expressed wishes of the mayor.
>
> The seven policemen were killed by a bomb. The identity of the bomb-thrower was never established, yet this minor flaw didn't prevent Chicago from using the "riot" to do itself great discredit.
>
> After a general panic, in which a police captain manufactured evidence, eight persons were put on trial, and the story of the trial still sends shudders through persons with

a sense of justice. Four men were hanged, not so much for what they did or didn't do as for their offbeat views.

In October 9, 1886, the *Knights of Labor,* a weekly labor journal published in Chicago, carried on page 1 the following announcement: "Next week we begin the publication of the lives of the anarchists advertised in another column." The advertisement, carried on page 14, read:

THE STORY
OF
THE ANARCHISTS
TOLD
BY THEMSELVES.

PARSONS SPIES FIELDEN SCHWAB
FISCHER LINGG ENGEL NEEBE

The only true history of the men who claim
that they are
CONDEMNED TO SUFFER DEATH
For exercising the right of Free Speech.

Their association with Labor, Socialistic and Anarchistic
Societies, their views as to the aims
and objects of these organizations, and
how they expect to accomplish them;
Also their connection with the Chicago
HAYMARKET AFFAIR
Each man is the author of his own story,
Which will appear only in the
KNIGHTS OF LABOR
During the Next Three Months.

The following week, October 16, 1886, the *Knights of Labor* carried the first part of the autobiography of Albert R. Parsons which was completed on October 23. Spies' autobiography ran in the issues of November 6 and 13; Fischer's in that of November 20 and 27; Engel's in the issue of December 4; Schwab's in that of December 11 and 18; Fielden's in the issues of February 19, 26, and March 5, 1887, and Neebe's in the issue of April 30. There the series ended, with no explanation of why Lingg's autobiography was not included. On September 17, 1887, the *Knights of Labor* announced that it had published the lives of the anarchists separately and each autobiography could be obtained for ten cents or all complete for fifty cents. It listed the autobiographies that were available as those of Spies, Engel, Parsons, Fielden, Fischer, Schwab and Neebe. Then on October 8, 1887, the journal carried the heading: "Introduction to the Story of the Anarchists," and the explanation: "The following was written by Capt. W.P. Black, Chief Counsel, as an introduction to the story of the anarchists. It seems to the publishers that it may have some influence in deciding the fate of these men, and therefore we publish it now."

Evidently it was planned to publish the autobiographies, with Black's introduction, in book form, but nothing came of the project. The complete text of the autobiographies of the seven Haymarket victims and Captain Black's introduction remained buried in the files of the *Knights of Labor*, and is reprinted now for the first time.

I made repeated efforts to locate the autobiography written by Lingg in libraries and historical societies throughout the United States. But to no avail. However, this past summer while visiting the German Democratic Republic, I located in the library of the Institute of Marxism-Leninism in Berlin, the files of *Alarm*, the anarchist paper published in Chicago. Copies of this paper are available in the United States but only scattered issues exist for late 1888 and early 1889. The Berlin library, however, has a complete file of *Alarm,* and in the issues of December 29, 1888, January 5, 12, 1889, I found the autobiography of Lingg. Thus the present volume contains the autobiographies of all the Haymarket men.

The style of the autobiographies varies. It is turgid, as in Neebe, pedantic, as in Fischer, or labored, as in Engel, while that of Parsons, Spies and Fielden is often eloquent. The defects are to be expected from men who were writing in what was not their first language. (Except for Parsons and Fielden, the authors of these autobiographies were of German birth, or of German descent, and received whatever education they had in Germany.) What all contributed, regardless of style, is an important picture of conditions in Europe and America which caused these men to be drawn into the radical movement, and, in several of the autobiographies, a detailed account of their activities in this movement. All contributed, too, a courageous and strong pleading for a cause close to their hearts, a firm belief in the "iniquities" of capitalism and in the justice of the anarchist society which they hoped to achieve.

The speeches of these men in court have been often reprinted in most modern languages. Now with the reprinting of their autobiographies we have a more nearly complete picture of America's first labor-revolutionary martyrs.

In the main, the text of Captain Black's introduction and of the autobiographies is reproduced as it appeared in the *Knights of Labor* and *The Alarm.* However, obvious typographical errors have been corrected though foreignisms have not been altered. For the sake of readability, long stretches of text have been broken into paragraphs.

I am indebted to the staffs of the Tamiment Institute Library of New York University and of the Chicago Historical Society for having placed their files of the *Knights of Labor* at my disposal. I am also indebted to the library of the Institute of Marxism-Leninism in Berlin for placing their file of *Alarm* at my disposal and furnishing me with a photostatic copy of the autobiography of Louis Lingg published in that paper.

The entire manuscript was read by Dr. Herbert Aptheker and his suggestions were most helpful.

Philip S. Foner
Lincoln University, Pennsylvania
September, 1968

2

Introduction by Capt. W.P. Black

"Thus it is, that no revolution in public opinion is the work of an individual or a single cause, or of a day. When the crisis has arrived the catastrophe must ensue; but its agents, through whom it is apparently accomplished, though they may accelerate, cannot originate its occurrence. Woe to the revolutionist who is not himself a creature of the revolution! If he anticipate, he is lost."—Sir Wm. Hamilton.[1]

To the king of old came a vision in the night season. Sleep, twin brother of death, the leveler, had fallen upon him for a time, bringing oblivion of state and care; but at last his sleep fled away from the disturbing phantasia of his dream; yet so indistinct was the impression, so little understood its lesson, that the very vision was gone from him, when he rose from his troubled slumbering. In vain he appealed to and commanded his wise-men to tell alike his dream and its interpretation. Tell us your vision, was their cry, and we

(NOTES BEGIN ON PAGE 277)

will interpret its teaching. At last a foreigner, one of a captive and despised race, that dwelt in the midst of the people, came forward to meet the king's demand.

The vision was of an image burnishing and shining, whose appearance was of an armored man, with head of gold, breast and arms of silver, belly and thighs of brass, legs of iron and feet of iron and clay. What a fit object of worship and admiration—man panoplied with riches, honor, beauty and strength. Yet only man, with feet ever in contact with the earth, and infected with the weakness of his clay. The power of human devising, buttressed with all that human wisdom, skill or craft could command, but having its origin from the human planning and owing its endurance to selfish scheming. That this mighty image, emblem of the highest result of moral devising for the establishment of power, should come to naught before a stone cut out without hands, with no touch of human designing upon it which beat against the mighty image and ground it till all its riches and strength became as the dust of the summer thrashing floor, and were carried away by the winds; while the unwrought stone grew to fill the earth, might well oppress the monarch with some image. The object of his veneration became as naught before a power that knew no human law. Who but a captive could interpret such a vision—who but one of a people abject and despised divine the portent of its magic teaching? Human government with all its variations of condition, from the gold of the head to the clay of the feet. Its riches and poverty, power and oppression, glory and shame; its reverse forms and irregularities; to be overthrown by a kingdom of natural law and force, without artificial constraint, that should be one, and fill the whole earth. This was the story of the vision that broke from the lips of the captive seer, becoming the prophecy of the aspirations and endeavors of the common world.

But the vision has a double teaching, not only does it present the thought of all governments constituted on the basis of artificial restraints and man-made legislation, giving place to one universal state of society controlled by national law; but it also suggests a process for the substitution which history has thus far verified, viz.: the overthrow by force of the order to make room for the new. Destruction to clear the way for construction—revolution against the old preceding the evolution of the new—this is the teaching of the vision as well as the lesson of history. And still another thought is suggested in this chaldaic story, that for the new grows, if it be worthy to abide, by virtue of innate force; helped neither by arbitrary enactment nor by artificial conditions. The stone, taken from the rocky foundations of the world, rejected by the visitors, yet growing to fill the whole earth, is but a type of truth—of the true—which is self-existent, indestructible and at last all-subduing, finding expression to one finite comprehension in what we call natural law, which is for our discovery. In the proportion in which we can discover truth in its relations to social conditions and life, do we discern natural law; and in the measure of our observance of that law do we approximate the harmony of the relations of life in which artificial or arbitrary regulations of conduct become unnecessary. Such a state of society has been the dream of the poets, the philosophers, the seers of all ages, and it has also been the nightmare of every established order of society since history commenced the record of human governments, in which the law of activity, the motive of endeavor, the mainspring of enterprise, has been the unnatural desire for mastery. To the votary of the existing order, he who desires the true is but a disturbing visionary, while he who resolves upon the betterment of society is the obnoxious revolutionist.

It is a law of the activities of life that all people are divided by their own election into two classes: Conservatives and progressists, subjects and rebels. The one class yielding unfaltering obedience to the existing conditions of society, desire the preservation of the accustomed government, while the other class, with vision opened to the defects and inequalities marking the inter-relation of men, long for a better order, and by this innert yearning of the spirit are often driven into open rebellion. The former is, as a rule, the major class. Whether it be that centuries of government wherein the many have been in subjection to the few have resulted in a preriatal *[sic]* disposition of obedience, or whether it be that a natural love of ease and a selfish hope that in some way and at some time ourselves may pass from the servile to the ruling class, from the popular ranks of the man who are the slaves of existing conditions to the limited class who, by fortuitous circumstances, are promoted to place and distinction; certain it is that the greater number of every people are predisposed to quiescence under established regulations of society, even when those regulations are recognized as unjust or felt to be harsh. "All experience hath shown," declared the revolutionary patriots of 1776, "that mankind are never disposed to suffer, while evils are sufferable, than to right themselves by abolishing the forms to which they are accustomed."[2] Very grave, therefore, is the work he essays who would take issue with the form of society of his day. The task he sets before himself is full of difficulties and fraught with peril. Perhaps no language has furnished a more vigorous description of this than the German of Schiller,[3] who wrote:

> What is thy purpose? Hast thou fairly weighed it?
> Thou seekest ev'n from its broad base to shake

The calm, enthroned majesty of power,
By ages of possession consecrate—
Firm rooted in the rugged soul of custom
And with the people's first and fondest faith,
As with a thousand stubborn tendrils twined.
It is an unseen enemy I dread,
Who, in the hearts of mankind, fights against me—
Fearful to me but from his own weak fear.
Not that which proudly towers in life and strength
is truly dreadful; but the mean and common,
The memory of the eternal yesterday,
That ever warning, ever still returns,
And weighs to-morrow—for it weighed today.
Out of the common is man's nature formed,
And custom is the muse to whom he cleaves.
Woe, then, to him whose daring had profaned
The honored heirlooms of his ancestors!
There is a consecrating power in time,
And what is gray with years to man is godlike.
possession, and thou art in right;—
The crowd will lend the aid to keep it
Be in sacred.

Poetic picture, but historic verity. Every advance that the world has thus far known in the evolution of society, the revolution of governments, has been an advance achieved by the few against the many, but for the whole, and whose benefits have fallen to the common heritage of that portion of our race whose destiny was touched by the struggle. The crowd have lent their aid to conserve the accustomed order; but in spite thereof truth in its holy courage has triumphed, and another step in the stairway of events leading up the mountain of progress toward the star-crowned heights of the sublime and truly ordered being has been laid by heroic hands and cemented in the martyr blood of those devoted truly to the good of the people. Always there have been found those who were ahead of their age in their vision of truth and conception of righteousness in government, who have dared adversity and challenged death in their determination to speak the truth received and to teach and lead the people in its light. Is it ordered that our hearts, the hearts of the multitudes, reject the truth until we see it written with the warm heart's blood of some man who stands a courier of the advancing dawn? Is abstract truth indifferent to us, and we can become the children of the truth, and loving it, only when we behold it worshiped in the life-libations of some noble hearts? The fact we recognize that every reform in social relations has become established only after sacrifice has been exacted by the demon of disorder that sits enthroned in power and buttressed round by custom. It is because, and only because, generous souls become possessed of the passion of beneficence, that divine spirit of self-abnegation for others' good, that the world's history as a whole is a history of progress instead of retrogression, and the trend of what we call civilization rather toward truth and liberty than toward despotism and error. To these, who have thus spent themselves for the world's advancement, no truer, nobler words may be applied than those of Lowell:[4]

> Many loved truth, and lavished life's best oil
> Amid the dusts of books to find her,
> Content at last, for guerdon of their toil,
> With the cast mantel she hath left behind her;
> Many in said faith sought her;
> Many with crossed hands sighed for her;
> At life's dear peril wrought for her,
> So loved her that they died for her,

Tasting the raptured sweetness
Of her divine completeness.
Their higher instinct knew

Those love her best who to themselves are true,
And what they dare to dream of, dare to do,
They followed her and found her
Where all may hope to find,
Not in the ashes of the burnt-out mind,
But beautiful with danger's sweetness round her.
When faith made whole with deed,
Breathes its awakening breath
Into the lifeless creed,
They saw her plumed and mailed,
With sweet, stern face unveiled,
And all-repaying eyes look proud on them in death.

I do not mean, of course, that all rebels are right, or that all of those who have joined issue with the established order are benevolent in their motives or beneficent in action. Not every malcontent is of noble spirit, or takes up a just contest against the powers that be. But conceding that many who pose as reformers make but a sorry masquerade, while others who impeach the social order present no scheme for remedy that can command their crusade to the judicious; yet it remains beyond question that the faults of the present system are as obvious as they are grievous, and imperatively demand reform. It is apparent also to the student and dispassionate observer that the reform which must be effected, if adequate to the demands of the situation, must go to the roots of the established order as to effect a complete revolution thereof; and for this very reason it is found that every step in this direction meets with a fixed resistance.

The theory of past reforms in administration, upon which have been based the changes of government from absolutism to democracy, has been that the only panacea for existing disorder was political liberty. But much as may be claimed to have resulted of good from the world's advancement in this direction, the highest types of republican government, with universal enfranchisement and a substantially absolute political quality, serve only to show that political liberty does not insure a prosperous, happy or advancing condition of society as a whole. The most that can be truly said is that political liberty produces conditions that may prove favorable for the application of the true remedy for the social disorder.

That a grave disorder afflicts society, threatening its very life, who can doubt! It is evidenced in the abiding poverty of the great masses of the people, and the abounding suffering of a mighty host, neither the suffering nor the poverty being justly chargeable to any fault on the part of their victims, but both being a natural result of the operation of the forces and principles sanctioned and upheld by the society of today. Nor is it an answer to this impeachment to say that this suffering and poverty have always existed; for as certainly as that one ought to seek the purifying blood whose taint was manifested in ulcers and plague spots, rather than to say lightly: They have always been upon me; so surely ought society to address itself to the work always of preventing poverty and suffering by seeking and removing the causes of these disorders. If it be true that among the inalienable rights of every man is "the pursuit of happiness," then the society in which that man lives owes to that man the conditions which will make possible the fruition of the hope of a happy life, and will crown the earnest best endeavor of every man in that direction with an assured success. Nor is to be forgotten that with the increasing intelligence which is reaching the masses the conditions of their poverty and suffering are rendered more unbearable, and their consequent misery the more acute. It follows that political equality and its attendant conditions soften but quicken the abject anguish of the poor and miserable; and that some other remedy must be sought for, or the problem of human unhappiness abandoned as unsolvable.

This last is the alternative of the pessimist. There are not a few who hold to the view that the societary evils, the inequalities of condition, with all the resultant suffering, grew out of the fixed dispositions of humanity; and that as they have always existed in the past so will they always exist in the future. And the major portion of those who thus hold, it is feared, make this opinion a refuge for their own selfishness in deciding to essay either remedy or amelioration. It is inevitable, say they, and wherefore vex our souls or tax our brains and purses with vain efforts to meet the evil?

To this doctrine of hopelessness, two classes of society furnish at least theoretically an exception. The Christian speaks in his enunciation of the gospel of a coming kingdom of righteousness, peace and joy, under the personal sovereignty of Christ, the kingdom of Daniel's interpretation of the vision. It is probable that very few, however, of those holding this creed feel as resting upon them any sense of duty to bring about the answer to their traditional prayer. "Thy kingdom come, thy will be done on earth as it is in heaven." "The poor always ye have with you," is often quoted, not because of the duty enjoined by the great teacher, to relieve the oppressed, minister to the sick and help the afflicted, but as though it were a prophecy that had in it some way a divine justification of conditions, which result confessedly from the infirmities and selfishness of humanity. The other class, who look forward to a condition of universal happiness as the heritage of humanity, to be possessed when the heirs know and assert their rights, strangely enough are almost universally unchristian in creed, though not in practice. The socialist, as the latter-day agitator, while generally a materialist, yet insists that the evils pregnant in society result, not from uncontrollable dispositions to evil, tainting the entire body of the people and rendering them incapable of deliverance, but from conditions which are susceptible of changes, doctrines which should be corrected and forces which should be brought into subjection to an enlightened theory of societary life. Whether they are right or wrong, can only be demonstrated finally by a fair experiment upon their theory, but meantime, at least, its purpose is exalting and its demand of a fair trial is emphasized by the confessed failure of the present system and order.

It is no part of the purpose of an introduction such as this, to go into any extended analysis or defense of socialism—and this will not here be attempted. The pages of this volume will themselves furnish cogent arguments upon the vital questions of modern society, and food for thought for every candid and inquiring reader. There is need here for nothing more than a suggestion. The ultimate of socialistic doctrine is claimed to be anarchism. Perhaps, to be exact, it should rather be said, that anarchists claim that their views are the ultimate of socialism. Certain it is, that no one becomes an anarchist save as he advances in the study of socialism as a science, and that very many of the most advanced and able socialists become anarchists in doctrine. But what is said we must allow them to define their own doctrines, declare their own position, rather than take the description of their views and purposes from their enemies. Perhaps no more intelligent and suggestive definition of their position is to be found anywhere than from the pen of Michael Schwab, in his autobiography. He says:

"Anarchism is order without government. We anarchists say that anarchism will be the natural outgrowth of universal co-operation (communism). We say that when poverty has vanished and education is common property of the people then reason will reign supreme. We say that crime will belong to the past, and that erring can be righted by other means than those of today. Most of the crimes of our day are engendered directly by the system of today, the system which creates ignorance and misery."

Stop a moment! Consider this definition, and let us ask ourselves if there is anything in such a teaching to justify our resentment or provoke our fears. That it has an import of offense to the property system of today must, of course, be conceded; for the basis of all this social agitation is the thesis: That with property enough in the world (the product of human labor applied to natural forces and the resources of the earth, which was originally a common heritage of the race), for the comfortable support and reasonable maintenance of all human beings, want and misery have fallen, (and this chiefly to the laborers who produce by their efforts that aggregation of natural products which men call wealth), because of the undue appropriation, through superior force, astuteness, or the application of prior accumulations for the purpose of further increase, of the results of the labor of the many by the few; and it is the project of socialism to restore the resources of nature to the common heritage, and to assume to the general body of the people the means of production, prohibiting private ownership either of natural resources (land, mines, water-power, etc.), or the instrumentalities of production, including all kinds of machinery, and making such industries as mining, transportation, etc., the enterprises of the state. This is not the confiscation of private treasure, or the prohibition of private property; but it is a means to prevent private accumulations, save as the direct result of personal industry and labor, economy and thrift; and it proposes an end to the system which has given us as its types the millionaire and the pauper, the corporation invested by legislative grant with the prerogations and powers of government itself, and who makes, but does not share its dividends. Capitalism may well discern in socialism a spectre that coming to power, will prove its nemesis; but to the great body of the people the project of socialism is not necessarily threatening, and we may fearlessly consider its complaints and promises. While anarchism is not a process, but a possible result of processes, a condition that may obtain as a sequence of the application in society of the doctrines of socialism, and that is only hateful to the selfish, terrible to the timid, because its predicate is the complete overthrow of the present system, the abolition of the present order.

But the position of the advanced socialist and the anarchist is that he does not produce the overthrow he predicts, is not responsible for the disorder he foresees, violence being foretold by him as the armed opposition of the established order to the execution of the sentence pronounced against it by the enlightened judgment of a socially educated people; the resistance of "the classes" to the impending abolition of those privileges so long exercised by them that at last they are claimed and defended as rights, which even the majority may not abrogate; and disorder being recognized as the result of this struggle which must intervene before natural right, triumphing over human selfishness becomes the order of a new system of society, where men may live righteously ungoverned from without. It is true that there is in man a natural disposition to precipitate the catastrophe through which reform is anticipated; but so long as the prophet of the reform confines to advice, to preparation for resistance of the attack which he foresees, and which all experiences proves will surely come before a surrender of the privilege will be made, or a deprivation of privilege acquiesced in, he cannot be justly accused of sedition, or of bringing on the conflict for whose inevitable coming he prepared. Still the very prophecy serves, in the nature of things, to hasten the event; and it is perhaps, therefore, not wholly unnatural that where disturbed by the vision of a seer we involve in our resentment the prophet whose words forecast the downfall of our selfish prosperity.

The men who tell their stories in the following pages are men whose lives have become involved in the social ferment, the agitation of which is about us all. They present a striking group. While six of them are Germans, or of German descent, one is a typical American, and the other a thorough Englishman. All are, in the fullest sense of the word, self-made men. Each could have far better served his own selfish interests by adapting himself to the existing order of society and seeking his own advancement in service of capital. How each was led to the adoption of the special views which he now champions, and the results thereof, is the story which is told, and which does not here need even summary. Perhaps even better than in their life stories their special views are evidenced by the speeches which they respectively made in court when asked if they had aught to say why sentence of death should not be pronounced upon them. These masterly utterances received from us neither comment nor commendation. Life and utterance alike plead for these men, and these autobiographies and speeches are put before the public in the hope that a perusal of them may prove not only of interest but of profit, and may lead candid thinkers to a dispassionate consideration of the cause for which they have lived and plead and are ready, if needs must, to die.

To the American reader two questions will occur. Is the scheme these men espouse practicable? Is there occasion with us for this agitation? Much will be found in this book to be considered in determining these questions—questions which each must answer for himself. But as we sit at ease and ponder these themes as matters of investigation, let us remember that there is a great multitude to whom they are matters of vital interest, and who will hold the consideration of these questions until a conclusion is reached and with whom a conclusion means action. There is a maladjustment of society that bears most hardly upon that class of our people which constitute the majority. In view of this condition he is no patriot who sings paeans to the praise of our country and its institutions, its form of government and conditions of society, but rather he who inquires after a remedy recognizing the wrong. Five years ago the writer of these lines concluded a lecture on socialism with these words:

Let us not be alarmists; but neither let us shut our eyes to the signs of the times, our ears to the mutterings of the multitudes. The miserable man whose rags will scarcely shut out from his grinning flesh the splashings of the millionaire's barouche as it dashes by him filled with richly-attired people, all unmindful of his distress and sore need, the very horses kept in a comfort far surpassing anything he can hope for, and who creeps to his tenement home, in garrett or basement it may be, to see his wife and children suffer for lack of sufficient food and warmth, albeit he may have toiled all day, or sought vainly for employment, will listen with heart-bitterness to the whisperings (is it fiend or angel?) which tell him that these things proclaim a wrong in urgent need of righting. The winds that buffet him, the cold that pinches and the hunger that gnaws at his flesh, and at that of those he loves, will emphasize this theme; and if it can at the same time be truthfully said to him that there is no hope for him from above—that earth's mighty ones will yet more and more use their power to fortify their pride and establish their arrogance—and that the alone chance of his deliverance is in his own right arm, put forth to shake the pillars of the state when his poverty is so mocked and made light of, he may prove indeed but a blind Samson, seeing no way clearly before him to deliverance and sure to perish in the overthrow he precipitates; but with the wailing of his babe in his ears, with the picture of his hopeless and enduring misery about him, he will one day join his comrades, in anguish in the travail and carnival of utter despair, in which will perish the thrones of a power malign to him, that the people may learn the necessity, in the ordering of life, of a loving consideration for and helpfulness of the poor, who are earth's multitudes. So reads the lesson of the world. Shall we of this land learn by the experience of others, or shall we wait our own?

W.P. Black.
Christmas, 1886.

3

Autobiography of Albert R. Parsons

In compliance with your request I write for publication, in the *Knights of Labor,* the following "brief story of my life, a history of my experience and connection with Labor, Socialistic and Anarchistic organizations, and my views as to their aims and objects and how they will be accomplished, and also my connection with the Haymarket meeting of May 4, 1886, and my views as to the responsibility for that tragedy."

Albert R. Parsons was born in the city of Montgomery, Ala., June 24, 1848. My father, Samuel Parsons, was from the State of Maine and he married into the Tompkins-Broadwell family, of New Jersey, and settled in Alabama at an early day, where he afterward established a shoe and leather factory in the city of Montgomery. My father was noted as a public spirited, philanthropic man. He was a Universalist in religion and held the highest office in the temperance movement of Louisiana and Alabama. My mother was a devout Methodist, of great spirituality of character, and known far and near as an intelligent and truly good woman. I had nine brothers and sisters; my ancestry goes back to the earliest settlers of this Country, the first Parsons family landing on the shores of Narragansett Bay, from England, in 1632. The Parsons family and their descendants have taken an active and useful part in all the social, religious, political and revolutionary movements in America. One of the Tompkins', on my mother's side, was with Gen. George Washington at the battle of Brandywine, Monmouth and Valley Forge. Major Gen. Samuel Parsons, of Massachusetts, my direct ancestor, was an officer in the Revolution of 1776, and Capt. Parsons was wounded at the battle of Bunker Hill. There are over 90,000 descendants from the original Parsons family in the United States.

My mother died when I was not yet two years old and my father died when I was five years of age. Shortly after this my eldest brother, William Henry Parsons, who had married and was then living at Tyler, Tex., became my guardian. He was proprietor and editor of the Tyler *Telegraph;* that was in 1851, '52, '53. Two years later our family moved West to Johnston county, on the Texas frontier, while the buffalo, antelope and Indian were in that region. Here we lived, on a ranch, for about three years, when we moved to Hill county and took up a farm in the valley of the Brazos river. My frontier life had accustomed me to the use of the rifle and the pistol, to hunting and riding, and in these matters I was considered quite an expert. At that time our neighbors did not live near enough to hear each other's dog bark, or the cocks crow. It was often five to ten or fifteen miles to the next house. In 1859, I went to Waco, Texas, where, after living with my sister (the wife of Maj. Boyd) and going to school, meantime, for about a year, I was indentured an apprentice to the Galveston *Daily News,* for seven years, to learn the printer's trade.

Entering upon my duties as a "printer's devil," I also became a paper carrier for the *Daily News,* and in a year and a half was transformed from a frontier boy into a city civilian. When the slave-holder's rebellion broke out in 1861, though quite small and but thirteen years old, I joined a local volunteer company called the "Lone Star Greys." My first military exploit was on the passenger steamer Morgan, where we made a trip out into the Gulf of Mexico and intercepted and assisted in the capture of U.S. Gen. Twigg's army, which had evacuated the Texas frontier forts and came to the sea coast at Indianapolis to embark for Washington, D.C.

My first military exploit was a "run-away" trip on my part for which I received an ear pulled from my guardian when I returned. These were stirring "wartimes" and, as a matter of course, my young blood caught the infection. I wanted to enlist in the rebel army and join Gen. Lee in Virginia, but my guardian, Mr. Richardson, proprietor of the *News,* a man of 60 years, and the leader of the secession movement in Texas, ridiculed the idea, on account of my age and size, and ended by telling me that "it's all bluster anyway. It will be ended in the next sixty days and I'll hold in my hat all the blood that's shed in this war." This statement from one whom I thought knew all about it, only served to fix all the firmer my resolve to go and go at once, before too late. So I took "French leave" and joined an artillery company at an improvised fort at Sabine Pass, Texas, where Capt. Richard Parsons, an older brother, was in command of an infantry company. Here I exercised in infantry drill and served as "powder monkey" for the cannoneers.[5] My military enlistment expired in twelve months, when I left Fort Sabine and joined Parson's Texas cavalry brigade, then on the Mississippi river. My brother, Maj. Gen. W.H. Parsons (who during the war was by his soldiers invested with the sobriquet "Wild Bill,") was at that time in command of the entire cavalry outposts on the west bank of the Mississippi river from Helena to the mouth of the Red river. His cavalrymen held the advance in every movement of the Trans-Mississippi army, from the defeat of the Federal General Curtis on White river to the defeat of Gen. Banks' army on Red river, which closed the fighting on the west side of the Mississippi.[6] I was a mere boy of 15 when I joined my brother's command at the front on White river, and was afterward a member of the renowned McInoly scouts under Gen. Parson's orders, which participated in all the battles of the Curtis, Canby and Banks campaign.

On my return to Waco, Texas, at the close of the war, I traded a good mule, all the property I possessed, for forty acres of corn in the field standing ready for harvest, to a refugee who desired to flee the country. I hired and paid wages (the first they had ever received) to a number of ex-slaves, and together we reaped the harvest. From the proceeds of its sales, I obtained a sum sufficient to pay for six months' tuition at the Waco university, under control of Rev. Dr. R.B. Burleson, where I received about all the technical education I ever had. Soon afterwards I took up the trade of type-setting, and went to work in a printing office in the town. In 1868 I founded and edited a weekly newspaper in Waco, named *The Spectator.* In it I advocated, with General Longstreet,[7] the acceptance, in good faith, of the terms of surrender, and supported the thirteenth, fourteenth and fifteenth constitutional amendments, and the reconstruction measures, securing the political rights of the colored people.[8] (I was strongly influenced in taking this step out of respect and love for the memory of dear old "Aunt Ester," then dead, and formerly a slave and house servant of my brother's family, she having been my constant associate, and practically raised me, with great kindness and a mother's love.) I became a Republican, and, of course, had to go into politics. I incurred thereby the hate and contumely of many of my former army comrades, neighbors, and the Ku Klux Klan.[9] My political career was full of excitement and danger. I took the stump to vindicate my convictions. The lately enfranchised slaves over a large section of the country came to know and idolize me as their friend and defender, while on the other hand I was regarded as a political heretic and traitor by many of my former associates. The *Spectator* could not long survive such an atmosphere. In 1869 I was appointed traveling correspondent and agent for the Houston *Daily Telegraph*, and started out on horseback (our principal mode of travel at that time) for a long tour through northwestern Texas. It was during this trip through Johnson county that I first met the charming young Spanish Indian maiden who, three years later, became my wife.[10] She lived in a most beautiful region of country, on her uncle's ranch, near Buffalo Creek. I lingered in this neighborhood as long as I could, and then pursued my journey with fair success. In 1870, at 21 years of age, I was appointed Assistant Assessor of United States Internal Revenues, under General Grant's administration.[11] About a year later I was elected one of the secretaries of the Texas State Senate, and was soon after appointed Chief Deputy Collector of United States Internal Revenue, at Austin, Texas, which position I held, accounting satisfactorily for large sums of money, until 1873, when I resigned the position. In August, 1873, I accompanied an editorial excursion, as the representative of the Texas *Agriculturist* at Austin, Texas, and in company with a large delegation of Texas editors, made an extended tour through Texas, Indian Nation, Missouri, Iowa, Illinois, Ohio, and Pennsylvania, as guests of the Missouri, Kansas & Texas railway. I decided to settle in Chicago. I had married in Austin, Texas, in the fall of 1872, and my wife joining me at Philadelphia we came to Chicago together, where we have lived till the present time. I at once became a member of Typographical Union No. 16, and "subbed" for a time on the *Inter-Ocean,* when I went to work under "permit" on the *Times.* Here I worked over four years holding a situation at "the case." In 1874 I became interested in the "Labor question," growing out of the effort made by Chicago working people at that time to compel the "Relief and Aid Society," to render to the suffering poor of the city an account of the vast sums of money (several millions of dollars) held by that society and contributed by the whole world to relieve the distress occasioned by the great Chicago fire of 1871.[12] It was claimed by the working people that the money was being used for purposes foreign to the intention of its donors; that rings of speculators were corruptly using the money, while the distressed and impoverished people for whom it was contributed, were denied its use. This raised a great sensation and scandal among all the city newspapers, which defended the "Relief and Aid Society," and denounced the dissatisfied workingmen as "communists,[13] robbers, loafers," etc. I began to examine into this subject, and I found that the complaints of the working people against the society were just and proper. I also discovered a great similarity between the abuse heaped upon these poor people by the organs of the rich and the actions of the late Southern slave holders in Texas toward the newly enfranchised slaves, whom they accused of wanting to make their former masters "divide" by giving them "forty acres and a mule,"[14] and it satisfied me there was a great fundamental wrong at work in society, and in existing social and industrial arrangements.

From this time dated my interest and activity in the

labor movement. The desire to know more about this subject led me in contact with socialists and their writings, they being the only people who at that time had made any protest against or offered any remedy for, the enforced poverty of the wealth producers and its collateral evils of ignorance, intemperance, crime and misery. There were very few socialists or "communists" as the daily papers were fond of calling them, in Chicago at that time. The result was, the more I investigated and studied the relations of poverty to wealth, its causes and cure, the more interested I became in the subject. In 1876, a workingmen's congress of organized labor met in Pittsburgh, Pa. I watched its proceedings. A split occurred between the conservatives and radicals, the latter of whom withdrew and organized the "Workingmen's Party of the United States."[15] The year previous I had become a member of the "Social Democratic Party of America." This latter was now merged into the former. The organization was at once pounced upon by the monopolist class, who, through the capitalist press everywhere, denounced us as "socialists, communists, robbers, loafers," etc.

This was very surprising to me, and also had an exasperating effect upon me, and a powerful impulse possessed me to place myself right before the people by defining and explaining the objects and principles of the workingmen's party, which I was thoroughly convinced were founded both in justice and on necessity. I therefore entered heartily into the work of enlightening my fellow men. First, the ignorant and blinded wage-workers who misunderstood us, and secondly, the educated labor exploiters who misrepresented us. I soon unconsciously became a "labor agitator," and this brought down upon me a large amount of capitalist odium. But this capitalist abuse and slander only served to renew my zeal all the more in the great work of social redemption.

In 1877 the great railway strike occurred;[16] it was July 21, 1877, and it is said 30,000 workingmen assembled on Market street near Madison, in mass meeting.[17] I was called upon to address them. In doing so, I advocated the programme of the workingmen's party, which was the exercise of the sovereign ballot for the purpose of obtaining state control of all means of production, transportation, communication and exchange, thus taking these instruments of labor and wealth out of the hands or control of private individuals, corporations, monopolies and syndicates. To do this, I argued, that the wage worker would first have to join the workingmen's party. There was great enthusiasm, but no disorder during the meeting. The next day I went to the *Times* office to go to work as usual, when I found my name stricken from the roll of employes. I was discharged and blacklisted by this paper for addressing the meeting that night. The printers in the office admired secretly what they termed "my pluck," but they were afraid to have much to say to me. About noon of that day, as I was at the office of the German labor paper, 94 Market Street (organ of the workingmen's party—the *Arbeiter-Zeitung*, printed tri-weekly), two men came in and accosting me said Mayor Heath wanted to speak to me. Supposing the gentleman was downstairs, I accompanied them, when they told me he was at the mayor's office. I expressed my surprise, and wondered what he wanted with me. There was great newspaper excitement in the city, and the papers were calling the strikers all sorts of hard names, but while many thousands were on strike there had been no disorder. As we walked hurriedly on, one on each side of me, the wind blew strong and their coat tails flying aside, I noticed that my companions were armed. Reaching the city hall building I was ushered into the Chief of Police's presence (Hickey) in a room filled with police officers. I knew none of them but I seemed to be known by them all. They scowled at me and conducted me to what they called the mayor's room.

Here I waited a short while when the door opened and about thirty persons, mostly in citizens dress, came in. The chief of police took a seat opposite to and near me. I was very hoarse from the outdoor speaking of the previous night, had caught cold, had had but little sleep or rest and had been discharged from employment. The chief began to catechise me in a brow-beating, officious and insulting manner. He wanted to know who I was, where born, raised, if married and a family, etc. I quietly answered all his questions. He then lectured me on the great trouble I had brought upon the city of Chicago and wound up by asking me if I didn't "know better than to come up here from Texas and incite the working people to insurrection," etc.? I told him I had done nothing of the sort or at least I had not intended to do so, that I was simply a speaker at the meeting, that was all. I told him that the strike arose from causes over which I, as an individual, had no control; that I had merely addressed the mass meeting advising to not strike but go to the polls, elect good men to make good laws and thus bring about good times. Those present in the room were much excited and when I was through explaining some spoke up and said "hang him," "lynch him," "lock him up," etc., to my great surprise holding me responsible for the strikes in the city. Others said it would never do to hang or lock me up. That the working men were excited and that act might cause them to do violence. It was agreed to let me go.

I had been there about two hours. The Chief of Police as I rose to depart took me by the arm, accompanied me to the door where we stopped. He said, "Parsons, your life is in danger, I advise you to leave the city at once. Beware. Everything you say or do is made known to me. I have men on your track who shadow you. Do you know you are liable to be assassinated any moment on the street?" I ventured to ask him who by and what for? He answered: "Why, those board of trade men would as leave hang you to a lamp post as not." This surprised me and I answered, "If I was alone they might, but not otherwise." He turned the spring latch, shoved me through the door into the hall, saying in a hoarse tone of voice, "Take warning," and slammed the door to. I was never in the old rookery before. It was a labyrinth of halls and doors. I saw no one about. All was still. The sudden change from the tumultuous inmates of the room to the dark and silent hall affected me. I didn't know where to go or what to do. I felt alone, absolutely without a friend in the wide world. This was my first experience with the "powers that be," and I became conscious that they were powerful to give or take one's life. I was sad, not excited. The afternoon papers announced in great headlines that Parsons, the leader of the strikers, was arrested. This was surprising and annoying to me, for I had made no such attempt and was not under arrest. But the papers said so. That night I called at the composing room of the *Tribune* office on the fifth floor partly to get a night's work and partly to be near the men of my own craft, whom I instinctively felt sympathized with me. The men went to work at 7 p.m. It was near 8 o'clock as I was talking about the great strike, and wondering what it would all come to, with Mr. Manion, Chairman of the Executive Board of our union, when from behind some one took hold of my arms and jerking me around to face them, asked me if my name was Parsons. One man on each side of me took hold of one arm, another man put his hand against my back, and began dragging and shoving me toward the door. They were strangers. I expostulated. I wanted to know what was the matter. I said to them: "I came in here as a gentleman, and I don't want to be dragged out like a dog." They cursed me between their teeth, and, opening the door, began to lead me downstairs. As we started down one of them put a pistol to my head and said: "I've a mind to blow your brains out." Another said: "Shut up or we'll dash you out the windows upon the pavements below." Reaching the bottom of the five flights of stairs they paused and said: "Now go. If you ever put your face in this building again you'll be arrested and locked up." A few steps in the hallway and I opened the door and stepped out upon the sidewalk. (I learned afterward from the *Tribune* printers that there was great excitement in the composing room, the men threatened to strike then and there on account of the way I had been treated; when Joe Medill,[18] the proprietor, came up into the composing-room and made an excitable talk to the men, explaining that he knew nothing about it and that my treatment was done without his knowledge or consent, rebuking those who had acted in the way they had done. It was the opinion of the men, however, that this was only a subterfuge to allay the threatened trouble which my treatment had excited.) The streets were almost deserted at that early hour, and there was a hushed and expectant feeling pervading everything. I felt that I was likely to fall a pitiless, unknown sacrifice at any moment. I strolled down Dearborn street to Lake, west on Lake to Fifth avenue. It was a calm, pleasant summer night. Lying stretched upon the curb, and loitering in and about the closed doors of the mammoth buildings on these streets, were armed men. Some held their muskets in hand, but most of them were rested against the buildings. In going by way of an unfrequented street I found that I had got among those whom

I sought to evade—they were the First regiment, Illinois National Guards. They seemed to be waiting for orders; for had not the newspapers declared that the strikers were becoming violent, and "the Commune was about to rise!" and that I was their leader! No one spoke to or molested me. I was unknown. The next day and the next the strikers gathered in thousands in different parts of the city without leaders or any organized purpose. They were in each instance clubbed and fired upon and dispersed by the police and militia. That night a peaceable meeting of 3,000 workingmen was dispersed on Market street, near Madison. I witnessed it. Over 100 policemen charged upon this peaceable mass-meeting, firing their pistols and clubbing right and left. The printers, the iron-molders, and other trades unions which had held regular monthly or weekly meetings of their unions for years past, when they came to their hall-doors now for that purpose, found policemen standing there, the doors barred, and the members told that all meetings had been prohibited by the Chief of Police. All mass meetings, union meetings of any character were broken up by the police, and at one place (Twelfth Street Turner hall), where the Furniture-Workers' Union had met to confer with their employers about the eight-hour system and wages, the police broke down the doors, forcibly entered, and clubbed and fired upon the men as they struggled pell-mell to escape from the building, killing one workman and wounding many others.

The following day the First regiment, Illinois National Guards, fired upon a crowd of sight-seers, consisting of several thousand men, women, and children, killing several persons, none of whom were ever on strike, at Sixteenth street viaduct.[19]

For about two years after the railroad strike and my discharge from the *Times* office I was blacklisted and unable to find employment in the city, and my family suffered for the necessaries of life.

The events of 1877 gave great impulse and activity to the labor movement all over the United States, and, in fact, the whole world. The unions rapidly increased both in number and membership. So, too, with the Knights of Labor. In visiting Indianapolis, Ind., to address a mass-meeting of workingmen on the Fourth of July, 1876, I met the State Organizer, Calvin A. Light, and was initiated by him as a member of the Knights of Labor,[20] and I have been a member of that order ever since. That organization had no foothold, was in fact unknown, in Illinois, at that time. What a change! Today the Knights of Labor has nearly a million members, and numbers tens of thousands in the State of Illinois. The political labor movement boomed also. The following spring of 1877 the Workingmen's Party of the United States nominated a full county ticket in Chicago. It elected three members of the Legislature and one Senator. I received as candidate for County Clerk, 7,963 votes, running over 400 ahead of the ticket. About that time I became a member of local assembly 400 of the Knights of Labor, the first Knights of Labor assembly organized in Chicago, and, I believe, in the State of Illinois. I also served as a delegate to district assembly 24 for two terms, and was, I think, made its Master Workman for one term.

I have been nominated by the workingmen in Chicago three times for Alderman, twice for County Clerk, and once for Congress. The Labor party was kept up for four years, polling at each election from 6,000 to 12,000 votes. I was in 1878 a delegate to the national convention of the Workingmen's Party of the United States, held at Newark, N.J. At this labor congress the name of the party was changed to "Socialistic Labor party." In 1878, at my instance and largely through my efforts, the present Trades

Assembly of Chicago and vicinity was organized. I was its first President and was re-elected to that position three times. I remained a delegate to the Trades Assembly from Typographical Union No. 16 for several years. I was a strenuous advocate of the eight-hour system among trade unions. In 1879 I was a delegate to the national convention held in Allegheny City, Pa., of the Socialistic Labor party, and was there nominated as the Labor candidate for President of the United States. I declined the honor, not being of the constitutional age—35 years. (This was the first nomination of a workingman by workingmen for that office in the United States.)

During these years of political action every endeavor was made to corrupt, to intimidate, and mislead the Labor party. But it remained pure and undefiled; it refused to be cowed, bought, or misled. Beset on the one side by the insinuating politician and on the other by the almighty money-bags, what between the two the Labor party—the honest, poor party—had a hard road to travel. And, worst of all, the workingmen refused to rally en masse to their own party, but doggedly, the most of them, hugged their idols of Democracy or Republicanism, and fired their ballots against each other on election days. It was discouraging.

But the Labor party moved forward undaunted, and each election came up smiling at defeat. In 1876 the *Socialist,* an English weekly paper, was published by the party, and I was elected its assistant editor. About this time the Socialist organization held some monster meetings. The Exposition building on one occasion contained over 40,000 attendants, and many could not get inside. Ogden's grove on one occasion held 30,000 persons. During these years the labor movement was undergoing its formative period, as it is even now. The un-American utterances of the capitalist press—the representatives of monopoly—excited the gravest apprehension among thoughtful working people. These representatives of the moneyed aristocracy advised the use of police clubs, and militia bayonets, and gatling guns to suppress strikers and put down discontented laborers struggling for better pay—shorter work-hours. The millionaires and their representatives on the pulpit and rostrum avowed their intention to use force to quell their dissatisfied laborers. The execution of these threats; the breaking up of meetings, arrest and imprisonment of labor "leaders;" the use of club, pistol, and bayonet upon strikers; even to the advice to throw hand-grenades (dynamite) among them—these acts of violence and brutality led many workingmen to consider the necessity for self-defense of their persons and their rights. Accordingly, workingmen's military organizations sprang up all over the country.

So formidable did this plan of organization promise to become that the capitalistic Legislature of Illinois in 1878, acting under orders from millionaire manufacturers and railway corporations, passed a law disarming the wage-workers. This law the workingmen at once tested in the Courts of Illinois, and afterward carried it to the Supreme Court of the United States, where it was decided by the highest tribunal that the State Legislatures of the United States had a constitutional right to disarm workingmen. Dissensions began to rise in the Socialist organizations over the question of methods. In the fall and spring elections of 1878–79–80 the politicians began to practice ballot-box stuffing and other outrages upon the Workingmen's party. It was then I began to realize the hopeless task of political reformation. Many workingmen began to lose faith in the potency of the ballot or the protection of the law for the poor. Some of them said that "political liberty without economic (industrial) freedom was an empty phrase." Others claimed that poverty had no votes as against wealth; because if a man's bread was controlled by another, that other could and, when necessary, would control his vote also. A consideration and discussion of these subjects gradually brought a change of sentiment in the minds of many; the conviction began to spread that the State, the Government and its laws, was merely the agent of the owners of capital to reconcile, adjust, and protect their—the capitalists'—conflicting interests; that the chief function of all Government was to maintain economic subjection of the man of labor to the monopolizer of the means of labor—of life—to capital.

These ideas began to develop in the minds of workingmen everywhere (in Europe as well as America), and the conviction grew that law—statute law—and all forms of Government (governors, rulers, dictators, whether Emperor, King, President, or capitalist, were each and all of the despots and usurpers), was nothing else than an organized conspiracy of the propertied class to deprive the working class of their natural rights. The conviction obtained that money or wealth controlled politics; that money controlled, by hook or crook, labor at the polls as well as in the workshop. The idea began to prevail that the element of coercion, of force, which enabled one person to dominate and exploit the labor of another, was centered or concentrated in the State, the Government, and the statute law, that every law and every Government in the last analysis was force, and that force was despotism, an invasion of man's natural right to liberty.

In 1880 I withdrew from all active participation in the political Labor party, having been convinced that the number of hours per day that the wage-workers are compelled to work, together with the low wages they received, amounted to their practical disfranchisement as voters. I saw that long hours and low wages deprived the wage-workers, as a class, of the necessary time and means, and consequently left them but little inclination to organize for political action to abolish class legislation. My experience in the Labor party had also taught me that bribery, intimidation, duplicity, corruption, and bulldozing grew out of the conditions which made the working people poor and the idlers rich, and that consequently the ballot-box could not be made an index to record the popular will until the existing debasing, impoverishing, and enslaving industrial conditions were first altered. For these reasons I turned my activities mainly toward an effort to reduce the hours of labor to at least a normal working day, so that the wage-workers might thereby secure more leisure from mere drudge work, and obtain better pay to minister to their higher aspirations.

Several trades unions united in sending me throughout the different States to lay the eight-hour question before the labor organizations of the country. In January, 1880, the "Eight-Hour League of Chicago" sent me as a delegate to the national conference of labor reformers, held in Washington, D.C. This convention adopted a resolution which I offered, calling public attention of the United States Congress to the fact that, while the eight-hour law passed years ago had never been enforced in Government departments, there was no trouble at all in getting through Congress all the capitalistic legislation called for. By this national convention Richard Trevellick, Charles H. Lichtman, Dyer D. Lum, John G. Mills, and myself were appointed a committee of the National Eight-Hour Association, whose duty it was to remain in Washington, D.C., and urge upon the labor organizations of the United States to unite for the enforcement of the eight-hour law.[21]

About this time there followed a period of discussion of property rights, of the rights of majorities and minorities. The agitation of the subject led to the formation of a new organization, called the International Working People's Association. I was a delegate in 1881 to the labor congress which founded the former, and afterward also delegate to the Pittsburgh (Pa.) congress in October, 1883, which revived the latter as a part of the International Working People's Association, which already ramified Europe, and which was originally organized at the world's labor congress held at London, England, in 1864. I cannot do better than insert here the manifesto of the Pittsburgh congress which clearly sets forth the aims and methods of the International, of which I am still a member, and for which reason myself and comrades are condemned to death. It was adopted as follows:

TO THE WORKINGMEN OF AMERICA.

Fellow Workmen: The Declaration of Independence says:

" * * But when a long train of abuses and usurpations, pursuing invariably the same object, evinces a design to reduce them (the people) under absolute despotism, it is their right, it is their duty to throw off such government and provide new guards for their future security."

This thought of Thomas Jefferson, was the justification for armed resistance by our forefathers, which gave birth to our republic, and do not the necessities of our present time compel us to re-assert their declaration?

Fellow-workmen, we ask you to give us your attention for a few moments. We ask you to candidly read the following manifesto issued in your behalf; in behalf of your wives and children; in behalf of humanity and progress.

Our present society is founded on the exploitation of the propertyless by the propertied. The exploitation is such that the propertied (capitalist) buy the working force body and soul of the propertyless, for the price of the mere cost of existence (wages), and take for themselves, i.e., steal the amount of new values (products) which exceeds the price, whereby wages are made to represent the necessities instead of the earnings of the wage laborer.

As the non-possessing classes are forced by their poverty to offer for sale to the propertied their working forces, and as our present production on a grand scale enforce technical development with immense rapidity, so that by the application of an always decreasing number of human working force, an always increasing amount of products is created; so does the supply of working force increase constantly, which the demand therefore decreases. This is the reason why the workers compete more and more intensely in selling themselves, causing their wages to sink of at least on the average, never raising them above the margin necessary for keeping intact their working ability.

Whilst by this process the propertyless are entirely debarred from entering the ranks of the propertied, even by the most strenuous exertions, the propertied, by means of the ever-increasing plundering of the working class, are becoming richer day by day, without in any way being themselves productive.

If now and then one of the propertyless class become rich it is not by their own labor, but from opportunities which they have to speculate upon, and absorb the labor product of others.

With the accumulation of individual wealth, the greed and power of the propertied grows. They use all the means for competing among themselves for the robbery of the people. In this struggle generally the less-propertied (middle-class) are overcome, while the great capitalists, par excellence, swell their wealth enormously, concentrate entire branches of production as well as trade and intercommunication into their hands and develop into monopolies. The increase of products, accompanied by simultaneous decrease of the average income of the working mass of the people leads to the so-called "business" and "commercial" crises, when the misery of the wage-workers is forced to the extreme.

For illustration: The last census of the United States shows that after deducting the cost of raw material, interest, rents, risks, etc., the propertied class have absorbed—i.e., stolen—more than five-eighths of all products, leaving scarcely three-eighths to the producers. The propertied class being scarcely one-tenth of our population, and in spite of their luxury and extravagance, and unable to consume their enormous "profits", and the producers, unable to consume more than they receive—three-eighths—so-called "over-productions" must necessarily take place. The terrible results of panics are well known.

The increasing eradication of working forces from the productive process annually increases the percentage of the propertyless population, which becomes pauperized and is driven to "crime," vagabondage, prostitution, suicide, starvation, and general depravity. This system is unjust, insane and murderous. It is, therefore, necessary to totally destroy it with and by all means, and with the greatest energy on the part of every one who suffers by it, and who does not want to be made culpable for its continued existence by his inactivity.

Agitation for the purpose of organization; organization for the purpose of rebellion. In these few words the ways are marked which the workers must take if they want to be rid of their chains; as the economic condition is the same in all countries of so-called "civilization," as the government of all monarchies and republics work hand in hand for the purpose of opposing all movements of the thinking part of the workers; as finally the victory in the decisive combat of the proletarians against their oppressors can only be gained by the simultaneous struggle along the whole line of the bourgeois (capitalistic) society, so, therefore, the international fraternity of people as expressed in the International Working People's Association presents itself a self-evident necessity.

True order should take its place. This can only be achieved when all implements of labor, the soil and other premises of production, in short, capital produced by labor, is changed into societary property. Only by this presupposition is destroyed every possibility of the future spoilation of man by man. Only by common, undivided capital can all be enabled to enjoy in their fullness the fruits of the common toil. Only by the impossibility of accumulating individual (private) capital can everyone be compelled to work who makes a demand to live.

This order of things allows production to regulate itself according to the demand of the whole people, so that nobody need work more than a few hours a day, and that all nevertheless can supply their needs. Hereby time and opportunity are given for opening to the people the way to the highest possible civilization; the privileges of higher intelligence fall with the privileges of wealth and birth. To the achievement of such a system the political organizations of the capitalistic classes—be they monarchies or republics—form the barriers. These political structures (states), which are completely in the hands of the propertied, have no other purpose than the upholding of the present disorder of exploitation.

All laws are directed against the working people. In so far as the opposite appears to be the case, they serve on one hand to blind the worker, while on the other hand they are simply evaded. Even the school serves only the purpose of furnishing the offspring of the wealthy with those qualities necessary to uphold their class domination. The children of the poor get scarcely a formal elementary training, and this, too, is mainly directed to such branches as tend to producing prejudices, arrogance and servility; in short, want of sense. The church finally seeks to make complete idiots out of the mass and to make them forgo the paradise on earth by promising a fictitious heaven. The capitalistic press on the other hand, takes care of the confusion of spirits in public life. All these institutions far from aiding in the education of the masses, have for their object the keeping in ignorance of the people. They are all in the pay and under the direction of the capitalistic classes. The workers can therefore expect no help from any capitalistic party in their struggle against the existing system. They must achieve their liberation by their own efforts. As in former times a privileged class never surrendered its tyranny, neither can it be expected that the capitalists of this age will give up their rulership without being forced to do it.

If there ever could have been any question on this point it should long ago have been dispelled by the brutalities which the bourgeois of all countries—in America as well as in Europe—constantly commits as often as the proletariat anywhere energetically move to better their conditions. It becomes, therefore, self-evident that the struggle of the proletariat with the bourgeois will be of a violent, revolutionary character.

We could show by scores of illustrations that all attempts in the past to reform this monstrous system by peaceable means, such as the ballot, have been futile, and all such efforts in the future must necessarily be so, for the following reasons:

The political institutions of our time are the agencies of the propertied class; their mission is the upholding of the privileges of their masters; any reform in your own behalf would curtail these privileges. To this they will not and can not consent, for it would be suicidal to themselves.

That they will not resign their privileges voluntarily we know; that they will not make any concessions to us we likewise know. Since we must then rely upon the kindness of our master for whatever redress we have, and knowing that from them no good may be expected, there remains but one resource—FORCE! Our forefathers have not only told us that against despots force is justifiable, because it is the only means, but they themselves have set the immortal example.

By force our ancestors liberated themselves from political oppression, by force their children will have to liberate themselves from economic bondage. "It is, therefore, your right, it is your duty," says Jefferson—"to arm!"

What we would achieve is, therefore, plainly and simply:

First—Destruction of the existing class rule, by all means, i.e., by energetic, relentless, revolutionary and international action.

Second—Establishment of a free society based upon cooperative organization of production.

Third—Free exchange of equivalent products by and between the productive organizations without commerce and profit-mongery.

Fourth—Organization of education on a secular, scientific and equal basis for both sexes.

Fifth—Equal rights for all without distinction to sex or race.

Sixth—Regulation of all public affairs by free contracts between autonomous (independent) communes and asso-

> ciations, resting on a federalistic basis.
>
> Whoever agrees with this ideal let him grasp our outstretched brother-hands!
>
> Proletarians from all countries unite!
>
> Fellow-workmen, all we need for the achievement of this great end is ORGANIZATION and UNITY!
>
> The day has come for solidarity. Join our ranks! Let the drum beat defiantly the roll of battle: "Workmen of all countries unite! You have nothing to lose but your chains; you have the world to win!"[22]
>
> Issued by the Pittsburgh Congress of the "International Working People's Association" on October 16, 1883.

In all these matters here enumerated, I took an active, personal interest. October 1, 1884, the International founded in Chicago *The Alarm,* a weekly newspaper, of which I was elected to the position of editor, and I have held that position until its seizure and suppression by the authorities on the 5th day of May, 1886, following the Haymarket tragedy. In the year 1881, the capitalist press began to stigmatize us as Anarchists, and to denounce us as the enemies of all law and government. They charged us with being the enemies of "law and order," as breeders of strife and confusion. Every conceivable bad name and evil design was imputed to us by the lovers of power and haters of freedom and equality.

Even the workingmen in some instances, caught the infection and many of them joined in the capitalist hue and cry against the anarchists. Being satisfied of ourselves that our purpose was a just one, we worked on undismayed, willing to labor and to wait, for time and events to justify our cause. We began to allude to ourselves as anarchists, and that name which was at first imputed to us as a dishonor, we came to cherish and to defend with pride. What's in a name? But names sometimes express ideas; and ideas are everything.

What, then, is our offense, being anarchists? The word *anarche* is derived from two Greek words *an,* signifying no, or without, and *arche,* government; hence anarchy means no government. Consequently anarchy meant a condition of society which has no king, emperor, president or ruler of any kind. In other words anarchy is the social administration of all affairs by the people themselves; that is to say, self government, individual liberty. Such a condition of society denies the right of majorities to rule over or dictate to minorities. Though every person in the world agree upon a certain plan and only one objected thereto, the objector would, under anarchy, be respected in his natural right to go his own way. And when such person is thus held responsible by all the rest for the violation of the inherent right of any one how then, can injustice flourish or wrong triumph? For the greatest good to the greatest number anarchy substitutes the equal right of each and every one. The natural law is all sufficient for every purpose, every desire and every human being. The scientist then becomes the natural leader, and is accepted as the only authority among men. Whatever can be demonstrated will by self interest be accepted, otherwise rejected. The great natural law of power derived alone from association and co-operation will of necessity and from selfishness be applied by the people in the production and distribution of wealth, and what the trades unions and labor organizations seek now to do, but are prevented from doing because of obstruction and coercion, will under perfect liberty—anarchy—come easiest to hand. Anarchy is the extension of the boundaries of liberty until it covers the whole range of the wants and aspirations of man—*not* men, but *Man.*

Power is might, and might always makes its own right. Thus in the very nature of things, might makes itself right whether or no. Government, therefore, is the agency or power by which some person or persons govern or rule other persons, and the inherent right to govern is found wherever the power or might to do so is manifest. In a natural state, intelligence of necessity controls ignorance, the strong the weak, the good the bad, etc. Only when the natural law operates is this true, however. On the other hand when the statute is substituted for the natural law, and government holds sway, then, and then only, power centers itself in the hands of a few, who dominate, dictate, rule, degrade and enslave the many. The broad distinction and irreconcilable conflict between wage laborers and capitalists, between those who buy labor or sell its products, and the wage worker who sells his labor (himself) in order to live, arises from the social institution called government; and the conflicting interests, the total abolition of warring classes, and the end of domination and exploitation of man by man is to be found only in a free society, where all and each are equally free to unite or disunite, as interest or inclination may incline.

The anarchists are the advance guard in the impending social revolution. They have discovered the cause of world-wide discontent which is felt but not yet understood by the toiling millions as a whole. The effort now being made by organized and unorganized labor in all countries to participate in the making of laws which they are forced to obey will lay bare to them the secret source of their enslavement by capital. Capital is a thing—it is property. Capital is the stored up, accumulated savings of past labor, such as machinery, houses, food, clothing, all the means of production (both natural and artificial) of transportation, and communication,—in short the resources of life, the means of subsistence. These things are, in a natural state, the common heritage of all for the free use of all, and they were so held until their forcible seizure and appropriation by a few. Thus the common heritage of all seized by violence and fraud, was afterwards made the property—capital—of the usurpers, who erected a government and enacted laws to perpetuate and maintain their special privileges.

The function, the only function of capital is to appropriate or confiscate the labor product of the propertyless, non-possessing class, the wage-workers. The origin of government was in violence and murder. Government disinherits and enslaves the governed. Government is for slaves; free men govern themselves. Law, statute, man-made law is license. Anarchy—natural law—is liberty. Anarchy is the cessation of force. Government is the rulership or control of man by men. In the name of law—by means of statute law—whether that control be by one man (*mon*-arche) or by a majority (*mob*-arche). The effort of the wage-slave (now being made) to participate in the making of laws will enable them to discover for the first time that a human *law*-maker is a human humbug. That laws, true, just and perfect laws, are discovered, *not* made. The law-making class—the capitalists—will object to this, they (the capitalists) will remonstrate, they will fight, they will kill, before they permit laws to be made, or *repealed,* which deprive them of their power to rule and rob. This fact is demonstrated in every strike which threatened their power; by every lock-out, by every discharge, by every black-list. Their exercise of these powers is based upon force and every law, every government in the last analysis is resolved into force.

Therefore, when the workers, as they are now everywhere preparing to do, insist upon and demand a participation in, or application of democratic principles in industrial affairs, think you the request will be conceded? nay, nay: The right to live, to equality of opportunity, to liberty and the pursuit of happiness is yet to be acquired by the producers of all wealth. The Knights of Labor, unconsciously stand upon a State Socialist programme. They will never be able to seize the state by the ballot, but when they do seize it, (and seize it they must) they will abolish it. Legalized capital and the state stand or fall together. They are twins. The liberty of labor makes the state not only unnecessary, but impossible. When the people—the whole people—become the state, that is, participate equally in governing themselves, the state of necessity ceases to exist. Then what? Leaders, natural leaders, take the place of the overthrown rulers; liberty takes the place of statute laws, of license; the people voluntarily associate or freely withdraw from association, instead of being bossed or driven as now. They unite and disunite, when, where and as they please. Social administration is substituted for governmentalism, and self-preservation becomes the actuating motive as now, minus the dictation, coercion, driving and domination of man by man.

Do you say this is a dream! That it is the millennium! Well, the crisis is near at hand. Necessity, which is its own law, will force the issue. Then whatever is most natural to do will be the easiest and best to do. The workshops will drop into the hands of the workers, the mines will fall to the miners and the land and all other things will be controlled by those who possess and use them. This will be, there can then be no title to anything aside from its possession and use. Only the statute law and government stand to-day as a barrier to this result, and all efforts to change them failing, will inevitably result in their total abolition.

Anarchy, therefore, is liberty; is the negation of force, or compulsion, or violence. It is the precise reverse of that which those who hold and have power would have their oppressed victims believe it is.

Anarchists do not advocate or advise the use of force. Anarchists disclaim and protest against its use, and the use of force is justifiable only when employed to repel force. Who, then, are the aiders, abettors and users of force? Who are the real revolutionists? Are they not those who hold and exercise power over their fellows? They who use clubs and bayonets, prisons and scaffolds? The great class conflict now gathering throughout the world is created by our social system of industrial slavery. Capitalists could not if they would, and would not if they could, change it. This alone is to be the work of the proletariat, the disinherited, the wage-slave, the sufferer. Nor can the wage-class avoid this conflict. Neither religion nor politics can solve it or prevent it. It comes, as a human, an imperative necessity. Anarchists do not make the social revolution; they prophesy its coming. Shall we then stone the prophets? Anarchists do not use or advise the use of force, but point out that force is ever employed to uphold despotism to despoil man's natural rights. Shall we therefore kill and destroy the Anarchists? And capital shouts "yes, yes! exterminate them!"

In the line of evolution and historical development, anarchy—liberty—is next in order. With the destruction of the feudal system, and the birth of commercialism and manufacturies in the Sixteenth century, a contest long and bitter and bloody, lasting over a hundred years, was waged for mental and religious liberty. The Seventeenth and Eighteenth centuries, with their sanguinary conflicts, gave to man political equality and civil liberty, based on the monopolization of the resources of life, capital—with its "free laborers," freely competing with one another for a chance to serve king capital and "free competition" among capitalists in their endeavors to exploit the laborers and monopolize the labor products. All over the world the fact stands undisputed that the political is based upon, and is but the reflex of, the economic system, and hence we find that whatever the political form of the government, whether monarchical or republican, the average social status of the wage-workers is in every community identical. The class struggle of the past century is history repeating itself, it is the evolutionary growth preceding the revolutionary denouement. Though liberty is a growth, it is also a birth, and while it is yet to be, it is also about to be born. Its birth will come through travail and pain, through bloodshed and violence. It cannot be prevented. This, because of the obstruction, impediments and obstacles which serve as a barrier to its coming. An anarchist is a believer in liberty, and as I would control no man against his will, neither shall any one rule over me with my consent. Government is compulsion; no one freely consents to be governed by another, therefore there can be no just power of government. Anarchy is perfect liberty, is absolute freedom of the individual. Anarchy has no schemes, no programmes, no systems to offer or to substitute for the existing order of things. Anarchy would strike from humanity every chain that binds it, and say to mankind: "Go forth! you are free. Have all; enjoy all."

Anarchism nor anarchists either advises, abets, nor encourages the working people to the use of force or a resort to violence. We do not say to the wage-slaves: "You ought, you should use force." No. Why say this when we know they must—they will be driven to use it in self-defense, in self-preservation against those who are degrading, enslaving and destroying them?

Already the millions of workers are unconsciously Anarchists. Impelled by a cause the effects of which they feel but do not wholly understand, they move unconsciously, irresistibly forward to the social revolution. Mental freedom, political equality, industrial liberty!

This is the natural order of things; the logic of events. Who so foolish as to quarrel with it, obstruct it, or attempt to stay its progress? It is the march of the inevitable; the triumph of the MUST.

The examination of the class struggle demonstrates that the eight-hour movement was doomed by the very nature of things to defeat. But the International gave its support to it for two reasons, viz: First, because it was a class movement against class domination, therefore historical and revolutionary and necessary; and secondly, because we did not choose to stand aloof and be misunderstood by our fellow workers. We therefore gave it all the aid and comfort in our power. I was regularly accredited under the official seal of the Trade and Labor Unions of the Central Labor Union, representing twenty thousand organized workingmen in Chicago to assist them in the organization of Trades and Labor Unions, and do all in my power for the eight-hour movement. The Central Labor Union, in conjunction with the International, publishes six newspapers in Chicago, to wit: One English weekly, two German weeklies, one Bohemian weekly, one Scandinavian weekly and one German daily newspaper.

The trade and labor Unions of the United States and Canada having set apart the first day of May, 1886, to inaugurate the 8-hour system,[23] I did all in my power to assist the movement. I feared conflict and trouble would arise between the authorities representing the employers of labor and the wage-workers, who only represented themselves. I know that defenseless men, women and children must finally succumb to the power of the discharge, blacklist and lockout and in consequent misery and hunger enforced by the militiaman's bayonet and the policeman's club. I did not advocate the use of force. But I denounced the capitalists for employing it to hold the laborers in subjection to them and declared that such treatment would of necessity drive the workingmen to employ the same means in self defense.

The labor organizations of Cincinnati, Ohio, decided to make a grand eight-hour demonstration of the 8-hour work-day. On their invitation I went there to address them and left Chicago on Saturday, May 1, for that purpose. Returning on Monday night I reached Chicago on the morning of Tuesday, May 4th, the day of the Haymarket meeting. On arriving home, Mrs. Parsons, who had theretofore attended and assisted in several large mass meetings of the sewing girls of the city, to organize them for the eight hour work day, suggested to me to call a meeting of the American Group of the International for that evening, in order to make arrangements, *i.e.*, appropriate money for hall rent, printing hand-bills, provide speakers, etc., to help to organize the sewing women for 8 hours. I left home about 11 A.M., and, not being able to get a hall, finally published an announcement that the meeting would be held at 107 Fifth avenue, the office of the *Alarm* and *Arbeiter Zeitung*. We had often held business meetings at the same place. Late in the afternoon I learned, for the first time, that a mass meeting had been called at the Haymarket for that evening, the object being to help on the 8-hour boom, and to protest against the police atrocities upon 8-hour strikers at McCormick's factory the day before, where it was claimed six workmen had been shot down by the police and many others wounded. I did not fancy the idea of holding the meeting at that time, and said so, stating that

I believed the manufacturers and corporations were so incensed at the 8-hour movement that they would defend the police in coming to the meeting to break it up, and slaughtering the work people. I was invited to speak there, but declined, on the ground that I had to attend another meeting that night.

About 8 o'clock P.M., accompanied by Mrs. Holmes, Mrs. Parsons and my two children (a boy six years old and a girl four years old) we walked from home to Halsted and Randolph streets. There we observed knots of people standing about, indicating that a mass meeting was expected. Two newspaper reporters, one for the *Tribune* the other for the *Times,* whom I recognized, were strolling around, picking up items, and observing me they inquired if I was to speak at the Haymarket meeting that night. I told them that I was not. That I had to attend another meeting and would not be there, and the ladies, the children and myself took a street car for down town. Reaching the place of meeting of the American group of the International, it was at once called to order and the objects of the meeting were stated to be how best to organize the sewing women of the city in the speediest manner. It was decided to print circulars, hire halls and appoint organizers and speakers, and money was appropriated for the purpose, when about 9 o'clock a committee entered the meeting and said there was a large mass meeting at the Haymarket but no speakers except Mr. Spies, and they were sent over to request Mr. Fielden and myself to come there at once and address the crowd.

We adjourned in a few moments afterwards and went over to the Haymarket in a body, where I was introduced at once and spoke for about an hour to the 3,000 persons present urging them to support the eight-hour movement and stick to their unions. There was little said about the police brutalities of the previous day, other than to complain of the use of the military on every slight occasion. I said it was a shame that the moderate and just claims of the wage-workers should be met with police clubs, pistols, and bayonets, or that the murmurs of discontented laborers, should be drowned in their own blood. When I had finished speaking and Mr. Fielden began, I got down from the wagon we were using as a speaker's stand, and stepping over to another wagon nearby on which sat the ladies (among them my wife and children), and it soon appearing as though it would rain, and the crowd beginning to disperse and the speaker having announced that he would finish in a few moments; I assisted the ladies down from the wagon and accompanied them to Zepf's hall, one block away, where we intended to wait for the adjournment and the company of other friends on our walk home. I had been in this hall about five minutes and was looking towards the meeting, expecting it to close every moment, and standing nearby where the ladies sat, when there appeared a white sheet of light at the place of meeting, followed instantly by a loud roar. This was at once followed by a fusillade of pistol shots (in full view of my sight) which appeared as though fifty or more men had emptied their self-acting revolvers as rapidly as possible. Several shots whizzed by and struck beside the door of the hall, from which I was looking, and soon men came rushing wildly into the building. I escorted the ladies to a place of safety in the rear where we remained about 20 minutes. Leaving the place to take the ladies home we met a man named Brown (who was well known to us) at the corner of Milwaukee avenue and Desplaines street, and asking him to loan me a dollar, he replied that he didn't have the change, whereupon I borrowed a five-dollar gold piece from him. We then parted, he went his way and we started towards home. (This man Brown told of the circumstance the next day that he had met and loaned me $5. He was at once arrested and indicted for conspiracy and unlawful assembly, thrown into prison, where he has lain ever since.)

The next day, observing that many innocent people who were not even present at the meeting were being dragooned and imprisoned by the authorities, and not courting such indignities for myself I left the city, intending to return in a few days, and publishing a letter in the newspapers to that effect. I stopped at Elgin two days in a boarding-house, when I went from there to Waukesha, Wis., a place noted for its beautiful springs and health-giving waters, pure air, etc. At this summer resort I soon obtained employment first at carpentering and then as a painter, which occupations I pursued for seven weeks, or until my return and voluntary surrender to the Court for trial. I procured the Chicago newspapers every day, and from them I learned that I, with a great many others, had been indicted for murder, conspiracy and unlawful assembly at the Haymarket. From the editorials of the capitalist papers every day for two months during my seclusion, I could see that the ruling class were wild with rage and fear against labor organizations. Ample means were offered me to carry me safely to distant parts of the earth, if I chose to go. I knew that the beastly howls against the Anarchists, the demand for their bloody extermination, made by the press and pulpit, was merely a pretext of the ruling class to intimidate the growing power of organized labor in the United States. I also perfectly understood the relentless hate and power of the ruling class. Nevertheless, knowing that I was innocent and that my comrades were innocent of the charge against them, I resolved to return and share whatever persecution labor's enemies could impose upon them. Consequently, on the night of June 20th, I left Waukesha. At 4:30 A.M., June 21st, I boarded a St. Paul train at the union depot at Milwaukee, and arrived in Chicago at 7:30 or 8 o'clock, and repaired to the house of Mrs. Ames at 14 S. Morgan street.

I sent for my wife, who came to me, and a few minutes later I conveyed word to Captain Black, our attorney, that I was prepared to surrender. After an affectionate parting with my noble, brave and loving wife and several devoted friends, who were present, I at a little past 2 o'clock p.m. June 21, accompanied by Mrs. Ames[24] and Mr. A.H. Simpson to the court house entrance, was there joined by my attorney, Capt. Black. We walked up the broad stairway, entered the court then in session, and standing before the bar of the court announced my presence and my voluntary surrender for trial, and entered the plea "not guilty." After this ceremony was over I approached the prisoner's dock, where sat my arraigned comrades Fielden, Spies, Engel, Fischer, Lingg, Neebe and Schwab, and shaking hands with each as I took a seat among them. After the adjournment of the court I was conveyed with the others to a cell in the Cook county bastille, and securely locked up.

What of the Haymarket tragedy?

It is simple enough. A large number, over 3,000 of citizens, mostly workingmen, peaceably assemble to discuss their grievances, viz: The eight-hour movement and the shooting and clubbing of the McCormick and lumberyard strikers by the police of the previous day.

Query. Was that meeting, thus assembled, a lawful and constitutional gathering of citizens? The police, the grand jury, the verdict, the court, and the monopolists all reply: "It was not."

After 10 o'clock, when the meeting was adjourning, two hundred (200) armed police in menacing array, threatening wholesale slaughter of the people, there peaceably (the mayor of Chicago and others who were present testified so before the jury) assembled, commanded their instant dispersal, under the pains and penalties of death.

Was the act of the police lawful and constitutional? The police, the grand jury, the verdict, the court, and the monopolists all reply: "It was."

Some person (unknown and unproven) threw a dynamite bomb among the police. Whether it was thrown in self-defense or in furtherance of monopoly's conspiracy against the 8-hour movement is not known.

Was that a lawful, a constitutional act? The ruling class shout in chorus: "It was not!"

My own belief, based upon careful examination of all the conditions surrounding this Haymarket affair, is that the bomb was thrown by a man in the employ of certain monopolists, who was sent from New York city to Chicago for that purpose, to break up the eight-hour movement, thrust the active men into prison, and scare and terrify the workingmen into submission. Such a course was advocated by all the leading mouth-pieces (newspapers) of monopoly in America just prior to May 1. They carried out their programme and obtained the results they desired.

Is it lawful and constitutional to put innocent men to death? Is it lawful and constitutional to punish us for the deed of a man acting in furtherance of a conspiracy of the monopolists to crush out the eight-hour movement? Every "law and order" tyrant from Chicago to St. Petersburg cries, "Yes!"

Six of the condemned men were not present at the meeting at the time of the tragedy, two of them were not present at any time. One of the latter was addressing a mass-meeting of 2,000 workingmen at Deering's Harvester works, in Lake View, five miles away. The other one was at home abed, and knew not of the affair till the next day. His verdict is fifteen years in the penitentiary. These facts stand unquestioned and undenied before the court. There was no proof of our complicity with or knowledge of the person who threw the bomb, nor is there any proof as to who did throw it. The whole question as to who did the deed is resolved upon motive. What motive controlled the person who did the deed?

The rapid growth of the whole labor movement had, by May 1, given the monopolists of the country much cause for alarm. The organized power of labor was beginning to exhibit unexpected strength and boldness. This alarmed King money-bags, who saw in the Haymarket affair their golden opportunity to make a horrible example of the Anarchists, and by their dreadful fate give the discontented American workingmen a terrible warning!

This verdict is the suppression of free speech, free press and the assemblage of people to discuss their grievances. More than that, the verdict is the denial of the right of self-defense; it is the condemnation of the law of self-preservation in America.

As to the responsibility for the Haymarket tragedy? You have heard the side of the ruling class. I now speak for the people—the ruled. The Haymarket tragedy was the immediate result of the blood-thirsty officiousness of Police Inspector Bonfield. Mayor Harrison (commander in chief of police) was present at this meeting, and testified before the court that he heard the speeches and left just before its adjournment and went to the police station and advised Bonfield that everything at the meeting was peaceable and orderly. The mayor left for his house. Soon thereafter, Bonfield thirsting for promotion and the blood money which he knew that monopolists were eager to bestow, gathered his army and marched them down upon a peaceable, orderly meeting of workingmen, where he expected to immortalize himself by deeds of carnage and slaughter that would put to shame a horde of Apache Indians. Had he not done such brutal things before with the striking streetcar Knights of Labor, Trades Unionists and other workingmen? Why not repeat it that night also? He had received the plaudits of the capitalistic press for such acts done on other occasions. Why not again?

But Police Inspector Bonfield was only a willing agent, not the dastardly principal in this outrage. He held plenary power and obeyed what he knew to be the express desire of his masters—the money kings—who want to suppress free speech, free press, and the right of workingmen to assemble and discuss their grievances. Let the responsibility for the Haymarket tragedy rest where it belongs, to wit: Upon the monopolists, corporations and privileged class who rule and rob the working people, and when they complain about it discharge, lock-out and black-list them, or arrest, imprison and execute them. The Haymarket tragedy was, undoubtedly, the work of a deep laid monopolistic conspiracy originating in New York City and engineered by the Pinkerton thugs. Its object was to break down the eight-hour movement and Chicago was selected by these conspirators as the best place to do the work because Chicago was the center of the movement in the United States. Now, what are the facts about the conspiracy against the eight-hour movement which has resulted in breaking it down and consigning us to the executioner?

Just prior to the time set apart to inaugurate the eight-hour work day, (the latter part of April, 1886,) the New York *Herald,* in reference to the question, said:

> "Two hours, taken from the hours of labor, throughout the United States by the proposed eight-hour movement,

> would make a difference annually of hundreds of millions in values, both to the capital invested in industries and existing stocks."

Now what did this mean? It meant that the issue of the hour with the New York and Chicago Stock Exchanges, Board of Trade, and Produce Exchangers in every commercial and industrial center, was how to preserve the steadiness of the market and maintain the fictitious values of the four-fold watered stocks, then listed and then rapidly shrinking in value under the paralyzing influence of the impending eight-hour demand of the united army of labor. Hundreds of millions in money were at stake. What to do to save it? Clearly, the thing to do was to stop the eight-hour movement. The New York *Times* came promptly forward with its scheme to save the sinking market values. Accordingly, just four days before the grand national strike for eight hours and only one week before the Haymarket tragedy, the New York *Times,* one of the leading organs of railroad, bank, telegraph and telephone monopoly in America, published in its issue of April 25, 1886, an editorial on the condition of the markets, the causes of existing decline and panicky symptoms, in which it said

> The strike question is, of course, the dominant one and is disagreeable in a variety of ways. A *short* and *easy* way to settle it is urged in some quarters, which, is to indict for conspiracy every man who strikes, and summarily lock him up. This method would undoubtedly strike a wholesome terror into the hearts of the working classes.
>
> Another way suggested is to pick out the labor leaders, and make such examples of them as to scare the others into submission.[25]

The sentiment was echoed at once by the New York *Tribune,* which said: "The best policy would be to drive the workingmen into open mutiny against the law."

The organs of monopoly (including the Chicago press), all over the United States took up the cry, and re-echoed the diabolical scheme. Something must be done to trump up charges against the leaders.

The first of May arrives, the great eight-hour strike is inaugurated. Forty thousand men are standing out for it in Chicago. Chicago is the stronghold of the movement, and 40,000 more threaten to join in the demand. An eight-hour mass meeting is held on the Haymarket, Tuesday, May 4. A bomb is thrown, several policemen killed, the leaders are arrested, indicted for conspiracy and murder, and seven of them sentenced to death. What's the result? It worked as the monopolists said it would. The labor leaders are "picked out and made such examples of as to scare the others into submission." Strikers were "summarily locked up. This method would undoubtedly strike a wholesome terror into the hearts of the working classes," said the *Times.*

The eight-hour strike is broken and the movement fell to pieces, all over the country.[26]

Commenting on the business situation on the 8th day of May, 1886, four days after the Haymarket tragedy, Bradstreet, in his weekly review, said, as telegraphed through the Associated Press and published in all the Chicago papers: "Of the 325,000 men who struck for eight hours, about 65,000 have gained it. Chicago was the center of the strike, but the movement all over the country has greatly weakened in the past few days. Stocks were very much depressed the first two days of the week (the 3rd and 4th of May, the days of the McCormick and Haymarket trouble), but have recovered their strength the last days of the week." The eight-hour strike is practically ended, since the Haymarket affair in Chicago.

The desired result was attained. Prices of stocks, bonds, etc., were restored. It was accomplished by the fatal Haymarket bomb.

Who threw the bomb? Who inspired its throwing? John Philip Deluse, a saloon-keeper, living in Indianapolis, Indiana, makes an affidavit, supported by the affidavits of two other men, who were present, and witnessed and heard it (all three men well-known citizens of Indianapolis), that a stranger stepped into his place on Saturday, May 1, with a satchel in his hand, which he placed upon the bar while he ordered a drink. The stranger said he came from New York City, and was on his way to Chicago. He spoke of the labor troubles. Pointing to his satchel he said: "I have got something in here that will work. You will hear of it." Turning at the door as he went out, he held up his satchel and pointing to it again, said, "You will hear of it soon."

The prediction of the man came to pass. It was heard round the world. The description of this man tallies exactly with that given by the witness Burnett, who saw him throw the bomb at the Haymarket.

The leaders, as well as many others, not at the meeting of the Haymarket, were arrested and punished, the others "scared into submission," and it resulted as the New York *Times* said, viz: "This method will undoubtedly strike a wholesome terror into the hearts of the working classes."

The conspiracy to bring about this result originated among the monopolists of New York City, at Pinkerton's headquarters.

Was Police Inspector Bonfield, and States Attorney Grinnell a party to it? Was the millionaire "Citizen's Association" of Chicago a party to it? They have, I understand, supplied unlimited sums of money to bring about our conviction. I solemnly believe all these men were either parties to the Haymarket tragedy, or to the conspiracy for our conviction. This conclusion is irresistible, when taken in connection with the admitted fact that, to bring about our conviction, the constitution and the law has been ruthlessly trampled under foot.

Without fear, or favor, or reward, I have given the untiring energies of the past ten years of my life to ameliorate, to emancipate my fellow wage-slaves from their hereditary servitude to capital. I do not regret it; rather while I feel the satisfaction of duty performed, I regret my inability to have accomplished more than I have done.

During these ten years (from 1876 to 1886) I have traversed the states of Nebraska, Iowa, Kansas, Missouri, Wisconsin, Illinois, Kentucky, Maryland, Ohio, Michigan, Pennsylvania, and New York, sometimes under the auspices and direction of the Knights of Labor, at other times Trades Unions and socialist organizations. Covering this space of time I have addressed probably a half million workingmen and women, and organized, or assisted in organizing many labor organizations. No man can truthfully say I have ever yet betrayed a trust, violated a pledge, or swerved from my conception of duty in the labor movement.

I have worked for my living and supported myself since 12 years of age. I have made some enemies. My enemies in the southern states consisted of those who oppressed the black slave. My enemies in the north are among those who would perpetuate the slavery of the wage workers. My whole life has been sober and industrious; was never under the influence of liquor, was never arrested for any offense, and voluntarily surrendered for trial in the present case.

I married in 1872 and since 1873 have lived in Chicago with my family. In all my labors for the up-lifting and emancipation of the wage-worker I have had the earnest, honest, intelligent, unflagging support of that grandest, noblest, bravest of women—my loving wife. We have two children, a boy of 7 years, and a girl 4 years old.

For free speech and the right of assembly, five labor orators and organizers of labor are condemned to die. For free press and free thought three labor editors are sent to the scaffold. "These eight men," said the attorneys of the monopolists, "are picked up by the grand jury because they are the leaders of thousands who are equally guilty with them and we punish them to make examples of them for the others." This much for opinion's sake, for free thought, free speech, free press and public assembly.

This Haymarket affair has exposed to public view the hideous enormities of capitalism and the barbarous despotism of government. The tragedy and the effects of it have demonstrated first: That government is power, and statute law is license, because it is privilege. It has shown the people, the poor, the wage-slaves, that law, statute law is a privilege, and that privileges are for sale to those who can buy them. Government enacts law; the police, the soldier and the jailor at the behest of the rich enforce it. Law is license, the whole earth and all it contains has been sold to a few who are thus authorized by statute law, licensed to rob the many of their natural inheritance. Law is license. The few are licensed by law to own the land, the machinery, the houses, food, clothes and shelter of the people, whose industry, whose labor created them. Law is license; law, statute law, is the coward's weapon, the tool of the thief. By it humanity has ever been degraded and enslaved. By law mankind is robbed of its birthright, liberty transformed into slavery; life into death; the fair earth into a den of thieves and murderers. The untold millions, the men, women and children of toil, the *proletariat,* are by law deprived of their lives, their liberties and their happiness. Law is license; Government—authority—is despotism.

Anarchy, natural law, is liberty. Liberty is the natural right to do what one pleases, bounded and limited only by the equal right of every one else to the same liberty. Privileges are none; equal rights for all. Liberty, Fraternity, Equality.

The trial throughout was a travesty on justice. Every law, natural and statute, was violated in response to the clamor of the capitalist class. Every capitalist newspaper in the city, with one exception, called for our blood before the trial began, demanded our lives during the trial and since. A class jury, class law, class hate, and a court blinded by prejudice against our opinions, has done its work, we are its victims. Every juryman swore he was prejudiced against our opinions; we were tried for our opinions and convicted because of them. The jury according to its own statements since the verdict (they served nearly two months) entertained themselves each night with either card playing or they played the fiddle, the guitar, the piano, and "sang songs" and gave parlor recitations and theatricals. They had carriage rides at the expense of the people amounting to one hundred and forty dollars; and their board bill was $3.50 per day at a fashionable hotel amounting to over $2,300; they had a fine time, a very pleasant and merry time. Mr. Juryman Todd said he was a "clothing salesman and a Baptist." "Then," said he, "this was a picked jury, *they were all gentlemen.*" Of course, these gentlemen, who have a profound contempt for the vulgar, dirty working classes had to bring a verdict befitting gentlemen. So highly appreciated was their verdict that Chicago millionaires proposed and so far as any one knows did contribute a purse of ($100,000) one hundred thousand dollars to this jury as a reward for their verdict. The jury has besides been lionized, wined, dined, banqueted, and given costly presents, and sums of money, since the rendering of their verdict.

The influences which are at work forcing upon the people the social revolution arise out of the capitalist system. Necessity is the mother of invention; it is also the father of progress and civilization. The justification for the social revolution is recorded throughout all the pages of history. Our fathers proclaimed it in the immortal Declaration, July 4th, 1776, as follows:

> We hold these truths to be self-evident: That all men are created equal; that they were endowed by their creator with certain inalienable rights; that among these are life, liberty and the pursuit of happiness; that to secure these rights governments are instituted among men, deriving their just powers from the consent of the governed; that whenever any form of government becomes destructive of these ends, it is THE RIGHT OF THE PEOPLE TO ALTER OR ABOLISH IT.

Will the coming revolution be peaceable or violent?

But now, when the workingmen of American refuse to "give their consent to be any longer governed" by the profit mongers, labor exploiters, children slayers and home despoilers, they are at once put down, and kept down by the strong arm of military power, against their will and without "their consent," in the name of "law and order."

It is against this barbaric use of force, this violation of every natural right that Anarchists protest, and for protesting, die!

The only fact established by proof, as well as by our own admission, cheerfully given before the jury, was that we held opinions and preached a doctrine that is considered dangerous to the rascality and infamies of the privileged, law-creating class known as monopolists, to whom, with the prophets of old, we say:

> Go to, now, ye rich men, weep and howl for your miseries that shall come upon you. Your riches are corrupted and your garments are moth-eaten. Your gold and silver is cankered; and the rust of them shall be a witness against you; and shall eat your flesh as it were fire. Ye have heaped treasures together for the last days.—James V., 1–3

4

Autobiography of August Spies

"Barbarians, savages, illiterate, ignorant Anarchists from Central Europe, men who cannot comprehend the spirit of our free American institutions,"—of these I am one. My name is August Vincent Theodore Spies, (pronounced Spees). I was born within the ruins of the old robbers castle Landeck, upon a high mountain's peak (Landeckerberg), Central Germany, in 1855. My father was a forester (a government administrator of a forest district); the forest house was a government building, and served—only in a different form—the same purposes the old castle had served several centuries before. The noble Knight-hood of Highway robbery, the traces of which were still discernable to the remnants of the old castle, had passed away to make room for more genteel and less dangerous forms of plunder and robbery, as carried on in the modern dwelling under the present government. But while the people from old custom designate this and similar old ruins in the vicinity as "old Robber Castles," they speak with great deference of the present government buildings, in which they themselves are daily and hourly fleeced; they would even, I believe, fight for the maintenance of these *lawful* institutions.

How greatly these "Barbarians" differ from the intelligent American people! Tell the Americans to fight for the maintenance of our commercial robbing posts and fleecing institutions—tell them to fight for the protection of the *lawful* enterprises of our Board of Trade men; Merchant princes, Railroad kings, and Factory lords—would they do it? Alas, more rapidly, I fear, than those "Barbarians from Central Europe, who cannot comprehend the spirit of our free American institutions."

Viewed from a historic standpoint my birthplace is quite an interesting spot. And this is the only excuse I can offer for my selection of the place for said purpose. I admit I ought not have made the mistake, ought not have been born a *foreigner,* but little children, particularly unborn children, will make mistakes! However, I find no fault with such wise and intelligent men as Mr. Grinnell and *His* jury, for hanging men who were injudicious in the selection of their birthplace. Sins of this character deserve severe punishment; "society must protect itself against offenses of this kind."

But speaking of castle Landeck. Follow me there, reader, on a bright and clear day. We make our way up the old tower. Take care, or you will stumble over the debris. That? Oh, that is a piece of an old torture rack; we found it in one of the subterranean walks, together with several pieces of old ugly weapons, once used to maintain *order* among the victims. . . . but why do you shudder? The policeman's outfit of to-day is not quite so blunt and barbaric, it is true, but it is as effective and serves the same purpose. . . . So, now, take my hand, I'll help you on top of the ruin.

Look out for the bats. These winged lovers of darkness have great resemblance with kings, priests and masters in general; they dwell in the ruins of the "good old times," and become quite noisy when you disturb them or expose them to the light; adders, too, made this place their favorable habitation in former years and rendered it very dangerous for any one to place his sacrilegious foot upon this feudal monument; we killed them. They were the companions of the bats and owls; their fate has given the latter much uneasiness, and tears were entertained that something terrible would happen—that the ghosts of the old 'noble knights' and 'noble dames' would come back and avenge the ruthless annihilation of the venerable reptiles, but nothing of the kind has transpired, I need hardly add that the work of renovation was greatly impeded by these venomous creatures; since their extermination we have made remarkable progress. . . . You smile! Oh, no, I am not speaking of those other reptiles you seem to think of. But here, we have reached the top. Great view, is it not! Over there, about thirty minutes walk from here, (west) you see another ruin like this; that is castle Dreieck, and over there an equal distance (southwest) you see another one, Wildeck. And now look down in the fertile valleys, the beautiful meadows and fields and flourishing villages! Of the latter you can count a dozen, all located around this mount; and do you know that all these villages and others which have been laid waste during the thirty years war[27] were tributary to the robbers who ruled over them in these three castles? Yes, the people in these villages worked all their lives from early dawn till late at night to fill the vaults of those noble knights, who in return had the kindness to maintain *'peace and order'* for them. Par example: If one of these toiling peasants expressed his dissatisfaction of the existing order of things, if he complained of the heavy and unbearable tasks placed upon him, 'law and order' demanded that he be placed upon one of those racks you have seen a relic of, to be tortured into obedience and submission. 'Society had to protect itself against this class of criminals.' The noble knights had their Grinnells, Bonfields and Pinkertons[28] as well as their descendants have them today; and while they were less civilized than their descendants of our time, they got along wonderfully well. To accomplish their beneficent objects, they did not even require the assistance of a Chicago jury.

Many of the peasants were put to an ignominious death. Some of them would persist in their folly that it could not be the object of society nor the intention of Providence to have a thousand good people kill themselves in a laborious life for the glory, enrichment and grandeur of a few ungrateful, vicious wretches. Such dangerous teachings were a menace to society, and their promulgators were unceremoniously stamped out.

Not more than 200 feet from where we stand there is a perpendicular (chasm) hole of volcanic origin; it is about 8 feet in length and 3 in breadth; its depth has never been ascertained. The saying goes that scores of girls were cast into this terrible abyss by the valiant Knights during their reign of peace and good order! It is said that these benevolent "respectables" of ancient times kidnapped the pretty girls of the villages, carried them like birds of prey to their lofty abodes, and then when they got tired of them, or found "something better," disposed of them in this way. . . .

Oh, I see, you shake your heads incredulously! Have you never seen the dumping grounds of the modern knighthood in our large cities—a similar abyss? No? It is more frightful than the one I have told you about; its name is prostitution. . . . . . .

You don't believe the people would have borne all these outrages—? My friend, your rebellious spirit carries you away. The "orderly and good people" suffered these atrocities just as silently as our "law and order abiding workingmen" bear them today. I told you what happened to those who showed resistance!

My words make you sad, turn you pessimistic? Let me show you something else. Look through these two mounts; can you see a tower in the dim distance—yes? At the side of this tower are yet to be seen the ruins of the first chapel built in the realms of the old heathen, but free and liberty-loving Germans. It was founded by one of the apostles of St. Boniface, in the eighth century; his name was Lullus. With this chapel and others that soon followed the poison of Oriental servilism, the gospel of man's degradation, resignation and asceticism was first introduced. The old *Cherutker* and *Katten,* who had in mortal combat thrust the Roman eagle to the ground, were less successful in resisting the mind infecting poison of pestilential Rome; it came flowing in incessantly through the channels of the Christian church. It is true, the healthy and robust Germans were not an easy prey to the pessimistic belief of a debauched and dying race—(Rome) they never have been good Christians—but they became sufficiently infected to lose their consciousness and pride of manhood for a while, to fall into the despairing vagaries of the Orient, and as a natural consequence into serfdom. If life had no value, why then aspire to liberty . . . ? Friend, the ruins of yonder chapel is the monument of an epoch that gave birth to such robberburgs as the one we stand upon. The people would have razed these roosts to the ground long before they did, if the priest had not stood between them and "Law and Order." The priest is an essential indivisible part of the despot and oppressor; he is the conciliatory link between them and their victims. . . .

These two ruins, once sacred as the pedestals of social order, are prophetic monuments. Man will so stand upon the ruins of the present order and will say as you say now—"was it possible. . . . . !"

But now turn around—along this mountain chain, northeast, there, where the earth dips mistily into the horizon, the periphery of our view—do you see yonder gray spot, it looks like a small cloud? Yes? That's the Wartburg, you have heard of Wartburg. It was here, where Dr. Martinus Luther lived and worked, an instrument of the revolutionary forces; the revolutionary forces, my friend, that gradually had developed in these villages.[29]

It is our custom to attribute great movements to single individuals, as being their merit. This is always wrong and it was so with Luther. The Germanic race could not digest the Byzantinian philosophy as embodied in the Judaic and Christian teachings. The idea that this world was calculated to be simply a purgatory and our life a martyrdom was repulsive to them, was that servitude and despotism were growing from the seed of the new religion and developing, where once had been the habitation of liberty; developing at such a rate, that patience ceased to be a virtue. The rebellious spirit of the people, their animosity to the doctrine of self-abnegation, imposed upon them by the church, had been successfully calmed and suppressed by the priests for several centuries. But as the iniquities of the "nobility," and the domestic burdens of the people grew unbearable this spirit burst out in flames, and in Luther found a crystallization point.

From the Wartburg then the mighty wave of the reformation rolled forth. It was the Occident struggling in self-preservation against the Orient. The love of liberty which had been lying spellbound in the people's heart for generations, now flowed out in lucid streams; the magic spell was broken. . . . . . But the "nobility," while they wanted liberation from the despotism of the Roman Church, they liked the privileges the latter had given them; the patent to rob the peasants of their labor too well—they scorned the idea of the common people aspiring to economic freedom. Was not "spiritual liberty," a change of certain religious notions, enough for any common man? Luther soon became the tool of these cheating knaves, and wielded his pen in condemnation of the objects contended for by the people. He denounced the true and brave leaders of the people, the fearless Thomas Muenzer and his associates, worse than the Pope had denounced him shortly before.

And when the liberty-thirsty people finally took up their scythes and axes and forks, and drove the "noble Knights" from their robbers' roosts, it was Luther who brought about a vast conspiracy of the latter against the people.[30] It is characteristic that now all religious differences were set aside and all petty tyrants combined to subdue the people. Papist or Lutheran, all were instantly united in the crusade against labor. (America at this time presents an analogous spectacle: Republicans and Democrats "embrace each other as Nectar and Ambrosia," wherever labor rises for emancipation.)

Of course, the people were conspirators and incendiaries. Hear what Thomas Muenzer said: "Look you, the sediment of the soup of usury, theft and robbery are the Great, the masters, they take all creatures as their property, the fish in the water, the birds in the air; and the vegetation of the earth. And then they preach God's commandment to the poor; 'Thou shall not steal.' But this is not for themselves. They bone and scrape the poor farmer and mechanic until these have nothing left, then, when the latter put their hands on the sacred things, they are hanged. And

Doctor Liar says, Amen! The masters do it themselves, that the poor man hates them. The cause of the rebellion they won't abolish, how then can things change to the better. And I say this, I am an incendiary—let it be so!" No, these words were not spoken in Judge Gary's court! You make a mistake, reader, the language is not modern, it's 400 years old. . . . . . And the man who used it was in the right. He interpreted the Gospel, saying that it did not merely promise blessings in heaven, but that it also commanded the equality and brotherhood among men on earth. The champions of law and order and Christendom chopped his head off.

The rebels were victorious at first, but against the united vassals of their oppressors they could not stand. At the foot of this mount they were defeated, down there, where you see that big rock, surrounded by magnificent oaks, the battle for freedom was fought and, alas, lost. No, it was not lost, it was merely interceded by a temporary victory of the enemy.

The spirit of the Reformation was the "eternal spirit of the chainless mind," and nothing could stay its progress. Gibbets, stakes, tortures, and dungeons were of no avail. On the contrary, the blood of the martyrs only intensified the flame of liberty, until it sprang from land to land, kindling everywhere the discontent of the oppressed in its irresistible triumphant course.

These ruins still bear evidence of its tremendous force! The most momentous thing accomplished by this rebellious and lawless spirit, however, was the openings of the *new world*. The reformation gave birth to the young giant, America; it gave England a Cromwell and France a Richelieu.[31] Its fermenting force drove the Huguenots from France and the Puritans from England. But for the reformation and the persecution of its adherents, these early settlers of the western hemisphere would have remained in France and England as good and law-abiding citizens. As dangerous elements, society had to protect itself against them, and they fled over the Atlantic rather than to suffer martyrdom at home for their "advanced ideas."

The reformation, my friend, which started right here, in the country where four centuries later the "Barbarian Anarchists" came from, "who cannot comprehend the spirit of American institutions," etc. . . . . . . broke down the feudal barriers, which impeded human progress. It was asserted in a thirty year's war, that laid the continent desolate, that the exercise of free thought and opinion as well as scientific investigation should no longer be suppressed because they conflicted with religious superstition and dogma generally believed in and sanctified by custom. The "good and law-abiding" people were fanatically opposed to those in favor of that imperative change, and oceans of blood had to be shed in consequence. The ruins you see here wherever you turn your eyes bear witness of the terrible war that is not yet ended—the war for human emancipation and freedom, economic, political and religious. Every one of these ruins is a milestone on the path of social progress. At our feet lies the historic *chausee,* upon which Napoleon's victorious armies, much against the intention of their *grand empereur,* carried the seed of "Liberty, Equality, Fraternity" to the far east, and there opened a new perspective to the purblind eyes of the oppressed and down-trodden millions of our race. Aye, even now that seed is bringing forth good fruit. Russian dungeons, gibbets and Siberia bear witness.

Now, friend, before we retire from this retrospective view, look once more into the mirror of the past 1,000 years, observe closely the traces that lead from yonder chapel to this castle, from this castle to the Wartburg, from the Wartburg to the battlefield below here and to their ruins, and then follow them to England, France and America, follow them up to this day and then tell me, if you do not see the contours of the *future* reflected. . . . . You do! . . . . .

I have dwelled at great length in describing my (barbarian) birth place, but in so doing I have traversed in a general way over the history of 1,000 years. The present status of society is but the result of the struggle of human kind during this and preceding periods—yes, struggle! "You cannot reform the world by the sprinkling of rose oil," said Mirabeau,[32] and history proves the correctness of this statement. In no age did the rulers and despoilers of our race relinquish their hold upon the throat of their victims, until forced so—by logic and argument? No. . . . . . Blood, the precious sap was ever the price of liberty.

My years of childhood were pleasant. I played and studied. How different from the childhood of the offsprings of the average workingman in this "glorious, civilized and—according to Grinnell—enlightened country." The children of the *proletaire* have no youth; the spring of life has no sunshine, no blossoms, no flowers for them! If there is a discernible object in their existence it is that of *serving* to make life happy and pleasant for those who tread upon them. In my native land children *must* attend school daily from the age of 6 to that of 14; every child in that "Barbarian country" is thus compelled to attend school for 8 years, and cannot therefore be "utilized and made to pay" by either their parents or factory lords. In this enlightened country the children of the wage-workers do not attend school in the average more than two years; they learn just enough to serve as a piece of organic machinery, and as such they are "let out" to benevolent and Christian employers in their tenderest years.[33] Their vitality, which is needed for their own bodily and intellectual development, is in such wise tapped from the innocents and turned into gold for our "law and order" loving, respectable citizens. They die from consumption before they attain their maturity, or resort to whiskey, thinking thereby to restore their lost vigor. If they escape early destruction, their career is generally terminated in one of those charitable or reformatory institutes known as the insane asylum, the penitentiary, or poorhouse.

But woe to the wretch who condemns this order of things! He is an "enemy of civilization," and "society must protect itself against such criminals.". . . . There comes the star-spangled Mephisto, Bonfield, with his noble guards of "Liberty;" there comes the savior of the state, Grinnell, with the visage of a Sicilian brigand, there comes the hireling juror, and there comes the vast horde of social vultures. *Unisono* is the anathema. *Unisono* is the cry—"To the gallows!"

"Society" is saved, and "Liberty and order"—of the policeman's club—triumph! *Selah!*

I do not intend to say that the condition of the wage-workers in Germany is better than in this country, but I will say that I never saw such real suffering from want as I have seen in this country. And there is more protection for women and children in Germany than here.

(I was educated for a career in the government service forest branch.) As a child I had private tutors, and later visited the *Polytechnicum* in Cassel. At the age of seventeen my father died suddenly, leaving a large family in moderate circumstances. As I was the eldest one I did not feel justified in continuing my studies—they were expensive—and concluded to go to America, where I had and have now a number of well-to-do relatives. I arrived in New York in 1872 and upon the advice of my friends I learned the furniture business. The following year I came to Chicago, where I have resided ever since; though I may add that I have been away from the city occasionally for some time. Once, with the intention of settling in the country, I worked on a farm for a year. But seeing that the small farmers and renters were in a worse plight even than the city wage-workers, and that they were equally dependent, I returned to the city. I have also traveled over the Southern States to get acquainted with the country and people, and at another time, I joined an exploring expedition through Upper Canada, which failed.

When I arrived in this country I knew nothing of Socialism, except what I had seen in the newspapers, the "public teachers" (?), and from what I'd read I concluded that the Socialists were a lot of ignorant and lazy vagabonds "who wanted to divide up everything." Having come but very little in contact with people who earned their living by honest labor in the old country, I was amazed and was shocked when I became acquainted with the condition of the wage-workers in the new world.

The factory, the ignominious regulations, the surveillance, the spy system, the servility and lack of manhood among the workers and the arrogant arbitrary behavior of the boss and his associates—all this made an impression upon me that I have never been able to divest myself of. At first I could not understand why the workers, among them many old men with bent backs, silently and without a sign of protest bore every insult the caprice of the foreman or boss would heap upon them. I was not then aware of the fact that the opportunity to work was a privilege, a favor, and that it was in the power of those who were in the possession of the factories and instruments of labor to deny or grant this privilege. I did not then understand how difficult it was to find a purchaser for one's labor. I did not know then that there were thousands and thousands of idle human bodies in the market, ready to hire out upon most any conditions, actually begging for employment, I became conscious of this very soon, however, and I knew then why these people were so servile, why they suffered the humiliating dictates and capricious whims of their employers. Personally I had no great difficulty in "getting along." I had so many advantages over my co-workers. I would most likely have succeeded in becoming a respectable business man myself, if I had been possessed of that unscrupulous egotism which characterizes the successful business man, and if my aspirations had been that of the avaricious Hamster (the latter belongs to the family of rats, and his "pursuit in life" is to steal and accumulate; in some of their depositories the contents of whole granaries have often been found; their greatest delight seems to be possession, for they steal a great deal more than they can consume; in fact they steal, like most of our respectable citizens, regardless of their capacity of consumption). My philosophy has always been that the object of life can only consist in the enjoyment of life, and that the rational application of this principle is true morality.

I held that asceticism, as taught by the Church, was a crime against nature.

Now observing that the vast mass of the people were wasting their lives in drudgery, accompanied with want and misery, it was but natural for me to inquire into the causes. (I had up to that time never read a book, or even an impartial essay on Modern Socialism). Was this self-abnegation, this self-crucifixion of the people voluntary, or was it forced upon them, and if so, by whom?

About this time, while looking over my books in search of something, my attention was attracted by this passage from Aristotle:[34] "When, at some future age, every tool upon command, or by predestination, will perform its work as the art works of Daedalus did, who moved by themselves, or like the three feet of Hephaestos, who went to their sacred work spontaneously, when thus the weaver shuttles will weave by themselves, then we will no longer require masters and slaves."

Had this time, long ago anticipated by the great thinker, not come? Yes, it had. There were the machines. But master and slave still existed. The question arose in my mind, is their existence still necessary?

Antiporas, a Greek poet, who lived at the time of Cicero, had in a like manner greeted the invention of the water-mill (water power) as the emancipator of male and female slaves. "Oh, these heathens!" writes Karl Marx, after quoting the above; "they knew nothing of Political Economy and Christendom! They failed to conceive how nicely the machines could be employed to lengthen the hours of toil and to intensify the burdens of the slaves. They (the heathens) excused the slavery of *one* on the ground that it would afford the opportunity of human development to *another.* But to preach the slavery of the masses in order that a few rude and arrogant *parvenus* might become 'eminent spinners,' 'extensive sausage makers' and 'influential shoe black dealers'—to do this they lacked the specific Christian organ."[35]

I think it was in 1875, at the time the "Workingmen's Party of Illinois," was organized, when, upon the invitation of a friend, I visited the first meeting in which a lecture on Socialism was delivered. If viewed from a theoretical standpoint this lecture, delivered by a young mechanic, was not very impressive, but the substance. . . . . I will simply say that this lecture gave me the *passepartout* to the many interrogation marks which had worried me for a number of years.

I procured every piece of literature I could get on the subject; whether it was adverse or friendly to Socialism made no difference. In the beginning I was a visionary, an enthusiast. I believed as so many righteous people do today that the truth only required to be expressed, the argument only to be made to enlist every good man and woman in the good cause of humanity. In my youthful enthusiasm I forgot to apply the experience of historical progress to this particular case. But to my great sorrow I soon became convinced that the bulk of humanity were automatons, incapable of thinking and reasoning, altogether unconscious of themselves, simply tools of custom—

> For from the sordid is man made,
> Usage and custom he doth call his nurse.
>
> —*Goethe.*[36]

But nothing could discourage me. The study of French, German and English economists and social scientists soon made me view things differently than I had seen them in my first enthusiasm. Buckle's "History of Civilization," Karl Marx' "Kapital," and Morgan's "Ancient Society"[37] have probably had the greatest influence over me of any—I now became an attentive observer of the various social phenomena myself. The last ten years have been very favorable for such investigation as I sought. I found my favorite teachers corroborated everywhere.

I think it was in 1877 when I first became a member of the Socialistic Labor Party. The events of that year, the brute force with which the whining and confiding wage slaves were met on all sides impressed upon me the necessity of *like* resistance. The latter required organization. Shortly afterwards I joined the "Lehr und Wehr Verein," an armed organization of the workingmen, numbering about 1,500 well-drilled members. As soon as our patricians saw that the *canaille* were arming for defence to repel such scandalous attacks in the future as had been made upon them in 1877, they at once commanded their law agents in Springfield to prohibit workingmen from bearing arms. The command was obeyed.

The workingmen also went into politics, independent politics. I served as a nominal candidate myself several times, but when the noble patricians and the political *augurs* saw that they were successful in electing a number of their candidates, a conspiracy was organized to disfranchise them by fraudulent count and like methods. The workingmen thereupon left the ballot with disgust.

Although I have myself in past years advocated political action, I have never for an instant believed that thereby the social evils would be abolished or even that reforms, benefiting the workingmen, could thus be brought about,—I viewed "political action," simply and solely as a good means of propaganda. Believing, as I do, that the economic body, is the organism of society, the substructure of all social, political, and moral institutions and operations, I cannot but repel the idea that the foundation of society could be changed by alterations of it, or by a structure that rests upon it, and would tumble down the very minute the foundation was touched.

The economic emancipation in my opinion can be achieved through an economic struggle only, not through politics—although the latter may be one of the many forces of organization, necessary in the development of things to bring the final struggle to a focus. Indeed it looks so at the present time.

To enter into this question more thoroughly in a mere autobiography would lead us too far. But if your readers should desire to hear my views upon this subject, I shall gladly furnish you a special contribution.

As stated before, since my arrival in New York (1872 until 1879) I was engaged in the furniture business (upholstery). Being of a very independent disposition, I began to work for myself in 1876 by opening a small shop. In the same year my mother, three little brothers and one sister emigrated to this city, with whom I have lived ever since, and who were for some years dependent upon me. Nothing very eventful occurred during these years.

In the spring of 1880 the *Arbeiter Zeitung*, the German workingmen's organ, a paper which had been started in 1872 as a weekly, and which had since grown into an influential daily, was on the verge of bankruptcy. Mismanagement was the cause of it. I was called upon by the society to take the management, and shortly after was elected superintendent, and still later editor. The paper was saved, and has at this writing the largest circulation of any German paper in this city. The German workingmen are justly proud of their organ; it belongs to them as a class, and no one has a private interest in it. I hope our English-speaking friends may soon follow this example. An English daily workingmen's paper, owned and controlled by the workingmen is surely needed here.

The politicians tried to befriend themselves with me; looking for the support of the *Arbeiter Zeitung*. And when they failed as they always did, they began to hate me. The worst thing they could say against me was—"he is a fanatic." So demoralized and degraded have the champions of "free government" (for them!) become that in their judgment a man that is not in the market, who is not for sale, must necessarily be a fanatic!

One of the members of the grand jury which indicted us has issued a *pronunciamento* to the effect that we were mercenaries, who made money out of the labor agitation, was Banker E.S. Dreyer.[38] This same man was treasurer of the Democratic campaign committee during the last presidential campaign, during which said committee offered me $10,000 if I would agree to say nothing damaging of Cleveland. He certainly must have known this; and he must have also known that I morally "bounced" the man who made the offer (he happened to be a friend of mine) out of the office. This same man, Dreyer, about three years ago had sold a piece of property to the School Board for $32,000. The property was located on the corner of Cass and Illinois streets. The common council was about to ratify the bargain when I learned that the same lots had shortly before been offered for sale for—I think—$16,000. I made all the noise I could, an investigation proved the attempted "boodler," and the "job" was spoiled.

When I consider that such men as he have indicted and convicted me and my comrades for murder; when I consider that these are the men who raise the cry that we are "dangerous to society," I am reminded of the old dodge, "stop the thief!" But it is sad to reflect that the good people are so easily being led astray.

Among those whose wrath I have brought upon me are our governors, the good police. For years I have exposed their blackmailing practices, their brutalities and general "pursuits." If their deeds and behavior could not bear the light, it was not my fault! When about eleven and a half years ago I had the desk sergeant of the West Chicago Avenue station arrested for brutally outraging a young girl while in the station, and nearly killing her (Martha Seidel), the star-spangled libertines of the city swore dire vengeance. They have got it now, they think.

That I have made myself generally obnoxious to the extortionists and fleecers during my management of the *Ar-*

beiter Zeitung—this I need hardly add. To conclude with: I am proud of the enemies, and no less of the friends I have made.

I have been a member of the "Ameri-Kanische Turner Bund" for a long number of years.[39] Two years ago I was elected a delegate to the national convention of this powerful organization, and succeeded in having a socialistic plank inserted in the platform.

I was also a member of the Knights of Labor once—about three years ago—but the Assembly to which I belonged dissolved, and I never since have renewed my membership, principally, because I never liked secrecy or ceremonies in an organization.[40] But I have frequently lectured in meetings of "Knights," when invited.

As an oral agitator among the wage-workers, I have been very active. I was a delegate to the congress of the Revolutionary Socialists, held in this city, in 1881, and also a delegate to the congress of the International Working People's Association, held in Pittsburgh, in 1883.

I have addressed meetings in most of the industrial cities in the states. During the strike in the Hocking Valley[41] I visited that locality and spoke to enthusiastic meetings, notwithstanding the good Pinkertons who threatened to kill me and who attended the meetings with Winchester rifles.

My connection with the meeting on the Haymarket, on May 4th, 1886, did not go beyond that of an invited speaker. I had been invited to address the meeting in German, but no English speakers being present I spoke in English. The meeting had been called by the representatives of a number of Trades Unions. Those present were workingmen of all beliefs and views; they were not Anarchists, nor were the speeches anarchistic, they treated on the eight-hour question. Anarchism was not even referred to by anyone.

But Anarchism was good enough to serve as a scape-goat for Bonfield. This fiend, in order to justify his murderous attack upon that meeting, said "they were Anarchists." "Anarchists! Oh, horror!" The stupid mass imagined that "Anarchists" must be something very bad, and they joined in the chorus with their enemies and fleecers: "Crucify! Crucify!"

"Tis easy to astonish or appal
The vulgar mass which molds a horde of slaves."

All the pertaining to this matter may be found in my speech before my hangman Gary and his worthy assistants.[42]

In the cause of humanity and light,

Yours,

A. Spies.

5

Autobiography of Adolph Fischer

On the banks of the Weser, in Germany, almost seven miles above the place where its waters lose themselves in the North Sea, lies the old city, Bremen. In the middle ages Bremen was one of the free cities which formed the Hanseatic Union,[43] a combination famous because of its constant war against the free-booters and for its wealth and power. These cities monopolized the trade of the world in those days. Bremen is still one of the most important commercial centers of the European continent, and has today a population of about 140,000. This is the place of my birth. It would be of very little interest to the readers of this journal were I to extensively describe the history of my childhood. It is the same as that of the average child. Therefore I may only state that I attended school eight years and a half and that I sailed for the United States when a lad of fifteen. Soon after my arrival on these shores, I entered apprenticeship as compositor in the printing office of my brother, William B. Fischer, at Little Rock, Ark., at which place he published a weekly German journal. Since the termination of my apprenticeship I have been working at my trade in different cities of this country. In the month of June, 1883, destiny landed me in Chicago, where I have resided with my family hitherto, occupying a situation as compositor in the office of the *Arbeiter Zeitung* until arrested on the 5th of May for alleged participation in the Haymarket affair. I am a member of the German Typographical Union, which organization I joined in 1879 in St. Louis, Mo. At the latter place in 1881, I also entered into matrimonial engagement, the result being three children—one girl and two boys—who are with my wife in this city.

Being familiar with the doctrines of socialism from my earliest youth, I have held it my duty to spread these principles so dear to me whenever and wherever I could. What induced me to become a socialist, you may ask? This I will relate in a few words:

It happened during the last year of my school days that our tutor of historical science one day chanced to refer to socialism, which movement was at that time beginning to flourish in Germany, and which he told us meant "division of property." I am inclined to believe now that it was a general instruction given by the government to the patriotic pedagogues to periodically describe to their elder pupils socialism as a most horrible thing. It is, as is well known, a customary policy on the part of the respective monarchial governments of the old world to prejudice the undeveloped minds of the youth against everything which is disagreeable to the despots through the medium of the school teachers. For instance, I remember quite distinctly that before the outbreak and during the Franco-German war[44] we were made to believe by our teachers that every Frenchman was at least a scoundrel, if not a criminal. On the other hand, the kings were praised as the representative of God, and obedience and loyalty to them was described as the highest virtues.

Thus the minds of the children are systematically poisoned, and the fruits of this practice are made use of when the little ones become men and women. (Enough at the mentioned occasion our teachers told us that the socialists were a lot of drunkards, swindlers and idlers, who were opposed to work.) "The time draws nigh," that worthy said, placing his forefinger significantly alongside of his roman nose, "when you young men will have to earn your daily bread in the sweat of your brow. Some of you may acquire wealth, while others will be less fortunate. Now, these socialists—mark you, who are a lazy set of people—intend to forcibly make you divide with them everything you possess at the termination of every year. For instance, if you should call two pairs of boots your own, one of these socialistic scoundrels will kindly relieve you of one pair. How would you like this?" Certainly, we thought we did not like this at all. Neither would I consent to anything of that sort to-day. Most decidedly not. Such an arrangement, I fancied, would be absurd.

Now I knew it to be a fact that my father took part in socialistic meetings very frequently, and I wondered that day why he—whom I thought to be so good—should have intercourse with such a bad class of men, whose object it was to lead a lazy life and to make the sober, industrious working people, at the termination of each year, divide their earnings with them. When I reached home that day I intimated to my father what (according to what my teacher had told us) bad people the socialists must be. Much to my surprise my dear father laughed aloud and embraced me very affectionately. "Dear Adolph," he said, "if socialism is what your teacher explained it to be, why then the very same institutions which prevail now would be socialistic."

And my father went on to show me how, in fact, there were so many idlers and indolent people under the now existing form of society, who were residing in palatial houses and living luxuriously at the expense of the sober and industrious working people, and that socialism had the mission to abolish such unjust division. After this day I accompanied my father to socialistic gatherings, and soon became convinced of the truth of what he had said. I began to study. Wandering about the streets I often saw groups of hard-fisted men who were working in quarries and other places of toil, and handling heavy picks and clumsy shovels from early morning until late at night. Standing a little aside I would notice an elegantly dressed individual, smoking a Havana, and seemingly interested in the work of the toilers. The hands of the idler were covered with kid gloves, in the bosom of his snow-white shirt glittered a diamond pin, and from his vest dangled a valuable gold watch chain. You can guess, dear reader, who this gentleman was—the "employer." The busy toilers, notwithstanding the many hours of strained work, could scarcely earn enough to keep themselves and family from want. I saw they inhabited miserable hovels, and the pleasures and comforts of life were unknown to them. Their children were hollow-eyed and resembled fenceposts—covered with human skin more than human beings.

Following, on one occasion, the fine gentleman whom I had seen standing idly by, and who had commanded the workingmen, I saw him enter a wonderfully beautiful house—a palace. Costly pictures decorated the massive walls of its parlors, precious carpets covered the floors and golden chandeliers were suspended from the ceilings. The safes and pantries were bursting with its tempting contents, and the tables covered with choice wines and delicacies. In short, everything good and agreeable could be enjoyed here in abundance. This contrast between the busy toiler and the idle bystander did not fail to impress itself upon my mind, especially as I observed that these conditions existed everywhere and in all branches of industry. I perceived that the diligent, never resting human working bees, who create all wealth and fill the magazines with provisions, fuel and clothing, enjoy only a minor part of their products and lead a comparatively miserable life, whilst the drones, the idlers, keep the ware-houses locked up and revel in luxury and voluptuousness.

Was I wrong, or was the world wrong? I saw men who manufactured shoes and boots and had helped fill the store-houses with these products ever since their boyhood, and yet they lingered to leave their shanties after rainy weather for fear of getting wet feet, and in many cases the toes of their children's feet peeped speakingly out of the top of the shabby shoes. Bricklayers were busy building houses from sunrise until sunset for several decades, yet as I looked about me, I discovered but very few who called a house their own; they were bound to pay rent for the very same houses which they had built. The clothing stores I knew to be crammed with goods, but it was not a rare spectacle in my native city to see tailors walk about in the streets with pants patched to such an extent, that they resembled chess-boards. Whilst the journey bakers were half-roasting in the hot bake-house, sixteen out of twenty-four hours a day, their wives in many instances did not know where to get a loaf of bread. My father's neighbor worked in a butcher shop, but his wages were so low that his family could afford the luxury of one pound of meat only once a week—on Sunday. All these circumstances convinced me that "there must be something rotten in the state of Denmark," and it did not even require a profound thinker or a sorcerer to discover that the prevailing social institutions were based upon the extortion of one class by another.

But now, after I had come to this conclusion I wondered whether the workingmen were conscious of their real situation. I found that the overwhelming majority were not. Instead of hating those who enslaved them, they looked upon their masters as their benefactors. Many incidents which I observed proved this to be a fact. For instance, I remember visiting a cousin of mine one Sunday, who worked in a gigantic sugar refinery together with thousands of other men and women, the owner of said factory being a well-known millionaire. My cousin could not help at every occasion to speak in high terms of praise of his "benefactor," as he styled his employer. On this day especially he endeavored to make the generosity of his "benefactor" plausible to me. "Why," my enthusiastic cousin explained, clapping his hands, "besides employing so many people, who would otherwise be compelled to starve, he donates annually an enormous sum of money to charitable purposes, and, furthermore, he was so noble-hearted as to give employment to the widow and children of the two unfortunate working men who lost their lives last month by being crushed by the machinery." But ungrateful as I was I saw nothing noble in this. I had read in novels (secretly, my father having forbidden me such literature) that Schinderhannes (a noted German "outlaw"), and other famous highwaymen, had given part of their booty to the poor, and therefore I saw nothing extraordinary in the "charity" of my cousin's "benefactor." I not only thought so, but I also communicated my thoughts to my esteemed relative, who in return got very angry because of this comparison, and muttered something which sounded like "that lad is getting too smart."

This is only one example. Thus I found the brains of the

toilers to be molded everywhere. Oh, these stupid fools! They were slaves without knowing it. They stood still like innocent sheep while their masters sheared them. Aye, more than that, they looked upon them as their noble benefactors, who employed them for the reason of saving them from starvation.

Years have elapsed since the time of my first inquiries into the causes of social inequalities. I have traveled comparatively a good deal, and have come in contact with people of all classes, and was enabled to study and learn. The whole of life is but a school. That which is commonly called a school is merely an introduction into this practical school of life. A good many of the toilers, like myself, have profited by the lessons of the serious school of experience, they are beginning to discover the real causes of the diseases of society. The reigning classes do not like this a bit. The capitalists and profit-mongers are dependent on social diseases for their harvest. Without them they would be what physicians are without physical diseases. This being the case, they try to prevent the toilers, their slaves, to awake from their mental torpor. And what means do the human drones employ to accomplish their schemes, in other words, to keep the wage-slaves in ignorance?

Let us investigate the matter. From their earliest childhood the working men are being prepared for their destiny like the dancing bears brought up for the profession by his master. In the schools and churches they are told that it is the will of God that there should be rich and poor people. God knows and sees everything and nothing exists without His knowledge. The doings of the Almighty being wise and inscrutable, He has a special purpose in bestowing wealth and riches upon some of His children, whilst others perish in want of the indispensable necessities. Now, some narrow-minded people may think that this is very partial of God; but they are mistaken. For those who are seemingly neglected on this miserable earth, will be given the more recognition in heaven, so that everything will be balanced after all. Humility and meekness are qualities which are highly agreeable to God and therefore highly recommendable to the workingmen. Patience and obedience are also becoming to the toilers. Work and pray; for God Himself has demanded of sinful humanity to eat their daily bread in the sweat of their brow.

These and similar "advisers" do not fail to make an impression upon the susceptible mind of the child, and thus they pass into manhood being obedient, unassuming and ignorant slaves, without being aware of it. Being raised in ignorance they suspect no wrong, but believe that the form of society under which they live is the natural order of things. No wonder, therefore, that the dominating classes call these people "good, honest, law-abiding" workingmen. They have but *too much* reason to thus dominate them, for they are really as obedient as a flock of geese and as gentle as lambs.

But if these blind, ever-dreaming slaves would only glance behind the curtains they would discover that they are infamously duped. They would find that those who yell into their ears, "Work and pray," condescend to pray, indeed, but do not work, and that those who never tire of reminding the toilers of the "demand of God," that they should eat their daily bread in the sweat of their brow, do not apply this adage to themselves. To be sure, these hypocrites sweat some times, but not from work; they do so amid wild orgies and debauchery.

The capitalistic papers of this country sneered at a certain Indian chief; I think Red Cloud,[45] who, they reported, had said: "What we (the Indians) want is white men to plant our corn, hoe it, harvest it, and put it in to barns which they will build for us." Now, I cannot comprehend why the capitalistic press considers this utterance of Red Cloud as a peculiar one. Have not the capitalists put this very same idea into practice? Let us investigate. Instead of the words "white men," use the expression "workingmen," and it will read thus: "What we (the capitalists, the privileged class) want is workingmen to plant our corn, hoe it, harvest it, and put it into barns which they will build for us." Well, nevertheless, these conditions exist today. The wage-slaves really produce everything, and store their products away into warehouses which they build for their masters; and besides they build for them, also palaces such as Red Cloud never had on his programme. Yes; and the toilers do more than that; they decorate their masters with diamonds, and over-burden them with luxuries and riches of which Red Cloud never dreamed. Who can deny this fact?

In order to illustrate the existing social "order," I will draw the following parable:

A long time ago the forests of a tropical land were populated by a happy lot of monkeys. They lived together like a large family and quarreling and discontentedness were qualities totally unknown to them. For a livelihood they searched the surroundings for food for themselves and their young ones in a harmonious way and without grudge. They were happy, indeed. One day some cunning monkeys were overcome by a very smart idea. They erected fences around the best parts of the forests and forbade their fellow-monkeys to hunt for food inside of the hedged regions. They named these pieces of land "property." Now, the propertyless monkeys were in utter despair, for they did not know where to get food for themselves and families. They called upon the property-owners and complained of their impossibility of making a livelihood.

The propertied monkeys said unto them: "We may allow you to seek food on our property under the condition that you will give us half of the result of your labor." This offer the poor propertyless monkeys were compelled to accept, as there was no other way of making a living. No other choice was left open to them as either to accept or starve. The propertyless monkeys had to build large warehouses for their "employers," into which to store away their services as was sufficient to keep themselves and families alive. This was called "means." The property-owning monkeys became very wealthy, and were living in luxury and idleness. And why should they not? Did not the poor monkeys work for them, and thus enable them to be idle and yet debauch in abundance?

For a long time the working monkeys did not grumble, but were very obedient. Generations thus passed, and the monkeys thought that the "social institutions" could not be otherwise and that there had to be rich and poor monkeys, because these were the conditions which existed already when they were born. But the employers grew continually richer whilst the portion of the products of the workers, which they received as a compensation, were reduced to the lowest standard. Consequently the poor working monkeys were living in destitution and misery, notwithstanding the fact that the warehouses were filled with food. Discontentedness among the workers was the natural result of the growing wealth on one side and increasing poverty on the other. In order to keep the grumbling monkeys in subjection and maintain the respect for the existing institutions (which were called "law and order") the propertied classes hired numbers of able-bodied monkeys from the ranks of the propertyless classes. Those men were called police, sheriffs, militia, a. s. f.

Now, the dissatisfied monkeys assembled frequently

for the purpose of seeking remedy for the existing evils. As the opinions as to ways and means to secure better conditions were very different, they formed various organizations. Some of the workers aimed at "higher wages" and others wanted to work less time. Still another class of workers held that the "wage-system" should be abolished entirely. They said that the propertied monkeys had accumulated their riches by robbing the workers out of the major part of the results of their labor. Furthermore, they claimed that the wealthy classes had no right to monopolize the natural resources of existence and thereby force their fellow-monkeys into their services, but that the mother-earth and her products belonged to the monkey race in common. The monkeys who confessed the latter ideas were considered very dangerous by the privileged classes. "Law and order is endangered," the wealthy cried. "Those anarchists want to overthrow our glorious institutions and turn everything tipsy-topsy. We must do away with those blood-thirsty rascals, who want to take our property and who are undermining our free and glorious institutions." These propertied monkeys were also opposed to that part of the working monkeys who only demanded a larger compensation for their work; but their hate against those who wanted to abolish their privileges altogether was immeasurable.

The capitalistic press, and even numerous labor journals, define anarchism as murder, plunder, arson and outrage upon society in general. These "learned" journalists, or at least a majority of them thus defining anarchism, misrepresent the objects and aims of this teaching maliciously. Anarchism does not mean plunder and outrage upon society; contrarily, its mission is to outroot the systematical plunder of a vast majority of the people by a comparatively few—the working classes by the capitalists. It aims at the extermination of the outrages committed by the reigning classes upon the wage-slaves, under the name of "law and order." Murder, plunder, robbery, outrages. "Is an anarchist really the impersonation of all crimes, of everything dastardly and damnable?" The "International Working People's Association," the organization of the anarchists, has the following platform, which was agreed upon at the congress at Pittsburgh in October, 1883. Let this platform be the answer to the questions I have raised before:

1. Destruction of the existing class rule, by all means, i.e., by energetic, relentless, revolutionary and international action.
2. Establishment of a free society based upon cooperative organization of production.
3. Free exchange of equivalent products by and between the productive organizations—without commerce and profit-mongery.
4. Organization of education on a secular scientific and equal basis for both sexes.
5. Equal rights for all without distinction to sex or race.
6. Regulation of all public affairs by free contracts between the autonomous (independent) communes and associations, resting on a federalistic basis.

Does this sound like outrages and crime?

In the course of my observations I will dwell more thoroughly on the aims and objects of anarchy.

Many people undoubtedly long to know what the relationship between anarchism and socialism is, and whether these two doctrines have anything in common with each other. A number of persons claim that an anarchist cannot be a socialist, and a socialist not an anarchist. This is wrong. The philosophy of socialism is a general one, and covers several subordinate teachings. To illustrate, I will cite the word "Christianity." There are Catholics, Lutherans, Methodists, Baptists, Congregationalists, and various other religious sects, all of whom call themselves Christians. Although every Catholic is a Christian, it would not be correct to say that every Christian believes in Catholicism.

Webster defines socialism thus: "A more orderly, equitable and harmonious arrangement of social affairs than has hitherto prevailed." Anarchism is aiming at this; anarchism is seeking a more just form of society. Therefore every anarchist is a socialist, but every socialist is not necessarily an anarchist. The anarchists again are divided into two factions; the communistic anarchists and the Proudhon or middle-class anarchists.[46] The "International Working People's Association" is the representative organization of the communistic anarchists. Politically we are anarchists, and economically, communists or socialists. With regard to political organization the communistic anarchists demand the abolition of political authority, the state, we deny the right of a class or single individual to govern or rule another class or individual. We hold that, as long as one man is under the dictation of another, as long as one man can in any form subjugate his fellow man, and as long as the means of existence can be monopolized by a certain class or certain individuals, there can be no liberty. Concerning the economical form of society, we advocate the communistic or co-operative method of production.

As to the distribution of products, a free exchange between the organizations of productions without profitmongery would take place. Machinery and the means of production in general would be the common servant, and the products certainly the common property of the whole of the people. The *Proudhon* anarchists, however, although being opposed to the state and political authority, do not advocate the co-operative system of production, and the common ownership of the means of production, the products and the land.

In what respect do the social-democrats differ from the anarchists? The state socialists do not seek the abolition of the state, but they advocate the centralization of the means of production in the hands of the government, in other words, they want the government to be the controller of industry. Now, a socialist who is not a state-socialist must necessarily be an anarchist. It is utterly ridiculous of men like Dr. Aveling to state that they are neither state-socialists nor anarchists. Dr. Aveling has to be either one or the other.[47]

The term "anarchism" is of Greek origin and means "without government," or, in other words, "without oppression." I only wish that every working man would understand the proper meaning of this word. It is an absurd falsehood if the capitalists and their hired editors say that "anarchism" is identical with disorder and crime. On the contrary, anarchism wants to do away with the now existing social disorder, it aims at the establishment of the real—the natural—order. I think every sensible man ought to conceive, that where ruling is existing on one hand, there must be submission on the other. He who rules is a tyrant, and he who submits is a slave. Logically there can be no other outlet, because submission is the antithesis of rule. Anarchists hold that it is the natural right of every member of the human family to control ourselves. If a centralized power—government—is ruling the mass of people (no matter whether this government "represent the will of the majority of the people" or not) it is enslaving them, and a direct violation of the laws of *nature.*

Where laws are made there must be certain interests which cause their issue. Now every statute law, and consequently every violation thereof—crime—can be traced back to the institution of private property. The state protects the interests of the owners of private property (wealthy class), and therefore does not and *cannot* possibly protect the interests of the non-possessing people (the wage-workers), because the interest of both are of an opposite nature. The capitalists who have taken possession of the means of production—factories, machinery, land, etc.—are the masters, and the workingmen who have to apply to the capitalists for the use of the means of production (for which they receive a small compensation) in order to live, are the slaves. The interests of the capitalistic class are backed by the state (militia, sheriffs, and police) while the interests of the non-possessing people are not protected. Anarchists say that there should be no class interests, but that every human being should have *free access* to the means of existence and that the pantries of mother-earth should be accessible to all of her children. One part of the great human family has no right to deprive their brothers and sisters of their legitimate place at the common table, which is set so richly by generous mother-nature for all. Anarchists, as well as all other thinking people, claim, that in the present society, a great number of people are deprived of a decent existence.—*We demand the re-installation of the disinherited!* Is this a crime? Is this an outrage upon society? Are we therefore dangerous criminals, whose lives should be taken in the interests of the common good of society?

Yes, the anarchists demand the re-installation of the disinherited members of the human family. It is, therefore, quite natural that the privileged classes should hate them. Why, do not wrong-doing parties always hate those who disclose the natures of their transactions and open the eyes of their ignorant victims? Certainly they do. The anarchists are very much hated by the extortioners; indeed, they are proud of it. To them, this is a proof that they are on the right road. But the ruling classes very cunningly play the role of the thief, who, when pursued by his discoverers, cried out, "stop the thief," and by this manipulation succeeded in making good his escape.

The anarchists have proven that the existing form of society is based upon the exploitation of one class by another; in plain words, upon legalized robbery. They say that few persons have no right whatever, to monopolize the resources of nature; and they urge the victims, the toilers, to take possession of the means of production, which belong to the people in common, and thus secure the full benefit of their toil. Anarchists do not want to deprive the capitalists of their existence, but they protest against the capitalists depriving the toilers of their right to a decent existence. Should the communistic form of production prevail, the capitalists of to-day would not starve; they would be situated just as comfortably and would be just as happy (yea, happier than they are now) as the rest of the people. But certainly, they would have to take an active part in the production and be satisfied with their respective share of the results of labor, performed in common with their fellow-men.

The strongest bulwark of the capitalistic system is the ignorance of its victims. The average toiler shakes his head like the incredulous Thomas, when one tries to make plausible to him, that he is held in economic bondage. And this is so easily to be seen if one only takes the pains to think a little. Working at my trade alongside my colleagues, whom I tried to convince of my ideas, I used to tell them a story about some foxes: "Several foxes, in speculating about some scheme, which would enable them to live without hunting for food themselves succeeded at last in discovering one. They took possession of all the springs and other water-places. Now, as the other animals came to quench their thirst, the foxes said, unto them: 'The water-places belong unto us; if you want to drink, you must bring us something in return, you must bring us food for compensation.' The other animals were foolish enough to obey, and, in order to drink they had to hunt the whole day for food for the foxes, so that they themselves had to live very meagre." I asked one of my colleagues, who was prominent as a denunciator of socialism, what his opinion was concerning the just-mentioned story. He told that the animals who were thus swindled by the foxes were very foolish in obeying them, and ought to drive the latter away from the water-places. When I directed his attention to the fact that a similar practice was being cultivated in modern society, with the only difference that the role of the foxes was occupied by the capitalists, and the water-places were represented by the means of production, and that he (my colleague) was very inconsistent in condemning the one and defending the other, he owed me the answer. This, for instance, illustrates the ignorance and indifference of the average workingmen. In the case of the foxes, they see no more and no less than robbery in their schemes, whilst in the case of the capitalists they approve of their methods.

Many inconsistent objections to anarchism are being made by its opponents. Some people have the impression that in an anarchistic society, where there is nobody to govern and nobody to be governed, every person would be isolated. This is false. Men have implanted by nature an impulse to associate with their fellow men. In a free society men would form economic as well as social association; but all organizations would be voluntary, not compulsory. As I have asserted before, laws and the violation thereof, crimes, are attributed to the institution of private property, especially to the unequal distribution of the means of existence, to degradation and want. When the institution of private property will be abolished; when economic and social equalities will be established; when misery and want will belong to the past, then crime will be unknown and laws will become superfluous. It is a wrong assertion when people claim that a man is a criminal because of a natural disposition to crime. A man, as a rule, is but the reflex of the conditions which surround him. In a society, which places no obstacle in the road of free development of men, and which gives everybody an equal share to the pursuit of happiness, there will be no cause which will induce men to become bad.

The legalized private property system gives birth to crime and at the same time punishes it because it exists. The mother punishes her own child because it is born. Do away with the systems that produce evils and the latter will vanish. The removal of the cause is synonymous with the removal of the effects; but the social diseases will never be cured if you declare war against the victims and on the other hand defend the causes which produced them. If one has the small-pox it would not cure the disease if one would scratch the scabs off. The disease in this case is system of private-property, and the scabs its evil effects.

How will the anarchists realize their ideas? What means do they intend to employ to accomplish the realization of a free society? Much has been written and talked on this subject, and, as an avowed anarchist, I will in plain terms give my individual opinion to the readers of this journal. The "anarchism" itself does not indicate force; on the contrary it means peace. But I believe that everybody who has studied the true character of the capitalistic form of society, and who will not deceive himself, will agree with me that now and never will the ruling classes abandon their privileges peaceably.

Anarchism demands a thorough transformation of society, the total abolition of the private-property system. Now, history shows us that even reforms within the frame of the existing society have never been accomplished without the force of arms. Feudalism received its death blow through the great French revolution a century ago, which at the same time gave form to modern capitalism. Capitalism now is speedily attaining its most extreme character, that is, it is developing into monopolism. Wealth concentrates itself more and more in a few hands and the misery and poverty of the great mass of people is consequently enlarging in the same degree. The rich get richer and the poor poorer. Like the ruling classes in the eighteenth century, so the same classes at the eve of the nineteenth century are deaf to the complaints and warnings of the disinherited, and blind to the misery and degradation which surround their luxuriously outfitted palaces. The natural result will be that perhaps before the nineteenth century will wing its last hours the people will arise en masse, expropriate the privileged and proclaim the freedom of the human race. It is wrong if people assert that the anarchists will be responsible for the coming revolution. No, the drones of society are the parties who will have to answer to the charge of being the cause of the prospective uprising of the people; for the rich and mighty have ears and hear not, and eyes and yet see not.

To abolish chattel slavery in this country a long and awful war took place. Notwithstanding the fact that indemnification was offered for their losses, the slaveholders would not bestow freedom upon their slaves.[48] Now, in my judgment, he who believes that the modern slave-holders—the capitalists—would voluntarily, without being forced to do so, give up their privileges and set free their wage-slaves, are poor students. Capitalists possess too much egotism to give way to reason. Their egotism is so enormous that they even refuse to grant subordinate and insignificant concessions. Capitalists and syndicates, for instance, rather lose millions of dollars than to accept the eight-hour labor system. Would a peaceable solution of the social question be possible, the anarchists would be the first ones to rejoice over it.

But is it not a fact that on occasion of almost every strike the minions of the institutions of private property—militia, police, deputy sheriffs; yes, even federal troops—are being called to the scenes of conflict between capital and labor, in order to protect the interests of capital? Did it ever happen that the interests of labor were guarded by those forces? What peaceable means should the toilers employ? There is, for example, the strike? If the ruling classes want to enforce the "law" they can have every striker arrested and punished for "intimidation" and conspiracy. A strike can only be successful if the striking workingmen prevent their places being occupied by others. But this prevention is a crime in the eyes of the law. Boycott? In several states the "courts of justice" have decided that the boycott is a violation of the law, and in consequence thereof, a number of boycotts have had the pleasure of examining the inner construction of penitentiaries "for conspiracy" against the interests of capital. "But," says some apostles of harmony, "there is something left which will help us. There is the ballot." No doubt many people who say this are honest in their belief.

But scarcely did the workingmen participate in the elections as a class, many representatives of "law and order" advocate a limitation (in many instances even the total abolition) of the right of the proletarians to vote. People who read the Chicago *Tribune* and *Times* and other representative capitalistic organs, will confirm my statement. The propaganda among capitalists in favor of limiting the right to vote to taxpayers—property owners—only, is increasing constantly, and will be realized whenever the political movement of the workingmen becomes really dangerous to the interests of capital. The "Law and Order League" of capitalists recently organized all over the country to defeat the demands of organized labor, has declared that the workingmen must not be allowed to *obtain power over the ballot box.* They have so resolved everywhere.

The anarchists are not blind. They see the development of things and predict that a collision between the plebeians and patricians is *inevitable.* Therefore, in time for the coming struggle—*to arms!* If threatening clouds are visible on the horizon, I advise my fellow-man to carry an umbrella with him, so he will not get wet. Am I then the cause of the rain? No. So let me say plainly that, in my opinion, only by the force of arms can the wage slaves make their way out of capitalistic bondage.

The Haymarket meeting and its consequences.

I have mentioned in the course of this article before, that again and again, when conflicts between capital and labor occurred, militia, police sheriffs and Pinkertons have thrust their weight into the scale in the interest of capital. These interferences have in many cases resulted in most unprovoked slaughterings of workingmen and women, yes, even innocent children; and the capitalistic newspapers have in a beastly manner applauded these massacres of the "canaille." No single instance is known to me where the perpetrators have been punished for such dastardly and cowardly crimes. I need only to point to the atrocious actions of deputy sheriffs in East St. Louis last spring in killing seven or eight men, women and children without the slightest provocation; the perpetrators were not even indicted, much less tried. How the militia raved in Lemont,

Illinois, some time ago, the widows and orphans of the slain can tell; the murderers were not prosecuted for their crime, but highly praised for their "bravery."[49] Without any pretense whatever, militia men inaugurated a scene of horror in Belleville, Illinois, a few years ago; no punishment followed the outrage. In the various coal regions of this country hundreds of widows and orphans mourn over their husbands and fathers who have been slaughtered by the minions of capital. Would I name and give a description of all crimes thus committed in the name of "law and order," I would have to write a book as large as the bible. Chicago herself can sing a sad song about the outrages of her police. Scores of her citizens, who were mere spectators, had their skulls broken at the time of the last strike of the street-car employes, and several persons have lost their reason as a consequence of the merciless clubbing.[50] As a reward the leader of the clubbing hordes was advanced from a mere captain to inspector of police. Hundreds of other "American sovereigns" have had their ribs broken and are crippled every year without any provocation; by drunken and brutal despots of "law and order," and the grave-yards harbor the dead bodies of not a few workingmen, who were killed by the police, while endeavoring to secure a higher compensation for their toil.

On all these occasions the "International Working People's Association" has never failed to raise a protest against the outrages and to demand a conviction of the guilty parties. Now, the McCormick affair on the 3rd day of May led to the meeting on the Haymarket. In a meeting on the evening of the 3rd of May, in 54 West Lake street, of which Waller (who testified during the trial on behalf of the state) was chairman,[51] the meeting of the following night was arranged on the suggestion of Waller himself for the purpose of protesting against the brutal behavior of the police. The presiding officer (Waller) appointed me as a committee to look after the printing of hand-bills and the invitation of speakers, which duty I performed. On Tuesday the 4th of May, I had the hand-bills printed and distributed.

The meeting took place and was a very quiet and orderly one. Even several witnesses for the state testified that the speeches were of a more conservative character than those made by the speakers on previous occasions. I was present and listened to the speeches until about ten minutes past ten o'clock at which time dark clouds moved up, indicating a rain-storm. Fielden was speaking at this time, but Parsons interrupted him, making the remark that the people present had better adjourn to Zepf's hall, which was near by, on account of the threatening rain. Fielden, taking up his speech again, urged the audience to have patience for a few minutes yet, as he would have finished his speech in a short while, and then the listeners all could go home. I, however, in the company of a friend proceeded to Zepf's saloon, where a few moments later, Parsons put in an appearance also. I had been in the saloon scarcely four or five minutes, when we all heard the sound of an explosion, and simultaneous volleys of shots. Before I could realize what had happened, people came rushing into the saloon, apparently to seek shelter from the bullets, some of which whistled even through the saloon. Now, I comprehended the situation; but I had at first supposed that the police or the militia had attacked the meeting with a gatling gun, so tremendous was the report of the explosion. At once the doors of the saloon were locked, and thus I was compelled to remain in the building perhaps ten or fifteen minutes, before I succeeded in gaining the sidewalk and making my way home.

The first details of the real character of the occurrence

at the Haymarket, I learned the following morning, when I bought a morning paper on a Milwaukee avenue car on my way down town. On the same morning, about half past ten o'clock, I was arrested in the office of the *Arbeiter Zeitung,* 107 Fifth avenue, together with all other compositors of that paper, and I have breathed prison air ever since.

What caused the police to attack the meeting? Certainly not the attitude of the assembled people; for it was proven during the trial that the meeting had been an orderly one, and that there was no indication that trouble would arise from the gathering. Even Mayor Harrison, who was present, testified to that fact.[52]

A few months ago the Chicago *Times* compared the anarchists and socialists with the murdering and plundering bands of Apaches, and especially the "convicted" anarchists with Chief Geronimo and his staff. I, in return, ask of an unprejudiced public, whether this omen cannot with more justice be applied to the police, or at least to the commanders of the same. I think such a comparison would be more accurate. So be it then. The police-Apaches had spilled workingmen's blood already on Monday afternoon and at intervals on Tuesday; but they thirsted for more. On the night of the memorable 4th of May they lay crouching in their wigwams on Desplaines street. They would had rather surprised the meeting at the beginning; but Mayor Harrison was there and they did not wish the mayor to be an eye-witness of the intended Bartholomew night. With impatient strides chief Geronimo Bonfield measured his wigwam and said: "The trouble with these d - - - socialists is that they always have their wives and children with them. I wish I could have three or four thousand of them in a bunch, without their families, and then I would make short work of them."

(It was testified by a trustworthy person, during the

trial, that Bonfield used words to this effect.) Mayor Harrison had left the meeting at last and had gone home, but not until he had told Bonfield not to undertake an attack upon the gathering, because it was orderly and peaceable. But hark! hasty steps approach the wigwam! Who is it? Scouts (detectives). "Mighty chief," they exclaim, "if you want to make an attack, now is the time for you, for the meeting will soon adjourn. Fielden said just now that he would be through with his speech, and if you linger any longer the socialists will be on there way home!" (The police-station is only a block distance from the Haymarket). The eyes of the chief sparkle in delight, and he gives to his warriors the signal to march. Rapidly they approach the meeting. The braves, with one hand clenching their clubs, with the other their pistols, were just ready to commence their bloody work, when the deathly bomb came through the air with a known awful result. Who threw the missile? I do not know; I was not in the meeting at that time. But still I am sentenced to death!

There remains but little for me to relate, for I assume that the readers of this journal are familiar with the farce in Judge Gary's court room. I do not believe that there is a trial on record in this country which equals this trial with regard to unfairness and the use of all possible corrupt means, including perjury and bribery, in order to procure a conviction. The prosecution knew that I was in Zepf's saloon at the time of the explosion of the bomb, and five unimpeached and trustworthy witnesses, against whose character not a word could be said, testified to this fact. But Gilmer ascends the witness box and swears (for cash) with the dryest air in the world that he saw me in the alley together with Spies, who, he claimed, lit a match the moment the missile was thrown. Furthermore, this hired tool of Grinnell swore that Schnaubelt, whom he claimed to be the bomb thrower, was five feet eight inches tall, so that he (Gilmer) could look over his head.[53] Now, everybody who knows Schnaubelt will confirm that he is a man of more than medium height 6 feet and 2 inches tall! In this style the whole trial was managed. The defense had witnesses in the witness-box (not "ignorant, lying foreigners," as the state's attorney pleased to express himself, but "law-abiding and intelligent American-born citizens") to whom officials of the Desplaines street station had said on the evening of the trouble, that they better had stay away from the meeting, because blood would flow in the streets that night. But the court rejected their testimony as "not admissible."

Notwithstanding the false testimony which was manufactured by the state by the bushel, the court admitted in pronouncing the sentence, that "it was not proven that any one of the defendants was directly connected with the throwing of the bomb at the Haymarket, and also not, who threw the missile; but that defendants had for years advocated violence, which agitation had induced the perpetrator to commit the act at the Haymarket." Did you, unprejudiced reader, ever hear any similar words uttered by a court of justice? It is astonishing. If Judge Gary admits that it is not known who threw the bomb, what law authorizes him to put us to death, because he supposes that the unknown perpetrator was encouraged to commit the act by our teachings!

But, alas! I forgot one fact: Seven policemen have died and, therefore, seven somebodies must pay the penalty. Now, as the anarchists are hated by a great many people—on the one hand by the aristocrats and on the other by a number of foolish workingmen—the agents of the ruling class thought it the easiest way to capture the ones of their number who seemed to be the most "dangerous" to society, place a noose around their necks and let them hang until they are dead. Well, it remains to be seen whether the people of this country are so degraded as to permit the commission of a sevenfold judicial murder.

There is one factor which played a damnable part before, during and after the trial: *the capitalistic press.* I dare say that even the newspapers in despotic Russia and Germany are not so unfair, lying and hypocritical as the press of "the land of the free and the home of the brave." It would consume too much space were I to nail all the lies which have been manufactured and published by the press against us. But I will take this opportunity to show that I do not exaggerate when I speak of the hypocrisy of the capitalistic lying sheets. I will quote a few sentences from an article which appeared in a Chicago morning paper a few weeks after the Haymarket affair. This article was published as a rebuke of an order given by Mayor Harrison to all city officials, that reporters should be excluded from police stations and other centres when news items were to be had: "Carter's Big Scheme.—An Order that is a Boomerang and that may lead to Sensational Developments."

Here are a few quotations:

> "The force has paled it exceedingly fine on the press and the public," said a gentleman long identified with police matters yesterday. "The department has never had any love for the papers, but it would not do for the mayor to show his hand while the surprised people were busy swelling the cash testimonials to the police. I say the 'surprised people' deliberately, because that was the sentiment which actuated the men who made the contributions and bought bundles of tickets for the benefits. The papers made heroes of the police, and for a while it was fashionable to idolize them. For what? Simply because

they did not run. What they did was well enough done, but that was what they were paid for. They did nothing but their duty, and in their grateful surprise that they did that the people showered money upon them, *dragooned as they were by the papers, which gave up columns to their praise. But a good many things about the riots remain to be told, and now that the boys have been shut out the stories may come to the surface.* The policemen were not all as brave as lions by any means, and they were nearer being stampeded in Haymarket than any of them will now admit. Would you believe me if I were to tell you that when the race began after a bomb exploded a flying newspaper man dashed into a house near-by and *discovered a dozen officers frantically trying to barricade themselves in? Well, now, that is said to be the cold fact, and the reporter who is responsible for the statement can break into one of the big papers with it any morning.* That is by no means the only instance, I believe, and now that the season of heroics is past, the suppressed truth would not be unpalatable. It would be interesting to know, for instance, how many of the wounded policemen were shot by their panic-stricken comrades in the ranks. The hospital authorities have not been particular to tell just what sort of bullet wounds were made in the bodies of the officers, and I would not be surprised if it could be easily ascertained that bullets taken from the wounds would fit the regulation revolvers. When that kind of ammunition begins to be used by the reporters it may be that the old man will realize that his order is a boomerang."

I quote these extracts in order to show that the capitalistic press and the authorities know the real facts about the Haymarket affair, but are keeping them from the public. In thus threatening the police with sensational developments, the capitalistic newspaper "lets the cat out of the bag." It is an open secret that most of the policemen who were wounded from bullets, received them from their fellow-officers. The newspapers and police know this; but when a physician testified to this fact on the witness stand, they raised a howl. During the trial as well as ever since, the press gathers up all possible and impossible stories and lies which, could in any way harm us; but they keep their columns closed against any appeal for justice and fairness. Pharisees!

As the court as well as the states-attorney have plainly hinted, the verdict of death was rendered for the purpose of crushing the anarchistic and the socialistic movement. But I am satisfied that just the contrary has been accomplished by this barbarous measure. Thousands of workingmen have been led by our "conviction" to study anarchism, and if we are executed, we can ascend the scaffold with the satisfaction that by our death, we have advanced our noble cause more than we could have possibly done had we grown as old as Methusalah.

When I left my native country, my dear father (who died since) advised me to always utter fearlessly whatever I might hold to be the truth, and I have followed his advice faithfully.

I have given my honest opinions to the readers of the KNIGHTS OF LABOR, regardless of all possible consequences just as I have done when yet among the people, and until death closes my eyes and shuts my mouth forever, I shall continue to preach that which I think is right. I cannot do otherwise.

I know that it is impossible to convince professional liars, such as the hired editors of the capitalistic press, who are paid for crushing the truth. But I beg all the editors of labor journals as well as all honest, intelligent workingmen, not to ape the ridiculous attitude of the capitalistic press towards the doctrines of anarchism, as this has been the case hitherto, but to make anarchism an object of thorough study.

Adolph Fischer.

Artist's conception of scene at Haymarket.

THE STORY
OF
THE ANARCHISTS
TOLD
BY THEMSELVES.

:O:

PARSONS | SPIES | FIELDEN | SCHWAB
FISCHER | LINGG | ENGLE | NEEBE.

O

The only true history of the men who claim that they are

CONDEMNED TO SUFFER DEATH

For exercising the right of Free Speech.

:O:

Their association with Labor, Socialistic and Anarchistic Societies, their views as to the aims and objects of these organizations, and how they expect to accomplish them; Also their connection with the Chicago

HAYMARKET AFFAIR

Each man is the author of his own story,
Which will Appear Only in the

"KNIGHTS OF LABOR"

During the Next Three Months.

O

The Great Labor Paper
OF THE UNITED STATES.

A 16-PAGE WEEKLY PAPER.

Containing all the latest Foreign and Domestic Labor News of the day, Stories, Household Hints, etc.

A CO-OPERATIVE PAPER
OWNED AND CONTROLLED BY MEMBERS OF

THE KNIGHTS OF LABOR

And furnished for the small sum of
$1.00 PER ANNUM.

:O:

Address all Communications to
Knights of Labor Publishing Company,
163 Washington St., Chicago, Ill.

"The Law Vindicated—four of the Chicago anarchists pay the penalty of their crime."

Drawn by Robert Minor
From the Blast

"Lest We Forget."

6

Autobiography of George Engel

According to your wishes I have written the story of my life, hoping that many workingmen may profit by reading it.

I, George Engel, was born on the 15th day of April in the year 1836, in the city of Cassel, Germany, at that time the capital of Kerkessen. My father, a mason and bricklayer, Conrad Engel, died when I was 18 months old and left my mother, a very poor widow, with four little children. When I was 12 years old my mother died and left me to the mercy of the cold and cruel world. Two of my brothers were taken to an orphan asylum, I and another child were given to two poor families, which took care of us for 20 thalers (15 dollars) a year. I already knew what hunger meant, more, I learned what starvation was. When I was 14 the city quit paying for my sustenance and I was told that it was now time for me to learn a trade. And so it was. In Germany, common school education is compulsory and every child must go to school from the age of 7 to 14, and that 12 months in the year, only interrupted by the usual vacation. At 14 years the boy begins to learn a trade and goes to the Sunday School. There he is further educated in reading, writing, and arithmetic, drawing, etc. Nobody caring for me, I went around and found at last a shoemaker, who was willing to teach me the mysteries of shoe-making in four years, provided somebody would furnish me during that time with clothing and washing. Nobody was inclined to do me the favor, and having been apprenticed for two weeks, the shoemaker turned me out on the street. For some time I searched in vain for a master who was willing to have me for an apprentice, and then I gave it up. In explanation I will state that in Germany to a great extent, even up to the present day, an apprentice must pay to his master a certain sum for learning a trade, so that it is difficult for a poor lad to get apprenticed at all. I had lost all hope when I heard that certain of my school comrades had emigrated to America. I heard a good deal of the United States, which left on my mind the impression that there was a better chance for me in that country. But before I would leave the old country I must earn some money, and therefore I went to Frankfort-on-the-Main to try my luck there after having failed in Cassel.

As I had no money I had to travel on foot. Tired and footsore, after traveling several days, I finally reached Frankfort. Being without money I wandered during the day in the streets of the city, not knowing what to do. Night came. Hunger and cold drove me at last into a saloon. I asked the saloon-keeper for lodging and something to eat. I would work for it. But he arose angry and told me to get out as quick as I could. A citizen, who was in the room, pitied me, for I was then only 14 years old. He said he would learn me the trade of painting, if I was willing to go with him. Very thankful and glad, I said yes. I went with him, after taking a hearty meal, for which he paid. I was apprenticed according to the rules of the trade and I remember the years of my apprenticeship still with gratitude, for my master was a good and righteous man. After getting all the necessary information of the trade I went abroad, "traveled," for so is it by custom described to the mechanic. In the year 1863 I came to Bremen, after having worked in Mayence, Cologne and Duesseldorf. I read a good deal, but nothing of the socialistic literature. By and by I perceived something of the ways of the world and often thought about the difference between the rich and the poor. Till then I had lived easy-going and careless.

The newspapers in Bremen had much to say about the oppression of the inhabitants of Schleswig-Holstein by Denmark. A movement was going on to free these German brethren from the yoke of the Danish King, as it was put. I considered the struggle of my countrymen for something great and joined a regiment of volunteers. We were drilled by officers of the city of Bremen in the Turner hall. Later we marched to Altona in Schleswig-Holstein. But when the regular militia of Prussia and Austria came there our volunteer regiment was dissolved. Then the war between the German federation and Denmark broke out. The German brethren were freed from the Danish yoke only to come under the Prussian yoke.[54]

In those war times business was slow in Northern Germany and this brought me to Leipzig, which I left when the war of 1866 broke out.[55] I then worked in different cities. The year 1868 found me in Rehna, Mecklenburg-Schnerin, where I married. I started a business of my own. The development of the factory system in Germany swept most of the small manufacturers, without great means, out of existence. The struggle for life increased and it became hard to make a decent living. My intention to emigrate to America, which I had when a boy, came back. To make it short, the 8th day of January, of the year 1873, found me in Philadelphia. I took work in a sugar refinery. In May I worked again as a painter. In Philadelphia for the first time in my life, I heard something about serious labor troubles. The militia marched along the streets. They came from the coal mines, where they had "subjugated" some troublesome, starving miners. I watched them, when a bystander said to me: "Those scoundrels ought to be hung on the spot." That remark surprised me, for, at that time, being an "ignorant foreigner," I sang the praises of this "free and glorious" country. Scornfully looking at that man I asked him for the reason of his un-patriotic remark. He gave me reasons. Having been a manufacturer myself, although on a small scale, and knowing nothing of the labor question I was unable to comprehend him. I told him America was a free country, anybody could earn good wages if he wanted to, and save money besides; in short, I reiterated the well-known trash of the capitalistic newspapers.

It is true, I earned what was called good wages by ten hours daily work and laid by a little money for a rainy day. Well, the rainy days came soon enough. I became sick, my eyes suffered. My savings were soon gone. Doctors and medicine were dear. I had to support a wife and little children. As the physician very quickly perceived that I was poor and helpless, and that there was nothing to gain by curing me, he sent me to the German Aid Society. This society helped me along for some time by paying for a physician. But that was all. My family was starving, and I often did not know where to get bread for them. After a year's sickness I was cured and able to work again.

As soon as I earned money enough, I came to Chicago. Chicago is the place where I heard something of socialism for the first time in my life. In the year 1874, I worked in the Tembruth's wagon factory. There I got acquainted with a socialist. One day he showed me a newspaper, *Der Vorbote.* It was a small socialistic weekly paper in the German language, edited by Conrad Conzett, a Swiss typesetter, who is now working for the cause in Switzerland. I found the paper very interesting and saw that it contained great truths. I was delighted. In it was an advertisement of a meeting to be held by the "International Workingmen's Association" at 130 Lake Street, in the basement. I went to the meeting. About fifteen or seventeen men were present, a small branch of the I.W.A. These men made great sacrifices to uphold their paper. It was at that time astonishing to me, that men could without the least compensation work so eagerly for the cause of humanity. It struck me what a gigantic work it was to educate and organize the masses who created everything, only to be cheated by their exploiters out of the fruits of their labor. My health was good. I had plenty of work and was therefore able to buy socialistic books to study the social question. The first books I read were written by Ferdinand Lassalle, the organizer of the German workmen. Very soon I became convinced and enlisted in the cause. Since then I continued to work for it and strengthened my belief.

In the year 1876 I started a toy store. My wife is still engaged in the business. As a storekeeper I had more time which I could devote to reading. The more I read the firmer grew my convictions. I was glad to see that the socialistic doctrine gained more and more followers in the United States as the years passed by. After the shooting at Lehmann at the German Emperor in May and June of 1878, the government of that country made special laws against the socialists and dissolved their organization.[56] That was the reason that the Chicago socialists, members of the I.W.A. were also disbanded. All our members now entered the different labor organizations of the city and in a very short time we were able to organize the "Socialistic Labor Party of North America." Next year (1879) we polled 12,000 votes for the labor candidates. This was a great success, but it brought a horde of corrupt politicians into our ranks, who cared little or nothing for principle. Dissensions broke out and reduced our numbers considerably.

At the time of the national Greenback convention of Chicago, some of our members proposed a fusion with the Greenbackers, others held that to be treason to the socialistic principles.[57] In Chicago the anti-Greenback fusion faction was in the lead. Numerous quarrels ensued, split after split occurred and at last nothing but two or three socialistic societies were left, very small in numbers. The only substantial remaining gain was the *Arbeiter Zeitung*, (daily), the *Vorbote* (weekly) and the *Fackel* (weekly), all three German newspapers. Of course there were thousands of socialists in the city, although unorganized. They still believed in the ballot box, but when Judge Gardener refused to punish two ballot-box stuffers on the pretence that they were drunk, and that it was a righteous thing to cheat a communist out of his vote; these workingmen got disgusted with voting and began to reason about other methods in order to spread socialistic ideas. In the year 1882 the socialists began to rally again and found clubs all over the city, which declared themselves for the International Working People's Association, the American branch of which was founded in October, 1883, in the city of Pittsburgh, Pa. The principles of the I.W.P.A. are set forth in the "Pittsburgh Manifesto". I soon became an active member of the International. I belonged to the North West-Side Group, the mother group of other groups in the same part of the city.

On Sunday May 2, and May 3, 1886, I was present in meetings in which it was proposed to give aid to any strikers if the police or the Pinkertons should attack said strikers. On May 4, the evening of the Haymarket tragedy, I was at home playing cards, when Waller entered my house and told us of the occurrence on the Haymarket. I told him to go home, and very soon after, I went to bed myself.

That is the story of my life, and now some words about voting. The workingmen are going to vote again, but will they be able to keep the professional politicians out of their ranks? I doubt it.

At the time when the socialists of this city believed in the ballot I worked for our ticket very hard, but I found that the workingman is too innocent and unsuspecting, and is very easy made a prey by the crafty politicians. The ruling classes as a class are far more intelligent, cunning and unprincipled than the oppressed and exploited workingmen. They get a fine education and have time and leisure to learn all that is necessary to keep up their tyranny and to defraud the working classes, no matter how earnest and honest they may be. And, after all, what is the gain in voting?

The development of machinery renders workingmen more and more superfluous, puts them on the road and degrades others from skilled laborers to mere machine hands. The solution of the labor question is in co-operation; or, in other words, the abolition of private ownership of the means of production. There can be no question that the present owners of land and machinery never will give them up to the people without resistance. They guard their "proprietary rights" with great jealousy. The strikers and boycotters are met with the policeman's club, the rifle of the militia and the deadly bullets of the Pinkertons. These are straws which point out the direction which labor will have to go. The history of all times teaches us that oppressing classes always maintain their tyranny by force and violence. The American colonists did everything to gain their end peacefully but everything failed and they had to resort to force. The right vote is in my opinion a double-edged sword, a most dangerous weapon. It makes the wage slave believe that he is a free man, while his enemies use that illusion most effectively to his deception and enslavement.

And now some few words about the bomb-throwing. It is my firm belief to-day, that if the bomb had not been thrown by the unknown, at least 300 workingmen would have been killed or wounded by the police. The police were used to put an end to the eight-hour movement, and thereby save the capitalists of this city millions of profits on labor. The police, led by Bonfield, wanted to pose as petted champions of millionaires. It came out different, and that is what the police are so enraged about. They intended to slaughter the workingmen, but were disappointed.

The bomb demonstrated that in the future street fights are an impossibility. Anybody can make and use bombs. Bombs only cost from 5 to 10 cents a piece. These are facts and I can't help that. But because they are facts and give in revolutionary times all the great cities into the hands of the people, arose the cry that somebody must hang for it. Of course they can hang seven men, but these facts are not put out of the world by such proceedings. I am not for war, but I realize that a violent revolution will come, must come, not brought about by the workingmen, but by the capitalists. Workingmen are made poorer day by day, the abuses grow more and more, and in the same ratio the masses will become discontented and organize against oppression. And then the law factories will be put into operation. They will dissolve all political societies of workingmen, then they will do the same thing with trades unions and workingmen societies of every description. They will fill the prisons with labor agitators, and hang them by the dozen. And when the people will get enraged degree by degree, deeds of violence done by workingmen against their oppressors will increase and the whole land will be divided into two classes—the capitalists and the *slum* of the country on the one side—the latter (the mercenaries) hired by the money power, and the *proletarians*—the workingmen—on the other side, and then the overthrow of the existing order of society is at hand. Some day, not twenty-five years from now, the war will break out. There is no doubt about that in my mind. Therefore all workingmen should unite and prepare for the last war, whose outcome will be the end forever of all war, and will bring peace and happiness to all mankind.

George Engel.

7

Autobiography of Michael Schwab

Dear reader, please follow me on the always ready wing of imagination to Central Germany to halt on a Franconian hill, planted with vines. Near us, on the ridge of the hill, thunders the railroad train, down in the valley flows in many curves, idly, the yellow waters of the Main. On its left bank we behold a large plain consisting of green meadows with silver-shining brooks, dark-green forests of pure oak and beech; numerous gardens with vegetables of all kinds, and wheat, oats, barley and corn fields held in an undulating motion by a soft, zephyr-like breeze. Our view is only checked by the mountains of the Steiger-wald, the highest of which is the Schnamburg, about 800 feet above the level of the sea. On the right side of the river, where we have taken up our standpoint, there is hill after hill covered with vine branches. Most of the forests belong to Bavaria, of which Franconia is a part, some to the villages or towns that lie outstretched before us.

These woods are common property; they are taken care

of by the officials called foresters. Every year a certain number of trees and bush are hewn down and sorted into piles, after which the citizens repair to the woods and cast lots for the numbered piles. A certain part is kept back to defray expenses necessary for the cultivation of the forest, taxes, etc. On such an occasion—I was about 10—the lots were drawn from my hat. It would appear from this incident that I was a communistic criminal long before I ever heard the word communism. The custom dates from time immemorial. I am at a loss to understand why, for instance, cereals could not be raised in the same way. I know a village, near my birthplace, where every citizen gets a patch of garden land, that belongs to the community, upon which he can raise vegetables for himself and family. There is more communism in Europe than usually is supposed. "The relics of barbarism," cry the hired men of the capitalistic press. Nevertheless, is it not singular that just those towns, and villages, who hold a great percentage of land in common, are well to do, while in proportion as the common property of all is transformed into private property, *few* gain and the *majority* lose? I will state here that in Franconia there are some towns whose citizens are not only free from taxes, but they get—after all state taxes have been paid and the costs of the municipal government defrayed every year—a small sum paid out of the town treasury. For illustration: In Lower Franconia is a certain town of 2,000 inhabitants, which owns extensive sandstone quarries. They are worked for the common interest and as a consequence 400 families are happy. *This* according to the green babblers of the press, is *barbarism,* whose speedy suppression is a highly civilizing mission. Near Chicago are extensive quarries; they are private property. Certainly we find a few very rich in dividends there. But the citizens of these quarry towns? Aye, they are *so* happy, so happy indeed, that it sometimes becomes necessary to tone down their extensive happiness by a little dose of lead. *This is civilization!*

After this digression we will go back to our landscape.

Down on the river in a southern direction the hills recede into fertile plains. Here in a beautiful valley Kitringen is situated, the place where I was born on August 9, 1853. My mother came from a well-to-do peasant family and had, if I remember right, 9 brothers and sisters. All I recall of her is that she had a very good heart, and abhorred rough and vile language to such a degree as is seldom found among people of her class. She died when I was eight years old. My father was a small tradesman and kind and loving to me and my sister, the only children he had. He died in the year 1865. I went to the public school, as all German children are compelled to do. My early childhood was a happy one. I spent all spare time in summer roaming through fields, forests and meadows. The inhabitants of the town were partly of Catholic and partly of Protestant faith; there were also some outspoken unbelievers, who were always gazed at by the children with awe, mingled with curiosity. We believed, as we were taught in school, that there was somewhere a place full of fire and brimstone, called hell, where all sinners, that is protestants, and such people as claimed to know more than our fine priests, of whom four were very fat and one very haggard—but he was young and had but just commenced—were after death sent to everlasting roasting. Hell we feared, but I am grieved to admit that we did not very much care for heaven. But this may have been due to the unfortunate description of the place—it was likened to our church.

Certain it is that we were always glad when the service closed and that we considered it a great boon, if for some reason or other, we were allowed to stay away from church.

Yet I held that to admit this was a sin, a victory of Satan. Very often I locked myself into a room, fell on my knees and prayed for hours, without mentioning my pious exercises to anybody else. I was a young saint, but for all that I had no visions, and never did any miracles, although my mind was full of superstitious nonsense of holy men and women, who did strange things to save their souls. Some of them, like St. Franciscus, caught lice and put them in their clothes, being evidently much given to sport; others performed the wondrous feat of standing all their life long on columns, others demonstrated their idea of humanitarianism by detesting men or women, as the case might be; and still others illustrated the evil habit of cleanliness by never washing themselves. These are no sneers at the Roman-Catholic faith. Anyone, who will take the trouble, can find these things and much more carefully recorded in the life stories of the saints, written by the clergy for the edification of the faithful. Perhaps it is needless to say, that our priests did not resemble these saints at all. They were of clean habits, lived in neatly furnished residences and loved their Christian sisters—alas! loved them only too well.

But, of course, when a boy, I looked reverently to the priests. Although, they did not resemble my model Christians I respected them very much and believed everything they had the kindness to teach, or preach, implicitly.

The first serious misfortune which befell me was when my mother died. Four years later (1865) my father followed her. Our home was broken up, the house and other property was sold, and after all debts were paid, there remained some hundred dollars for each of the two children. A guardian, an uncle of mine, was appointed, and we had to make our home with him. He was a Christian in the better sense of the word. There was nothing sentimental about him, I never heard him utter a kind word, but I do not think that I ever again met with a man as scrupulously honest as he was. He considered it his duty to go to church every day, and accordingly he went, but he was no hypocrite. He was a man of duty, not of sentiment. The new order of things seemed to me terrible, but I soon got over it. I was now merely 13. It was 1866. In this year I was made a communicant.

Strange, too, in the same month in which this event happened, my tender faith was shaken so rudely that it never recovered. On the Sunday after Easter we were made church members. Next day the new communicants, their parents—in most cases only the female part—and our good shepherd, made an excursion to Dettelbach, where a wooden image of the holy mother of God, which was said to have done miscellaneous miracles, resided in a cloister-church. We set out on foot and walked the distance which was an hour and a half. The way led through pine woods. The time was passed delightfully. For say what you may, the Catholic priests are always men who understand the people; only such are selected for the profession. They had their holy and pious fun with the women and there was much merrymaking. The first thing we did when we arrived in D. was to visit the celebrated image, where we were made to swear with great solemnity that we would cast away reason forever, wherever said Satan did antagonize the articles of faith of the church. We did not know what we did; at any rate we acted under compulsion. Therefore our vow was null and void. The thirsty shepherds shortened the visit of honor to St. Mary as much as possible, and led their congregation to a saloon where the old heathen St. Bacchus, was arduously and deservedly venerated. We quit Mary's parlor half an hour after we had entered it, but Bacchus, more enchanting than the holy virgin, kept us for some hours. One of the holy men forgot that these heathen gods are treacherous tricksters after all, and was not careful enough as to the number of libations he offered to Lemele's and Jove's son and the hellish fire of Franconian wine made his walk less dignified than the occasion justified. He seemed to be all aglow; his eyes were sparkling and rolling; his hands described all sorts of geometrical figures in the air; his very hair stood up, a circumstance in which, no doubt, it was due that the clerical stovepipe involuntarily receded in a semi-circular way, leaving the impression of the "old-timer" during a spree.

The other shepherds were very sorry as they beheld his doleful condition. They caught him under his arms, and took him down to the river, where a large barge was waiting to bring the whole congregation back to Kitringen. The women—good souls—pitied the worthy reverend, but as they were themselves in a hilarious mood, they forgave him his woeful sins, as christian women always do. It was a fine evening. The barge was well filled with boys and girls, with women and men. Of the latter were few, among them the shepherds. *"In vine veritas"* says the Latin proverb (wine is truth), and the truth came out pretty strong from the consecrated lips of our unfortunate shepherd.

His unruly tongue meant mischief. One of his colleagues said: "Let us sing a hymn," whereupon one of the boys with a conspicuously long frock-coat stood up and howled the verses of the hymn—"Great God, we praise thee!" The musical feat was followed by the boys and girls, who repeated each line in a chorus. But the jolly priest was displeased with our incantation and interrupted the proceedings with disapproving remarks, such as: "Shut up your nonsense." "You, with your long frock-coat, keep your tongue," "I am sick of your singing." "I'll give you a sechser (5 cents) if you keep quiet," and so on. Then he began jesting with the women on board of the ship. I do not know whether this occurrence made any impression on my schoolmates, but I know that I could not help thinking that the reverend father did not believe in his own teachings. And from that day I began to doubt in earnest the truth of christianity. This sinner was a very talented man, and somewhat later published a book, in which he defended the doctrine of the infallibility of the pope. At present he is a Catholic bishop in Speier, Germany.

I was about 13 years of age at that time. I think it was four or five months later when Schiller's works fell into my hands. That was forbidden literature! Nevertheless, we pupils read and enjoyed them very much. Schiller, like all really great German classics, was a disbeliever in Christianity. A new world sprang into existence before my eyes. He simply carried me along. Till then I only had known of him by "selected" poems, that I saw in the school books. All our teachers told us about him and the other classics was, that they were great men, but their works were no proper reading matter for boys. They were well enough for grown up persons. After Schiller, I took to Goethe, the "Great Heathen," as well he was called by the priests, who undertook to enlighten us in the doctrines of the Catholic faith. Truth compels me to say that most of the pupils admired more the "Great Heathen" writings than his teachings of the "alone saving church." In school we had to learn Latin, Greek, German, geography, history, etc. We heard a good deal of the old slayers of tyrants—Aristolgelton, Harmodios, the two Brutus[58] and others, and they were praised very much for their patriotic deeds in our school books; somewhat remarkable in a monarchical country!

Of course, our king was, according to our teacher, a model king and not at all like Peisistratos, Tarinwins Luperbus or Caesar.[59] An exemplary king indeed he was, our

Ludwig, for he was at that time, already out of his senses. Whether it was intended or not, (of course not) but the fact remains that we all believed that it was the proper thing to kill tyrants at first sight. We did not know that some of our well beloved "fathers of our country" were even worse than the oppressors of ancient times. Greeks and Romans were our ideals. We heard so much of the eternal gods, that many of us had a longing for the time where they reigned instead of their grim descendent, the cold God of Christianity, who drove his merry predecessors from Olympus. Often enough the thought would arise in my mind, however hard I tried to banish it—"Will there in future time be still another God, one who will depose the God of the Christians just the same as he had deposed the Gods of the heathen?" Yet these thoughts I considered sinful and conscientious as I was, I mentioned them to my confessor. But lo! he was a poor warrior of the Ecclesia militants. All he told me was, that scholars of high reputation, kings and emperors had believed, and therefore a boy like me had no right to *think* about such matters. They had believed; could there be a more convincing argument why I should believe? He himself was not of an inquiring disposition, and what he said was probably his honest conviction. As I have stated before, I was a religious fanatic at the age of ten to twelve. The priests I viewed at that epoch as demigods, but, when I saw what they really were, men of the world in every sense of the word, the nimbus faded away, and their teachings lost their influence. The business, like many in which they went through their religious duties was shocking to me, when I commenced serving them as an acolyte. But after a time I fell in with them and lost my fanaticism. Then came the study of German, Greek and Roman classics. My faith dwindled and dwindled and when I was sixteen, instead of being a Roman Catholic, I was an atheist, that is, my faith was simply the belief in a personal God, and some years later I did not even believe that.

Circumstances, first of all, lack of means, compelled me to quit school and learn a trade. I selected the book-binding business, and was apprenticed to a book-binder in Wuerrburg, on the 5th of August, 1869. The change was rather hard for me. The master was one of those poor devils who struggle with all their might to eke out an existence, and who are destined to be crushed by capital. We worked thirteen hours a day in summer time and, in winter time fifteen to seventeen hours. Nearly every Sunday forenoon we worked also. He was a good workman, but at that time the fate of manufacturers without capital was already sealed. The good man said often enough, that he would earn more money as a journeyman and would work as such, but he was more independent as a "manufacturer." He died about four years later, killed, as I believe by over work. He was smaller than his new apprentice and square shouldered. One of his many troubles was that his wife was a little taller than he, and I never saw him side by side with her on the street. Many were the jokes his acquaintances had with him on that account. He was an enthusiast and was of the opinion that the priest-craft was the root of all evil. No wonder! Bavaria was, when he was young and later, ruled by clericals. He was 23 when he engaged himself to his wife, and 30 when he was allowed to marry her. Thirteen long years he had petitioned, till at last there was an opening for him in Wuerrburg.

At those times only a certain number of manufacturers were allowed for each city and only by marrying a widow or daughter, or buying out another master, it was possible to start up in business. Sometimes favoritism was shown by the officers. My good master had to wait thirteen years till he got a chance. No wonder he hated these institutions!

Now all this is changed. The change came soon after the little man's bold enterprise.

As an apprentice I lived a very solitary life, books, books, and nothing but books! I bound them and I read them. How often did I sit till 1 o'clock in the morning with my beloved classics! They were everything to me, and a great deal of my time I thus mentally spent in Italy and Greece. Religious books and pamphlets I studied, too, but they only tended to strengthen my disbelief in religious teachings.

In 1870 the German-Franco war broke out. Little did I then know of politics, but as I abhorred wholesale slaughter, my patriotism did not loom up to the highest pitch. After the battle of Sedan, Germany was overflooded with captured Frenchmen.[60] Wuerrburg got her share, 6,000 men. The whole population of the city being then only 40,000, every second grown man was certainly French. Our newspapers had depicted them as a sort of cannibals, but they behaved themselves as well as German soldiers. They were very polite and very fond of children. Some of them worked in the city as mechanics, others roamed about till evening came, when they had to repair to their barracks. And they too found out that the Germans were not barbarians.

The hate of nationalities is indeed an artificial device. It is a fact that the socialistic workingmen of France and Germany protested against the murderous war, before it had its terrible sway.[61]

Time passed on very rapidly, and I was no longer an apprentice. It was in March, 1892, I was working, when a law student who lodged with my employer went to the shop, picking up a newspaper and addressing me, he said: "I suppose you will become a socialist too?" I looked at him and said, "I don't know. What is a socialist anyhow?" He couldn't tell exactly, thought socialists were dissatisfied workingmen. He would not say they were wrong, but they made a good deal of trouble. Three of their leaders, Bebel, Liebknecht, and Hepner were just then in Leipzig on trial for "preparation for high treason," but there could be no conviction, everybody said, the accusation being simply ridiculous.[62]

That was the first time I ever heard anything of socialism. I read now the report of the trial and found to my astonishment that Bebel and Liebknecht were convicted by a jury of their political antagonists and sentenced to two years' confinement in jail. This occurrence called me back from the ancient Greeks and Romans to modern peoples, and I looked out for socialistic literature. My employer had a friend who was a socialist with heart and soul, and he furnished me with socialistic papers. In the same year the journeymen of the bookbinding trade formed a union and I became one of its members, and then for the first time I came in real contact with workingmen. It did not take long to make a socialist of me; the leaders of the union were socialists and worked for their principles. We gained by our union a reduction of the hours of labor from twelve to eleven hours a day, and a slight increase in wages. At that time there were two factions of socialists in Germany, the "General German Workmen's Association," and the "Social-Democratic Labor Party."

"The General German Workmen's Association" was founded by Ferdinand Lassalle. Lassalle was born 1825 and died August 31, 1864. His agitation among the German workmen was of short duration, one year and five months, but most remarkable. I doubt that there ever was an agitator who accomplished so much as he did in so short a time. A most phenomenal man. He was a scholar of great learning, which is conceded by his most bitter enemies, an orator of great power and a fascinating writer. He wrote two great works and besides a great many pamphlets.[63] The most difficult scientific problems were rendered comprehensible by him to the ordinary workman, and herein consisted his force.

In the year 1862 some labor leaders contemplated calling a labor convention. Some of them were of the opinion that politics were better let entirely alone by the workingman, others held the German workmen were destined to be the tail of the "Progressive party" composed chiefly of great and small manufacturers, merchants and professors. A committee went to the leaders of the "Progressive party" and asked for the privilege for the workmen to become members of the party organization. They were snubbed. Lassalle was known in Berlin as a scientific man, and a friend of men like Humboldt[64] and Bolkh. He lectured now and then, and his views were rather radical. The snubbed committee went to Lassalle and he gave his opinions in writing. This document was called "An open letter to the central committee for calling a general German workmen's convention in Leipzig." He counseled the workingmen to ask the right to vote for every person whether rich or poor, to inaugurate independent political action and free individual association for production with the help of the state. The convention which was held 1863 adopted these views.*

And from that time hence he led a life of almost incredible activity. The "General German Workmen's Association" was founded and gained members, especially in western Germany. The Berlin workmen reserved a cool attitude against the new movement. They never had 100

* The "open letter" is translated into English and was printed in New York. [Note in original]

members of the organization during his lifetime. Once he was arrested in a meeting; workmen spat on him and cheered the police! Well, all this has changed. Today the socialists are the strongest party in Berlin.[65]

Lassalle turned his guns against his own class, the bourgeoisie, and they made it pretty hot for him. All the newspapers slandered him and ran him down in a way which would do credit even to such experts as their Chicago colleagues. But he stood his ground well and gained his point. Of course they dragged him to the courts. As a learned scholar of the law he defended himself, and his speeches served as a most powerful means of propaganda. (But I nearly forgot that I am expected to write my own biography and not that of Lassalle.) The organization founded by Lassalle was centralistic, and he being president thereof. The presidents after him were no Lassalles; nevertheless the organization grew, although centralization was found wanting.

In the year 1869 former members of the "General German Workmen's Association," and others who held more progressive ideas, called a convention in Elswach in Thuringia. There the Social Democratic Labor party was born. Its principles were: abolition of class rule, abolition of the wage-system, and introduction of co-operative system to gain for the workman the full fruit of his labor; to strive for political liberty as a means to gain economic freedom, and farther, "the liberation of labor is neither local nor national but a social mission and therefore international." The new party had its stronghold in southern, the old one in northern Germany. There were now two socialistic parties, who fought each other, not only theoretically, but often enough, in the physical sense of the word. After some years these parties became convinced of the folly of their antagonism towards each other, and they united—(1876, convention, in Gotha).[66] The persecutions of the government against both parties had, moreover, made this coalition necessary. The new party was called "Socialistic Labor Party of Germany," and is still in existence, having at the present time 25 members in the Reichstag. The principles of this party do not differ from that of the former "Social Democratic Labor Party."

It was the "Social Democratic Labor Party" which I entered in 1872. Nothing of importance happened to me till the spring of 1874, when I left Wuerrburg to go abroad. Since the middle ages until quite recently it was customary for a young merchant to visit different cities for the purpose of acquiring useful knowledge in his trade. In former times it was compulsory with Journeymen-mechanics to travel. The law was abolished, however, some thirty or forty years ago, still the custom remained. Instead of law, dire necessity compels the workmen now-a-days to migrate from town to town, and it is not always the young mechanic who tramps along the dusty road, but, in many cases, it is the head of family or the gray-haired man, whom nobody wants to employ and who often perishes on a biting cold winter day on the road. These traveling mechanics are called "trades-fellows" (Journeymen).

In former times when the factory system and the railroads were little known in Germany, these "trades-fellows" were a different sort of people from what they are now. Many of them were sons of well-to-do people and had money enough to defray the expenses of their keep in the world; others made their way by "fighting," which strong-sounding term was used euphemistically for—begging. The peasants were always willing to help the poor journeyman along. This begging was by no means considered disgraceful—many an old manufacturer even to-day relates with delight and pride his former "fighting" exploits.

All this is altered now. Industrial progress made itself first known to the peasant by the from day to day increasing number of beggars, regular tramps, who were not weeks but months on the road. The number of "trades-fellows," tramps, vagabonds, etc., on great country roads is simply incredibly large. I remember myself once having sat down to rest near the city of Stuttgart, three or four others did the same thing. Just for fun we called halt to all traveling in the same direction, traveling journeyman and unemployed factory hands, and in less than an hour we had collected a force of thirty or forty men, most of them without a cent in their pocket, and they all had to make their living by begging. This was nothing extraordinary. Of course, this was near a great city, but it may serve to give an idea to what extent the German peasant has to suffer from the "reserve army" of the capitalists. Our industrial system needs this army first to enable the exploiter to "regulate" wages, second to have always workmen on hand for any emergency. With these people I now came in contact.

When I left Wuerrburg I went to Munich, from there, after two months stay, to Innsbruck. I was then in the spring of life and quite an enthusiast. You may imagine what impression the eternal snow-covered mountains of the grand Alps made upon me. In Tyrol I traveled on foot inasmuch as at that time no railroad led from there to Switzerland. After a perilous walk over the Arlberg Pass, which was covered with deep snow, I reached the valley in which the city of Bludenz is situated. There I took the train and went over to St. Gallen, and to Zurich, where I found work and stayed for some time.

Switzerland is the holy land for every liberty loving German. Zurich the Mecca of every German Republican, and indeed if there is an ideal republic, Switzerland is that one. What is the highly-praised constitution of the

United States compared with the constitution of this little republic! To begin with, the president of Switzerland is in fact only president of the meetings of a board of counsellors; he has no veto power, no monarchical authority. The people have the right reserved to themselves to cancel any law made by their lawmaking bodies, and no law is law until approved by the people at large. The people have the right of the initiative, i.e., propose laws to the representatives. Justly it is claimed that Switzerland has the best laws for the benefit of the toiler. Every able-bodied citizen is a member of the militia and bound to keep the necessary small fire arms at home. All that a democratic republic can give, Switzerland gives, yet in spite of all this, even in that model land of political freedom, there is want, misery and starvation. The freeholders, who were the creators of these free institutions are getting into bankruptcy, their sons and daughters are forced to sell their working capacity to the factory owner, and the once independent son of the Alps is forced to come down from the mountain, leave the farm where his forefathers lived and died, and descend from an independent mountaineer to a dependent factory slave.

Instead of the melodious tinkling of the bells of his cows, he now hears the task bell of the factory, that calls him to work. Instead of the splashing or roaring of the creeks and cataracts, the whispering of the air in the dark-green forests, he is treated to the clattering of noisy busy machines. Stout, big-chested, strong-limbed and with rosy cheeks he fell into the power of enslaving capital. Alas! it lasts not long till the cheeks lose their color, the limbs their strength and the freeman his independence. His offspring, growing up in unhealthy surroundings, are a different race—the race of exploited, wretched wage-slavers. "Work, work, work! to enrich some money-making spinner king," is the watchword for his daughters, whose youth and beauty is only a farther curse to make their life miserable and wretched. For the industrial ruler makes it a condition for granting the privilege of a job—for them to surrender their virtue or starve. This is a dark picture, but it is a feeble one and nothing but the truth. Switzerland taught me for the first time that political liberty without economic freedom is a mocking lie, a corpse without life.

After working for several months in Zurich I went, partly on boat and partly on foot, to the most beautifully situated city, Luzern on the "Vierwaldstaetter lake." Some months later I left for Bern, where I worked for the first time near one of those unfortunate girls, whose small pay compels them to make up the requisite balance by street walking. Rosa—this was her name—was already doomed when I first saw her. The expression of her face was sad, the eyes were sunken deep into their sockets, the cheeks were deadly pale and already had those fatal blue spots, which appear in the latter stages of consumption, and this woman had to work 11 to 12 hours a day and then solicit customers for lust, to banish starvation from herself and mother! And such cases as this are very numerous in all industrial centers of Europe, *and the United States!* What a terrible accusation against our Christian civilization! Later in my life I saw even more horrible crimes of this kind. At that time I commenced to hate the capitalistic system.

I left Switzerland in the year 1875. It was spring. I was young, and not inclined to sour and rust by staying too long in a city. This time I went on foot to see the fertile country, to observe the customs of the people, to admire the old cities of the Rhine with their magnificent cathedrals, and to taste the much lauded Rhine wine. I had money enough in my pocket to satisfy my modest desires.

This time I had many socialistic pamphlets with me, and my heart was full of socialism. Every traveler, if he was intelligent enough to be talked to, was very soon made to discuss socialism. It made no difference whether he was a "trades fellow" or a peasant; I dare say I made many converts. Other socialists employed the same means of propaganda; often enough other traveling workmen assisted me in the good work. The evening brought rest to the brotherhood of "trade fellows," and when I arrived at the inn I opened my bundle and gave them something to read. It consisted of all kinds of literature; what I had there were poems, novels, economic treatises, speeches—but all were socialistic.

In the cities we, agitators, went to the socialistic newspaper offices, got some old copies, which were distributed in the villages through which we passed. This kind of agitation is still going on in Germany. My next halting place was Glessen, in Upper Hessia. From there I went over to Hanover, Brunswick, and to Saxony, the most industrial province in Germany. In Meerane, one of the weaver towns, I stayed for a longer period, working at my trade. This was the place particularly suited for social studies, as there the capitalistic system reigns supreme. Inquiries revealed the fact to me, that in this town—as in all other German weaving towns—heads of families average from 6 to 8 marks ($1.25 to $1.75) a week! Of course the wife and children have to work, too, "to make ends meet."

Wage slavery is more horrible than chattel slavery! This capitalistic system is beautifully harmonious. It forces the wife to slave in the factory-hell, takes her away from her household work, the kitchen and the children. And lo! the rooms are so bare of furniture, that in some instances even beds are considered a luxury. The wages are so small that the people can well dispense with the cooking art; nor have they any time to transform eatables into meals. And last but not least, the children are brought up under the kind supervision of some foreman who works them for the glory of our civilization. Thank God, we have left the dark ages of barbarism behind us. It may be interesting for some readers to know how these people live. In the morning, very thin coffee with a slice of brown bread and fat (butter is too dear); at ten, a slice of bread and fat; at noon potatoes or vegetables, with or without a little soup-meat (in most cases without) or dumplings made of potatoes or flour; at four, brown bread and fat, and in the evening, coffee very thin and bread and fat. This is considered a good bill of fare, and they do not always get such luxurious meals. It is very painful for a stranger to note that "father" or "brother" "who has to work so hard" gets more and better morsels than the hungry children. Mother is always satisfied with very little.

The homes are simply crowded; kitchen, parlor and bedroom is one, every other room is stuffed with lodgers. Men and women sleep, often enough, in one room. I myself, have seen that. I have seen that girls 13, 14, or 15 years old would strip their clothes down to the waist and wash themselves in the presence of strangers. It was done without hesitation, without a sign of bashfulness, for there was no other room for them. The factory lord considers his working girls his mistresses. No, no, not that. He would not dare to ask from a mistress what he compels these unfortunates to do. When I was in Meerane, one of the lords had for his own and his friend's amusement, a ball where his most beautiful working girls had—but I can't coin words to relate the occurrence in decent phrases. After the ball was over, every girl received as wages of sin 25 cents. Dear Christian ladies, this is shocking, is it not? But it is the system that develops these things. How do the poor people bear them? Let me answer in the language of Heine, the German poet:[67]

With tearless eyes in despair and gloom,
Gnashing their teeth, they sit at the loom;
"Thy shroud we weave, Germany of old.
We weave into the curse three-fold.
We are weaving, weaving, weaving."

"A curse to the false God we prayed to in vain,
In our winter's cold in hunger and pain;
Our hope, our waiting all were for naught,
He fooled us, he mocked us, a terrible thought.
We are weaving, weaving, weaving."

"A curse to the king, the king of the rich,
For none of our misery his heart did reach;
He takes our money the very last cent,
To shoot us like dogs, his soldiers he sent.
We are weaving, weaving, weaving."

"A curse to the state, O false fatherland,
Shame and disgrace are cursed by thy hand;
Where blossoms are early broken by storm,
And in rot and in mould delights the worm.
We are weaving, weaving, weaving."

"The rattling loom, the shuttle's flight,
We are busy weaving day and night;
Thy shroud we weave, Germany of old,
We weave into it the curse three-fold.
We are weaving, weaving, weaving."

These are the sentiments of the people. Maybe that in reading these lines some American scribe or hypocrite, knocks his breast and squints his eyes, saying: "God, I thank thee, thank thee, that we Americans are not as other men are, extortioners, adulterers, or even as these German factory lords." To him I say: "My friend look around in this glorious republic and you will discover the same horrible state of affairs. Is it not true that only last month (November) a number of Brooklyn girls struck for their honor. They asked for protection against rape! And when the German weavers weave shroud for old Germany then the starving coal miners of Pennsylvania, Ohio, Illinois and other states dig the grave of Old America." *De te fabula naratur!*[68]

This story of German wrongs is the story of American wrongs. The government is only too willing to lend a helping hand to capitalistic oppressors. There are more striking workmen killed by American authorities per annum than in all despotic countries in Europe. Even in Chicago are whole quarters where people are starving and perishing by the score. Thousands of children are worked to death or perdition. Look about you and see it.

Of course not in every province of Germany is misery prevailing to such an extent, but they are coming to it. And the same is true of these United States.

Meerane is a socialistic stronghold, and I belonged there to a socialistic society, and founded a society myself called the "Red Club." This club's object was to educate speakers. As the summer drew near its end I made a long journey through Thuringia and northern Germany. That time I visited Berlin for a short time, after that I went to Hamburg and took work in one of the suburbs of the city.

The suburb is named Wandsbeck and is overwhelmingly socialistic. When I was there the election of a member for the German parliament took place. This was 1876. There was a split in the socialistic ranks. The most popular leader of the town seceded and put a candidate of his own in the field. The capitalists were jubilant. But discipline was so excellent there, that the secession candidate got only eight votes while the regular socialistic nominee got 800. In districts where the socialists are strong, election times are very exciting. Men, women and children are electioneering and attend the meetings. Much shouting and singing is done. On Sundays, groups of thirty or forty workingmen or shopkeepers—a good many of the latter are socialists—walk to the villages and stir the farmers and their hired men up.

After such and other preparations the day arrived, when the paper-battle commenced. I went with thirty other socialists to a village, and then the trouble of the good villagers commenced. Some of us repaired to the voting place—for in Germany also in America, those so well-known tricks are practiced. Others went from house to house and ran the candidates of the other party down, but the rich farmers held their hired men out of the way and marched them to the voting place, where they did not dare to vote for our candidate. In this village we got more than one-third of the votes, on a former occasion we had a majority. In the meantime it was pretty lively in the cities, Altona (100,000 inhabitants) and Wandsbeck. The police and the hussars were called out, but there was no riot. The capitalistic party hired coaches for voters, the socialists did the same thing. The coachmen of the former party had blue, those of the latter party had red badges. If it is true that a voter is a sovereign, then the voters of these places were certainly such, for not only free rides were furnished, but meals, and wine, and beer also, lodgings they did not provide, for the sovereign was deposed at 6 o'clock, p.m., when the polls closed. During the day men ran through the streets with poles on which there were mottoes like this, "Vote for the friend of the people, H.H." All the candidates styled themselves thus, and it was therefore pretty sure that a friend of the people would be elected. The women, especially our lady comrades developed an energy in dragging tardy voters to the polling places that was simply appalling. In the cities we had a clear majority, but weighed down by the country vote we had only a plurality, the main candidates had about 13,000 each, our candidate was in the lead. A third candidate had polled 100 votes and a new election was ordered, for in Germany an absolute majority is necessary for election. The socialists, as a rule, only took part in the elections for the parliament, for the election laws for other bodies gave the workingman no show. I found the registration lists, in which every vote was marked, and saw the tickets that were thrown out. I saw from the lists that all the stayaways were workmen, all the voters of the middle or upper classes had voted. One of the castaway tickets read thus: "I do not vote for Hartmann, nor for Herstein, I have elected one, and his name is Jesus Christ." It seems that Jesus Christ is in Germany ineligible.

When summer came, I commenced traveling again. I wanted to see Vienna. It took me four months to get there, for I was not in a hurry, and took a roundabout way on foot, on boat, and on railroad. In some towns, in Cologne and in Botzen (in Tyrol) I worked a short time, only to rest a little. This time I visited Westphalia, Rhenisch, Prussia and enjoyed the beautiful landscapes on the Rhine. From there I went to Bavaria and then to Tyrol. After wearisome marches I arrived in Botzen. The man for whom I worked was a Catholic, and had a clerical brother. Therefore he considered it his duty to make converts. Another journeyman was a Protestant and already member of the "Catholic Journeymen Society." Now as I was a former Catholic, he set at once to work to save my poor troubled soul, even of whose existence I wasn't quite sure. He commenced first by extolling his wife and himself, how their religion gave them peace and rest, and what holy and contented men and women their ancestors had been. A certain former official, his father-in-law was pictured as a model man of faith and goodness. But it was rather unlucky that the hired girl was in love with the half-converted I protested, and so it happened that we knew the sins of our employer, his wife and those of the dear relations better than our own. The highly respected official was an embezzler who had spent some years in the penitentiary, the good housewife could not cook a meal, and had married because she was told, that is as it must be, only having known her husband six weeks before they entered their holy partnership for life. Her mother did not dare to visit a certain place because she did, when a barmaid there, certain swinish things. The so much lauded peace and rest were all humbug, for he and his wife did not even like each other. Thanks to the hired girl we know all these facts. Armed with this useful knowledge all the bold assertions of the holy agitator seemed to us ridiculous.

I cared little for the man's religious notions, for in that respect very few men are sound—if they are—but when he told me that it was the custom in Botzen to work in winter time 14 instead of 12 hours, that, however, the custom did not allow to increase pay, I shook the dust from my feet and left.

The reader thinks it probably a horrible thing to work 14 hours a day, and it is; but it must be taken into consideration, that in such out-of-the-way towns, which are still deep in the mire of the middle ages, everything goes along in a slow way, and there is not much "deadworking" as in progressive, hurrying cities with shorter hours of labor. It is simply impossible to work as many hours with machines as without them. Without machines the workman stops here a minute, there a minute; goes slower now and then, and is careful not to overwork himself. The machine alters this. It does not stop for a minute, or run a little slower; it takes no considerations whatever. On it rattles, never tiring, never resting, and the workman is dragged along. Therefore the reduction of the hours of labor was a necessity.

From Botzen I went to Munich. It was summer. I was young, and as a great admirer of the grand Alps, I walked most of the way, in order to enjoy the always changing scenes. In my company was my fellow-workman of Botzen. As soon as we had left the mountains behind us, we took the train for the metropolitan city of Bavaria. We came there early in the morning. Near the depot we found a great many loungers, who slept in the corners and niches of the building. It was still night, but the pale moon was shining bright. We stood still, lost in contemplation. It was a part of the world we wanted to see. These poverty-stricken people before us had not even the little money to pay for one night's lodging, and so they put us up as best they could. We were not very long standing there, when two night constables appeared. Some of the poor wretches got up and left suddenly, others still slept on; they were rudely shaken up by the men of law and order, and carefully examined. After telling these proletarians, who like Jesus, "had not where to lay their heads," to move on, the constables stopped there, and we went, under the eyes of the law, towards the city. One was of a sentimental turn of mind. He said: "It's a rather painful duty to chase these unfortunates away, but we have to do it, or else risk our positions. You have no idea how many people in these hard times are unsheltered.

In Munich I stayed only one day. I had Vienna in my mind. I went over Salzburg to Linz, where I took the boat. It was later in the evening when we landed in the empire city of Vienna. There I worked for two manufacturers; one of them belonged to the slowly perishing manufacturers, killed by steam and machinery; the other to the prosperous manufacturers, growing by the same agencies.

Mr. Young was an old man, 70 years old, his wife 35. Once, years ago, he was doing well, but he did not understand the times. When machines made their appearance in the trade he did not appreciate their significance, lost customers, lost money, lost confidence in himself, and his first wife, who died rather in time. Then he tried to better his fortune by marrying again a peasant maiden of about 30, who had no attractions whatever, but a little money. This woman was attracted to this unhappy marriage by the glowing prospect of city life that existed in her fertile imagination. She had cause later on to repent her foolishness. Mr. Young was unable to call fortune back, although he worked as much as an old man can. The marriage gift went for a paper-cutter and other improvements of the small shop, but the needs of life compelled him to raise money and the cutter had to be sold for cheap cash.

Without capital, without the necessary machinery of a modern book bindery he could not take in work like his capitalistic competitors, and nevertheless, he was bound to struggle on or die with his wife and his three boys age one, five and twelve years. And a terrible struggle it was. He only had customers who could get no work done elsewhere, either on account of their scanty pay or because they were generally no good. One of his best customers was an author, one of those men who get on by contracting debts and swindling on a small scale. He published an almanac. It was a rather difficult job to get money out of him. After many visits, much begging, cajoling, threatening, and God knows what else, he designed to give up some dollars. If money run short Mr. Young and his family had nothing to eat, for the grocer had long ceased to give them victuals on credit. I have seen that they had no dinner at all, or some hours after on account of the scarcity of money. It was a terrible sight to behold the pinched faces and the hungry looking eyes of the poor boys of whom the oldest was an invalid. The old man was an optimist nevertheless, for there hardly passed a day, that did not smash some hope of his to pieces. The yellow peasant woman, his wife, was all despair and had lost all energy. She was always either crying or bewailing her fate. Shop, parlor, kitchen and partially bed room was all the same room. The shop etc., had two windows facing a yard, hardly a sunbeam found its way into this chamber of human misery.

The only thing to smile at there was a baptised Hebrew who came on a visit now and then, and held a mortgage on the scanty furniture, but the beds, the table and chairs, etc., were not worth the money he had loaned on them. As far as I could judge he was a kind hearted man, although ludicrous in the extreme. His chief pleasure was to talk about the rascality of the Jews and the high virtue of us Christians. This spoken in Jewish pronunciation from the lips of a typical Hebrew sounded oddly enough. After some weeks I left. I do not know what became of Mr. Young and his family afterwards. Such unhappy beings may be found by the thousand in every large city of Europe, yes even in our proud Chicago, not ten minutes walk from our crumbling court house. In Europe such families end either by slow or quick starvation, or they perish by murder or suicide, or the sheriff takes for some debtor everything from them. The glorious law as lawyers put it, allows that, and puts them on the street. Oh yes, we live in a very civilized Christian age!

After some weeks passing in compulsory idleness I got work in the magnificent shop of Mr. Gockel. He was a Tyrolere and good Catholic as far as business did not interfere with his holy faith. But I fear business left him little time to look out for his immortal soul. He was one of the model citizens of our capitalistic journalists, having started with nothing and having become a very prosperous business man. He was always working, mostly bookkeeping. His friends said that he was an amiable companion. If he talked to a workingman he always said something like Mr. H, please be so kind, etc. But his main object in life was to work, make others work, and to make money thereby. In the words of Judge Gary, Gockel "loved his home, his country and his property."

In his shop were about 25 men, 20 women and one apprentice. This apprentice was treated in a fearful manner. Not enough that his master cowhided him for every mistake he made, he asked it as a favor of the workingmen to abuse the boy in the same way. The workmen, be it said to their credit, refused to do it; although, the *law* gives them expressly the right to act as dastardly brutes. Nominally the working hours were ten, but there was always some extra hours put in, yes, I know that in one week 120 hours were worked, Sunday included. Three times in this memorable week, 36 consecutive hours. The model money maker stopped this only on account of its impracticability. Some of his hands fell down and were brought to the hospital, the others were so tired the next week that it was impossible for them to work as used to. His arrangement *did not pay in the long run* and so he abandoned it for another. The other scheme was the following: Ten hours a day and two to six hours over work every day, over work on Sunday eight hours. Nearly all the work was piecework, which was arranged in a way that the workman became exploiter himself. The model sublet certain quantities of work to a workman who was given two or three girls or men, who worked for him. The sub-contractor made usually fair wages by exploiting the other workers in a shameful manner. Of course he hurried them up to a terrible rate of speed. A girl would make by that kind of work from four to five guldens a week (1 gulden—50 cents), a workman 8 to 12, and the sub-contractor 15 to 20. It must be taken into consideration that meals and clothing are in Vienna to be had for a little over one-half the price they cost in Chicago.

To get the above wages the average overtime was necessary. If women were put on work by the hour they got only two-thirds of the wages men got for the same kind of work. Somebody stole here openly one-third of somebody's wages, besides the hidden theft called profit. As far as I am concerned, I was mostly let alone to work either by piece or by the hour. And Mr. Moneymaker seemed to like me in his sort of way. Only once a young girl was given me to do some work with me. Well, I had these impractical socialistic notions in my head, and held it to be a crime to coin money out of a fellow-creature, even if it was only a working girl "and paid her" over one half the money I had earned. Of course wages fell below average. It was certainly to my advantage that I was put to other work. The model was particularly great in showing his contempt for "his hands." But there were great differences. A poor man who had worked himself to an invalid—he was only 30—in his shop, and could certainly get no work elsewhere, was especially abused by him. As a rule he let those workmen alone who were liable to use violence in a given case. But it was another thing with girls, who never dared to reply to his insolent vicious remarks. The age of the girls ranged from 13 to 20; one woman was 40. She had a number of children from different men. When he became furious—at least once every day—he used epithets as "wenches," "jades," "whores," and the like. Some workmen and some girls, the old woman foremost, used to gloat very often over sexual brutalities and certain sicknesses, and some of the hearers were girls 13, 14, and 15 years old. Of course the learning in the moral atmosphere of such hell was not lost. Some years later the pupils were teachers, and who is going to cast the first stone at them? If decency would not forbid I might have made the picture even more graphic by using darker colors. A good many things I did not state on that account.

In the summer time I left Vienna for a last journey, and then I thought I would settle down somewhere. I went through southern Germany and Switzerland, and conceived at last the idea to emigrate to Australia. What I had seen of the world had made my heart ache, and I think that the main object of that plan was to flee from such horrible surroundings.

I was again in Saxony. It was the year 1879. In Plauen I got work in a blank book factory. The owner of the factory was a polite man, who never said a harsh word to anybody; but he had his prey, to be sure, and it was unnecessary for him to be insolent and rough. He knew well enough that he could get girls and men by the hundreds if he wanted them. There was no indecent language—no, nothing of that kind, oh, no! There was not even piece work. Two men worked always together, and it was the easiest thing in the world to find out who worked the quickest. Now to the list of wages. The foreman got $4.50, the average workman $2.50 to $3.00, the porter $1.75 a week for 12 hours daily labor. It was just enough for an average workman to live as an average $6.00 or $8.00 clerk lives. Of course the clerk has most of his money to expend for clothes. The porter was forced to marry to get along. This seems to be a joke, so it is but a grim one. To state it in a matter-of-fact way, he had to go into partnership with another person, who could cut his expenses down by washing, cooking, earning money for him and would raise children with him who, as soon as they could firmly stand upon their feet, would earn some pfennige. As to girls who earned from 75 cents to $1.50 a week and the majority of whom stood on their own hook, if they made it up somehow, who is going to blame them?

The plan to emigrate, which I entertained, was changed by me in so far as I contemplated now to go first to the United States, and I began to study the English Language. I boarded with a man who belonged to the so-called middle classes, who was even the owner of a house and garden—mortgaged, of course—and employed a weaver journeyman for the high sum of $1.75 a week. He was, of course, a capitalist. As they said in Plauen, Mr. S. gave very good board and so it was, considering the magnificent sum of $1.75 for board and lodging which I paid per week. Breakfast and supper, bread and lard and "blossom coffee," (the coffee is called that way because you can see through it the blossoms painted on the bottoms of the cup) then for lunch at 10 and 4 o'clock bread and lard, which was taken to the shop by the boarders, dinner, potato dumpling, a little piece of soup meat and some sort of vegetables, every other Saturday excepted, where dinner consisted of herring and potatoes. The latter dish was highly commented upon by outsiders, because in other boarding houses the herring dinner was in order every Saturday. The house was a two-storied new brick building, with a garret where four persons slept, two boarders and two sons of the landlord, but as once a girl came to visit her uncle, she and her cousin, the daughter of the house slept in the same room with the males, because all beds were filled except two in this room. The house and garden owner, the capitalist, an excellent man in his way, was a little ashamed, but he saw no other way and so he communicated the arrangement to us, asking us to behave ourselves, which we did. This is an illustration of crowding people in factory towns, and by no means are such arrangements seldom. In this house, as in many others there was no kitchen; one room is used for all purposes. In this room we all sat on the table in the evening. In one corner was a maid of about 28, busy embroidering with a tambour. This girl was at work when I came and when I left, Sunday as well as ordinary work day; what a refreshing sight for a hired man of the press; work, work, work! She never was idle and little complaining, the noise of the machine would not have allowed that. I remember her even singing. But on a certain evening, while I was grappling with English orthography, all of a sudden the machine stopped, and the girl cried aloud, "My God, My God! not one hour's rest in all these long years, nothing but work and nothing but work; late to bed and early up again to rattle on the machine, and only earn just enough to prolong this misery; why did I not die long ago, my God, my God!" and then she dropped her head and sobbed and wept. The good-hearted wife of the house owner and capitalist, who herself had little sunshine in her life, tried to console her. The capitalist himself was not at home; he was in the country peddling goods. After a while the embroideress dried her tears, sighed and went back to work again. Soon after that dramatic scene, I emigrated to America.

It was a beautiful morning when the *Weser,* on which

I had taken passage, landed in New York. As everybody knows, the harbor of New York affords a grand sight and as it is a well known fact that this city is as dirty as can be, anyhow in the neighborhood of the Castle Garden. I need not dwell further on my first impression of this country. I did not stay very long in New York, but after three days delay, I went to Chicago. In Germany, I had always been a member of my Union and of the socialistic party. Arrived in Chicago, I kept aloof from all organizations and led a solitary life. With all my energy, I commenced to study the English language. When I was so far advanced that I could understand books written in that language, I studied the history of the United States. Bancroft's was the best work among those I read[69] and then I turned to geography and labor statistics. Of course, these studies were continued during my seven years stay.

After passing the first year this way and having acquainted myself with the modes of bookbinding in this country in some shops, I went to Milwaukee, where I, after some months life in seclusion, became a member of the Socialistic Labor Party. Its principles differ in no essential point from those of the German social democrats, which I have stated. And now I changed my mode of life to the great astonishment of the lady with whom I boarded. Instead of keeping silent and non-committal, I began to talk to all the twelve boarders of socialism and went out a good deal in the evening. Some of the suddenly attacked workingmen resented, others said they knew everything about it, but their enthusiasm had cooled down forever. But I knew that there is no man on earth who can resist truth successfully, and commenced arguing again and again, till out of the twelve, six became members, and the others sympathized with the movement, always ready to help it along. From Milwaukee I went west and came so far as Durango in Colorado.

The first place I stopped was Kansas City. This city lies on the Kaw river, which at that time over flooded the lower part of the town. My comrade and I strolled down the river. The most exposed quarter was fast getting inundated, there the bulk of the Negro population lived. The huts were built from old lumber and logs. I must confess that in my native town the pigsties were of a better and more substantial build then these palaces of "American sovereigns," as American citizens are proud to call themselves, and these shanties were the homes of men in "the country of the brave and the free," in the sweet land of liberty! There were only Negroes mingled with some white trash—what did it matter anyhow! Farther up in the hills where the "aristocracy" lived there were fine residences. There lived some of the real sovereigns of America.

The people of the inundated districts carried their scanty furniture up hill and placed these in empty lots—how poor they were! From Kansas City I travelled by Denver and Leadville to Cheyenne, Wyoming Territory. There I worked for some time at my trade and led a very quiet life in the little town. There I made the acquaintance of a Mormon elder, who seemed to me rather confused in his ideas. In the evening I usually strolled to the cemetery, where I noticed for the first time in my life that even in death the poor were separated from the rich. In my half communistic native town in barbarism to such an extent conceived, that Catholics, Protestants, well-to-do people and poor men enjoying when dead, at least the earth in common, and they never get quarrelling about it. From Cheyenne I went to Denver, but as I could not get steady work there at my trade, I went farther west to Durango, which took me about two months, because I worked on the way as a farm hand to earn some money. As I could get in Denver no suitable work, I worked for some weeks as hod-carrier, and fell sick. I went back to Chicago where I worked nine months at my trade. On account of scarcity of work I had to stop. At a time when my ready cash was nearly exhausted, a friend of mine brought it about, that the editor of the *Arbeiter-Zeitung* employed me as a translator of the romance "Wanda Kryloff." Soon after that I was employed as a regular reporter, and later on as assistant editor of the *Arbeiter-Zeitung*, which position I occupied when arrested.

I cannot say truthfully that the book-binders of this city are in any way better paid than their German brethren. Their wages range from $5 to $25, most of them earn from $8 to $12 a week. Those who get higher wages are few, and might be termed the aristocracy of the trade. To get more than the average wage a man must display unusual skill or strength.

The kind reader who followed me so far, will perhaps think this Germany is real slave country, but that in this glorious republic things are different. Are they? Let us see. In Saxony a coal miner works eight hours a day and makes about $21 a month, the infamous truck system does not exist,[70] in fact is forbidden by law. In America the truck system is in vogue, and even if a legislature passes a law to suppress this form of robbery, the higher courts declare "it is the privilege of every American workingman to be swindled out of his wages by his employer; to take this privilege away from the toiler would rob him of his freedom, and by the eternal gods we shall not allow that." The superb structure of our liberal institutions must not be assailed. Yes, you may assail it in a windy political harangue. But when you set to work to change one of the many arrangements that have become obnoxious, a peremptory halt is called, and we are forceably reminded of Charles Dickens, "You touch the commons, and down comes the country."

According to the "first annual report of the Commissioner of Labor," American miners work 10 to 11 hours a day, and get from $25 to $50 a month. Of course the lower figures prevail. Out of 300 working days they work about 200. Now, as I know myself from the letters of miners from all over the country, even these figures are too high, although, even they show that the Saxonian miner is better off than the American. But this is not all. The workingmen of this country are "protected" by a high tariff and it is a matter of fact that the commodities of life in this country *are one-third dearer than in Germany.* There is no first-class industrial country on earth whose factory laws give so little protection to the workingman, as the factory laws of this country, with its "highest civilization." What the conditions of these miners is, is well-known. I merely call attention to the fact.

But not only the miners suffer, there are large classes of people who are in exactly the same or even in a condition far worse. It was in the winter of 1882–3 when the citizens' association or league, I don't remember exactly which, sent out a committee under the leadership of Joe Gruenhut and Architect Banman, to investigate the dwelling places of the working people of this city. The committee was accompanied by a swarm of reporters among them Paul Grottkau.[71] He was the first who went out with the committee. By his friends, G. is considered a cynic. When he came back he was deadly pale, greatly excited, he was not feeling too well. He said that he never would go out to see such terrible things again. He knew a good deal of Berlin and her misery, but such a condition of affairs did not exist there, not even in the poorest quarters.

The editor-in-chief sent me out, and I was horrified too,

but went with them every time. The health officer said that he would make no selections but we would go into homes promiscuously, as the same condition of things prevailed in nearly every house. We found single rooms where three or four families lived, we found dwelling places in such a condition, that the officer only took some of us to the second story for fear the ceiling would break through; we saw rooms where only light came in through rents of wall, where human beings slept on rotten straw or rags, where broken chairs and tables were luxuries, where fire was not in the stove although it was bitter cold, and three or four members of the family were sick, we observed water-closets full with excrement. The atmosphere in these "residences of sovereigns" was stifling and sickening. The parents looked hungry and starving, the children, if there were any, were on the road to eternity. Some of these people get their vegetables from the waste-barrel, others beg or buy offal of meat and make sausages out of that. Such is the condition of thousands in Chicago. No newspaper dare deny that, because they printed column after column at that time describing the misery of the unfortunates of Chicago. And all this can be found within four blocks of Wabash avenue. Nothing was done.

What is the difference between the Roman heathens and the American or European christians? The Romans held wild beasts to tear and devour fellow-beings, and applauded lustily. This was done in open daylight. Christian humanity, of course, is different. They train their fellow-beings by the existing order of things till they submit to perish secretly in poverty, hunger and dirt. Their tender feelings do not allow them to gaze upon their victims, and so the highly civilized and respectable citizen prefers to read about these cruelties in his paper, enjoying thereby his comfort all the better.

If the exploiting classes would take warning they might profit by the following story: Once there was a ruler over a certain city in Grecia major. He acted very arbitrarily and took all liberty away from the people. First he took all their arms, then they petitioned, but he did forbid that, and as they were of a very meek and timid character they submitted. But the tyrant was not satisfied even then. He commanded them to hold no meetings in the future. They obeyed. But the poor wretches talked in private about their grievances and lost grievances and lost liberties. As the tyrant heard that, he threatened death to everybody who would henceforth utter a single word. And as the citizens heard this, they went to the market place and wept, but did not say a word. And he, the tyrant, made his appearance and forbade their weeping also. And the citizens took up stones and stoned the oppressor till he was dead, and then they tore down his palace and killed his body guard. And after that, founded a free state and lived happy.

In your midst, ye well-to-do Americans, there is already a class who has lost all hope, who is submissive to everything; don't make the last fatal step! But you neither see nor hear; you will even forbid weeping and then the rats will come out of their holes and sound the chorus: "*Dies ira, dies illa sovet sadum in favillo.*"[72]

The prophet of misfortune is never welcome, and instead of doing away with the causes which hasten the day of judgment, they kill the prophet, adding a new cause to that already existing—accelerating their own ruin!

It was autumn of the year 1881, when I came back to Chicago. Inner dissensions had at that time nearly destroyed all socialistic organizations, although there were thousands of socialists in the city, and the organ of the German socialists, the *Arbeiter Zeitung,* was flourishing. There were radical socialists, their organization was the so-called German section; although called section, it was independent of the Socialistic Labor Party, to which it had belonged in former years; there was the so-called "English Section," which belonged to the Socialistic Labor Party, and there was an independent club called "Socialists of the Northside," composed of members of the two factions. All three organizations were not strong in members. I became a member of the "German Section" and also of the "Socialists of the Northside." I saw at once that the organization of the so-called German section was utterly impracticable, there were more officers during the latter days of its existence present at the meetings than other members. To reform this fossil was out of the question, and so the only way to get rid of it was to let it get weaker and weaker and then throttle it. In the Northside club things were different. There was weakness also, but that was weakness of early youth. In the German section it was that of old age.

The following spring we commenced a lively agitation on the Northside putting candidates in the field. In the 16th ward our candidate, Mr. Eisner, got about 400 votes. After the campaign was over the members of the club who belonged to the Socialistic Labor Party wanted the club to join the party. But the majority resolved to remain independent. Two former meetings of all the representative socialists of Chicago for the purpose of coalition had failed in their object. From the Northside club now a movement started whose aim it was to build up an entirely new organization. The central committee which sprung into existence when the unification of the factions had met with no success, was reorganized and a meeting of socialists resolved, on my motion, to form clubs like the Northside Club all over the city. It was hard work to do that, but it was done. I was one of the organizers and I attended many and many a meeting where only six to twelve persons were present, and always the same old faces!

There were meetings called and nobody except myself and the speaker were present. But we knew we were right and gave to five or six persons perhaps more carefully elaborate speeches than later to audiences of thousands. Slowly we gained a foothold and then we adopted constitutions. The original draught of the constitution was written by me. It was very simple. The object was propaganda of socialism, as laid down in the "Communistic Manifesto" by Marx and Engels. Every club was independent, as far as its own affairs went. Every twenty members were entitled to a delegate to the central committee. Every club had the right to adopt for its own business different rules, but in every instance the officers of the club were: A secretary, a financial secretary, librarian and three revisers. For special business, special committees were elected. It was a feature of our organization that no officer or speaker was allowed pay of any kind. Resolutions of the central committee were only binding for those clubs who approved of them. Every officer or delegate could be withdrawn as soon as his electors saw fit, it was not necessary to give reason for such a proceeding.

In the fall of 1883 we had established about twenty clubs in the city of Chicago, most of them prospering. At that time the radical wing of the socialists called a convention at Pittsburgh. Chicago was represented there. There the "International Working Peoples' Association" was founded. The only change that was made for Chicago was that clubs were called from that time "groups" and the central committee "general committee." There the "Pittsburgh Manifesto" was adopted. Later on most of the "groups" did away with minutes and lists of membership. The financial secretary recorded the members by numbers. This was done, besides other reasons, because some of our members were black-listed and persecuted. The minutes were abandoned, because our societies were debating societies, and it was deemed unnecessary to give an account of discussions in the next meetings.

Each member had to pay 10 cents a month to defray expenses for hall rent, advertisements, hand-bills, etc. There was no secrecy about the meetings. Several times I noticed policemen among the listeners. When I wrote down this "life" I strolled a good deal out of the way, picturing conditions from the life of the people, which I had opportunity to observe. There is nothing new in these observations, thousands make them and—maybe—are not influenced by them at all. They think, either, that these conditions are natural, self-evident, or they don't trouble themselves with any reflections at all. But it was different with me. My surroundings made me a nonbeliever and an anarchist, and therefore they are important as a part of the story of my life. If I had never seen life as it is, I never would have taken to foretelling the coming downfall of this murderous system, and might now cry out like the learned and the ignorant mobsters: "Hang the anarchists!" instead of sitting in the shadow of the gallows. Seeing the terrible abuses with my own eyes, seeing how girls become prostitutes, before they knew it, observing the slaughter of little ones, the killing of workingmen by slow degrees, corruption, misery, crime, hypocrisy, poverty, dirt, ignorance, brutality and hunger everywhere, and conceiving that all these things are the legitimate children of the capitalistic system, which, by establishing the right for single persons to possess the means of production and the land, makes the mass of the people wretched, I become a "kicker." For an honest and honorable man only one course was left, and I became an opponent to the order of things, and was soon called an anarchist.

What are my views? If we socialists, communists and anarchists held the views malicious or ignorant hirelings impute to us in their writings, we would simply be madmen who should be confined in an insane asylum forever. But if it were true that modern socialism, communism and anarchism were methodical madness, how could it be that these doctrines spread all over the world in so short a time? No doctrine whatever made so quick its mark around the world; no doctrine ever made so many converts in so few years! Our martyrs alone count hundreds of thousands in a score of years—men, women, yes even children. They perished in dungeons, in the wilderness, in the snow, and the mines of Siberia, under the tropical sun, they were driven from town to town, from country to country, outcast by their families, and some ended in madness brought about by persecutions such as only modern civilization could invent. Girls brought up in palatial mansions, with a life of ease and luxury before them; youths of rich and aristocratic parents worked as common factory hands, leading a life of misery, with no hope of ever gaining a reward, often enough despised and betrayed even by the class for whom they endured all this—only to preach the gospel of the saving of mankind—socialism, communism, anarchism. Of some of these heroes not even the names are known. Even one of your famous American poets—Joaquin Miller—could not help to say, in a poem written to the praise of that noble anarchist girl, Sophia Perowekaja, who was hung, that he would rather die with her at the gallows, than live as the Russian Czar.[73] There is certainly truth in an idea, which has such martyrs. If our doctrine was wrong, our enemies would state the facts and it would then be comparatively easy to show the absurdity of the same. I have been a socialist for 13 years, but never, never did I see our views correctly stated by a capitalistic newspaper. They fabricate windmills, call them socialism, communism and anarchism and begin fighting them.

The modern communist holds that labor is the fountain of all wealth and of all culture and that, because useful labor only is possible by association of all mankind, the fruits of labor belong to all mankind. Even land has no value except where it can be put into use by labor. No empty lot in a city would have the least value, if labor had not built around it houses and streets, if business was not going on near that lot. We know farther, that labor is not paid its full value; if this were the case, it would be unprofitable to employ labor and would not be done. Let one man work alone for himself, he never could grow rich, although even in such a case his knowledge would be the fruit of the work of others, the labor of generations. And because the latter is the case, the communist wants education, culture and knowledge for all. The land was common property thousands and thousands of years, and the private property system is—to speak historically—but of yesterday. And how was it introduced? Queen Elizabeth, that highly praised monster of murderous lust and brutality, for instance, had during her reign two millions of Irishmen killed in the usual way—battles, gallows, etc.—took their land and gave it to favorites. It is not for me now to give a history how the common lands in England were stolen and robbed, but it is a historical fact that it was acquired by the forefathers of the present owners by murder, arson, theft and lesser crimes.

Let the hired men of the press fill their columns with history of the crimes of land-robbing, if they dare. The sentence: "Property is robbery," is literally true—if you call robbery what the laws call so—of the property of the British landholders. The socialists and communists know farther that the capitalistic system requires always expansion. The so-called profits—that is, the fruit of the labor withheld by the employer—are transformed into capital, to gain for him new profits. New factories are built, more machines set to work, new markets are sought for, if necessary by war. More and more nations are drawn into competition. It begins to become difficult to find buyers for the goods, each nation, each corporation, each capitalist wages war against the other for supremacy. He who sells cheapest holds the market. But not only this is required; he who is first in the market, he who can supply the demand in any emergency quick and cheap, will win the battle.

This brings in speculation. The demand of the market is but limited, but the capitalists of all industrial countries are busy to glut it, to overflood it with the products of their factories. To come out all right from this insane race for money, it is necessary to supply cheap and quick, so as to leave other competitors behind. The greater the plant, the better the machines, the cheaper the workmen, the more probable is victory. The smaller manufacturer is soon driven from the contest and forced to close his establishment; new inventions of labor-saving machines throw workmen out of employment and compel these forces to look out for new work, as machines tend to transform skilled labor into common labor. The competition for work among workingmen grows to fearful dimensions and brings wages down to a minimum. But this in turn has its effect on production, and the battle wages more fearful than ever. But now reaction sets in. Millions of workmen are starving and leading the lives of vagabonds. Even the most ignorant wage slave commences to think. The common misery makes it clear to them that they must combine, and they do it. The great levellers, the machines, destroyed the guild pride of olden times. The carpenter feels that he has a common interest with the farm hand

and the printer with the hod-carrier, the German learns that his interest is that of the Negro, of the Frenchman, of the American, and passing I would like to state, that in my opinion it is the greatest merit of the order of the Knights of Labor to have carried out that principle in America in such an immense way.[74] The workingmen learn that the capitalistic system, although necessary for some time, must make room for universal co-operation, that the land and means of production must pass from the hands of speculators, private individuals into the hands of the producing masses; this is communism.

Any thinking man must concede that strikes, boycotts, co-operation on a small scale and other means will not and can not better the condition of the working-classes, even not so-called factory laws can bring the sought-for result about. It is true the workingman cannot help to use these insufficient means, often enough they are forced upon him. They must be looked on as means of education. Man learns by failures. A little baby who commences to stand on his feet, tumbles down many and many a time, before his limbs gain sufficient strength to walk. Many and many a time it tries to raise itself, till at last the great feat is accomplished. In all these fights, in striking, boycotting, going into politics, yes, even in street riots the young hercules collects strength to throttle the serpent—the capitalistic system. The workingman may be sometimes wrong, why not, the baby sometimes tries to raise itself by the means of the table-cloth, thus bringing down the dishes, but his impulse to raise is all right, and therefore the workman should continue to try raising his condition, even if he sometimes brings down the dishes.

Now as to anarchism. Anarchism is order without government. We anarchists say that anarchism will be the natural outgrowth of universal co-operation (communism). We say that, when poverty has vanished and education is common property of the people, that then reason will reign supreme. We say that crime will belong to the past and that erring brethren can be righted by other means than those of to-day. Most of the crimes of our days are engendered directly by the system of to-day, the system which creates ignorance and misery.

We anarchists do believe that the time is near at hand when the working people will demand their rights of their exploiters, and we further believe, that the slaveholders of today will rebel against the majority of the people, aided by the slums of the cities and duped people of the country. This struggle, in our opinion, is inevitable, and therefore we call to every honest man who lives not by the labor of his fellow-men to arm themselves. Should we be wrong in this respect, nobody would be more glad than ourselves, but history of the last year gives us right.

And now some words about the Haymarket affair: I was told in the morning of May 4, that in the evening a meeting would be held to protest against the outrages of the police, and called, in two notices in civil language, attention to the fact. In the evening the men of Deering reaper works, in Lake View, struck and called by telephone to the *Arbeiter Zeitung's* office of Mr. Spies, because he is well versed in both languages. I went over to the Haymarket meeting, which I was going to attend, and looked for Mr. Spies. Nobody had seen him, time was pressing, the men were waiting already an hour and a half, and so I concluded to go myself, which I did. Next day I saw from the paper what had occurred, and went down to the office. There I was told that Spies, I and others would be arrested. Mr. Spies and I waited nearly two hours for the detectives, and were then brought over to the Central Station, where Chief Ebersold saluted us with choice words from the dictionary of police politeness, dogs, curs, scoundrels, etc.

I am now done with this work and the only thing that is left, is to say that I am married since June 7, 1884, and father of two children. Our union is a happy one.

Michael Schwab.

8

Autobiography of Samuel Fielden

To the Editor: In accordance with a desire on your part that I should give you a history of my life for publication of your valuable paper, I have written the following incidents of my life, with the influences under which I was born and reared, hoping that they may not prove altogether uninteresting to my friends and readers of your paper.

I was born in the town of Todmorden, part of which is in the West Riding of Yorkshire and part in the East Riding of Lancashire, England. I was born in the Lancashire part. The town is like all towns in Lancashire—a manufacturing one. It lies in a beautiful valley, and on the hillsides are small farms; back about a mile are the moorlands, which could be made into fine farms, as the topography of the moors is more level generally than the inclosed land. But though thousands of starving Englishmen would be very glad to work them, they must be kept for the grouse and the gamekeeper and the gentry. Grouse sport for the privileged classes being esteemed of more importance than the happiness of thousands of human beings. The inclosed lands rent for about two pounds an acre (about $10). The farms are small, running from 10 acres to 60 acres, hardly any being larger than the latter figure. The farms are all dairy, the milk all being sold in town. There are numerous large mills in the town, Fielden Bros. being the largest; it contains about 2,000 looms.

Here I was born in the year 1847, on the 25th day of February. My father's name was Abram Fielden, he was one of a family of four sons and three daughters. They were of very powerful physique; my father stood nearly six feet in height; they were a family of hand-loom weavers, until the application of steam to weaving. This occurred when my father was hardly out of teens, and then they became steam-loom workers. My father became a foreman when quite young in the mill of Fielden Bros., where he worked until incapacitated by infirmities and age. He was a man of more than ordinary intelligence, and was generally acknowledged "to know a thing or two." There were very few that cared to cross swords with him in argument among those with whom he came in contact. I remember that when I was quite young he and a few more of the most intelligent of the factory kind of the place, instead of going to church on Sunday, would meet at our house and discuss politics, religion, and everything else. These discussions used to become quite warm, and carried on as they were in the rich Lancashire accent, they contained a peculiar charm. I used to wonder how they could know so much. Although I cannot recall anything that was said at this distance, yet I have no doubt that what I understood of these discussions have had an influence on my life and opinions.

My father was a peculiarly eloquent conversationalist, and the recital of the most ordinary incident from his lips bore the charm of romance. When the ten-hour movement was being agitated in England[75] my father was on the committee of agitation in my native town, and I have heard him tell of sitting on the platform with Earl Shaftesbury, John Fielden, Richard Otler, and other advocates of that cause. I always thought he put a little sarcasm into the word earl, at any rate he had but little respect for aristocracy and royalty. He was also a Chartist,[76] and I have heard him tell of many incidents connected with the Chartist agitation and movement. He was an earnest champion and admirer of the principles advocated by that noble but unfortunate Irishman, Fergus O'Connor.[77] I have heard him say that on the day the *Northern Star*, O'Connor's paper, was due, the people used to line the roadside waiting for its arrival, which was paramount to everything else for the time being. He was also one of the incorporators of the Consumer's Corporation society in the town of Todmorden and one of the managers of that society for a long time.[78] I remember that he used to go with the other managers and work in the warehouse of the store after he came home from his work at night. From a small room where these pioneers first stored and dispensed the few barrels of potatoes, a few barrels of flour, a barrel of molasses, one of sugar and a very limited supply of other articles, that society had risen to owning two stone buildings, where they conducted the business of the society in 1880, when I was there last, besides having branch stores in the outskirts of the town. He also owned some shares in some of the co-operative manufacturing establishments of the vicinity. He was also one of the managers of a local odd fellows' benevolent society, which flourished amazingly until in 1880 it owned some 50 or 60 houses and paid a very handsome rate to its sick members and also to the families of its deceased members.

In his family relations my father was very severe, at the same time he was kindhearted in the extreme. I remember one time that he was going to work after his dinner and a tramp fell in a fit at the bottom of the lane. He immediately picked him up and carried him some distance to our house, while the people at whose door he had fallen were wringing their hands with pity and compassion. He was a great lover of children, and the children of all the neighbors used to make common property of his knees. There seemed to be a sort of spontaneous freemasonry between him and every child that he came in contact with, but in his own house he was a very strict disciplinarian, but, notwithstanding this, there was hardly ever a father who was more idolized by his children than ours was. There was such a sense of justice and right in all his severity that when he grew older we appreciated his motives. I will relate one instance of his severity. On the hillsides in the vicinity of my home were small clusters of woods, and it seemed that here particularly the birds delighted to build their nests. These woods seemed to be full of nests in the summer time; in the more open places the wren would build its nest in some tuft of grass; the thrush would build its nest in the trees, and in the adjoining meadow the musician of the skies, the skylark, would build her nest. It used to be our delight as children to find these nests.

On the occasion I refer to my elder brother and my sister had been having a stroll some distance from home, and on their return had quarrelled, and in revenge for something my brother had done, my sister told my father that her brother had taken a young bird out of one bird's nest and put in the nest of another. I shall never forget the scene that followed: My father rose from the table, he advanced toward the trembling culprit, while we all thought that something terrible would take place. Not one of us, for our lives, dared utter a word; he seemed by a mighty effort to control himself, then in a voice trembling with suppressed anger he told my brother to get down on his knees and there beg pardon and promise to never do so any more. He then told him to go and take the bird back to its own nest, making my sister go with him to see that he did it. When I visited England in 1880 my sister and brother both asked me if I remembered the circumstance, and as we recalled the affair it was not with feelings of bitterness, but with honor and respect, that we discussed it. If severity to children, as some writers have said, be a vice, it will be admitted that vices of this kind lean to virtue's side.

If he ever had studied socialism I believe his strict sense of justice would have led him to adopt it; as it was he was a hater of all forms of affectation, deceit and hypocrisy; in politics of late years he was ostensibly a liberal—in reality a republican. He took a great deal of interest in the political agitations which have been going on, and having a fairly good memory he could discuss intelligently the political problems that have agitated his country during his lifetime. He was always a staunch supporter of every measure for the relief of the Irish peasantry from the greed of the foreign bloodsucker—the English landlord.

I well remember the intense interest he took in the disestablishment of the protestant established church in Ireland.[79] As I at that time was engaged in religious work I did not have as much time to go to the meetings which were held in my native town for the promotion of that measure, but I was still earnest-minded enough to attend some of them, and also frequently found myself defending the measure. When I did this in the presence of my religious associates some of them regarded this as worldly wisdom and unworthy of one who was thought to be solely occupied in furnishing a suite of rooms in the sky. But as

Satan is always on the alert, I suppose he used to get his oar in on me occasionally, and this was one of his brief triumphs. Also in the intense excitement consequent upon the movement for the extension of the franchise in 1866.[80] Such was my father.

Of my mother I cannot remember so much, as she died when I was a child of 10 years of age. I can remember her as small of stature, with dark eyes and hair, and with pleasing and regular features. I remember in the later years of her life she was a very devoted member of the primitive Methodist church. Her maiden name was Alice Jackson; the family to which she belonged was very poor, and I have often heard her and father tell on the cold winter nights, when the wind would shriek around the corners of the house, of the first meeting of herself and father. How that she was walking in her bare feet through the snow, carrying a basket which contained sand, which she was trying to sell to the poor people to sprinkle upon their stoneflag floors. You can imagine how poor a family must be when I tell you that this sand was sold for one-half penny (1 cent) a quart, and how much a child could carry in a basket, but they were compelled to put their children to this means of earning a few cents. The sand they procured from refuse piles at quarries and picking out the whitest scraps, then taking them home, and with a large stone beating them up into fine sand. I well remember how she used to take my father's rug and wrap it around her on class-meeting nights, and travel down the lonesome road which skirted to the top of the piece of woods which covered the side of the hill, to go on the coldest and roughest nights to her class meetings. Such was my mother.

I remember vividly the foreman under whom I worked in the cotton-mill coming to me and telling me that I was wanted at home, one summer afternoon. I instinctively knew what it was, for my mother was sick when I left home. With breathless haste and with beating heart I climbed the steep hill to find my mother dying. My father was walking the floor. He took me and led me to a chair on which he sat down and took me between the knees. He tried to tell me, what I already knew, that my mother was dying. But the words would not come, and he laid his cheek against mine until I released myself from him and rushed upstairs to the bedside of one who is every man's best and truest friend, and I saw the pale face of my mother. She was unconscious. She gasped for breath. Her breast heaved in the last throes of life. Words cannot describe my feelings. It seemed as though the bright summer day grew black, and my life seemed to be going out as that of the form before me was going. But I will not dwell upon this painful scene. Many of your readers have doubtless undergone similar experiences, but it had a wonderful effect upon me, and I have had the scene before my mind in all the pain and anguish in all my wanderings and all the changes that have occurred in my life. I do not recall it now for the first time. I do not think that there has ever been a day that I have not had it before me since the occurrence, and the words of Cowper,[81] in his lines on the death of his mother, come home to me very forcibly when he says:

> But while the wings of fancy still are free,
> And I can take such mimic views of thee.
> Time has but half succeeded in his theft,
> Thy self removed, thy power to soothe me left.

She was laid in the little churchyard at Walsdan Under the hill. On my visit to England in 1880, I went with an uncle of mine to see the grave. I knew the spot, but when we got to where we thought it should be, I experienced some difficulty in finding it. My uncle remarked, they have been selling graves between the graves as the place has filled up, and crowding bodies in between the others. I remarked they have crowded us while we live, and they are not satisfied but they must follow us to our graves, and make us move over there also to satisfy their greed. Since my visit home my father has also found a resting place there. He died Aug. 27, 1886, the present year. The Todmorden Adviser contained the following on Aug. 28, 1886: "Abraham Fielden, of Burnley, formerly of Todmorden, a moral force chartist, died at Burnley on Friday last and was interred at Walsden churchyard." I undoubtedly inherited from my father that hatred of shame and hypocrisy which I hope I possess to some extent; from my mother that sympathy that I find it impossible not to feel for every form of suffering and which has impelled me to try to do something toward alleviating it, and I believe now today that I was fortunate in having such a father and mother.

When I think of those who have no higher idea of human life than the desire to make money, that if my lines had fallen in different places I could do a great deal worse. But circumstances over which I had no control placed me under these influences, and whether there is any necessary connection between these influences and my subsequent opinions, the readers will decide for themselves.

I was born of these parents as I have said in the year 1847, of the years between my birth and my eighth year I of course know or remember but little. I have heard my father tell of myself, when I was but 3 years of age, and himself both having the malignant fever at the same time, and as our surroundings were not of the very best, we both occupied the same bed during our sickness. He always in after years, when referring to the circumstances, referred to me as the most patient child in sickness that he ever knew.

Perhaps I at that time and under those circumstances began to display the germs of that philosophical character which some people have given me credit for possessing in later years. When I was, as near as I can remember, in my sixth or seventh year, I went for about six months to a small school kept by a spinster lady; here I learned to read. I very early became a good reader, and after I had learned the rudiments I used to read all the advertisements that I could see on the dead walls and in the shop windows. In this way I became very proficient in that branch of the limited education I have been able to attain.

The house that we occupied stood in the midst of some meadows that were owned by two wealthy brothers, who were engaged in flour milling. Their mill was situated at the bottom of the hill. They need to cut the grass from these meadows and cart it down to their stables near the mill. During these days I was engaged in bringing the haymakers their ale and bread and cheese, which they used to indulge in during their morning and afternoon siestas. The people of the vicinage all being engaged in the mills, the men employed in the harvest were mostly strangers, who came from different parts of England and Ireland. I thus became somewhat acquainted with strangers, and perhaps thus laid the foundation which afterward developed into cosmopolitanism. These hay-fields had a peculiar charm for me, and years after, when I had grown to be a young man, I used to manage to get off from the mill for a week to work in these hay-fields with the men who came from Ireland to earn, by the hardest labor and the most abstemious living, the money to pay for their little holdings in their native country and the thatch above the heads of their wives and little ones. Thousands of these men are led this merry dance every year between the two countries, by this scheme. These men are compelled to harvest the crops in England for the privilege of living in their own country; for the money they earn in the English harvest the English landlord compels them to give up again, and his lordship brings it back again to England, until Pat comes again and harvests his crops for him. I accumulated the evidence for this charge by my contact with these men in the harvest fields, but I did not "tumble to the enormity of the racket" until I became a socialist.

When I arrived at the mature age of 8 years I, as was usual with the poor people's children in Lancashire, went to work in a cotton mill, and if there is any of the exuberance of childhood about the life of a Lancashire millhand's child it is in spite of his surroundings and conditions, and not in consequence of it. As I look back at my experience at the tender age I am filled with admiration at the wonderful vitality of these children. I think that if the devil had a particular enemy whom he wished to unmercifully torture the best thing for him to do would be to put his soul into the body of a Lancashire factory child and keep him as a child in a factory the rest of his days. I think that would satisfy the love of cruelty of his satanic majesty. The mill into which I was put was the mill established by John Fielden, M.P., who fought so valiantly in the ten-hour movement. It was then and is now conducted by his sons, Samuel, John and Joshua. The last was for some time member of parliament for the West Riding of Yorkshire.

I have read of John Fielden's description of the treatment of the pauper children that were shipped into the Lancashire mills from the unions of the large cities when Lancashire received its first great impetus as a cotton manufacturing center. And, horrible as it reads, it was hardly any worse than the treatment that was meted out to the innocents when I became acquainted with the sober side of life as a factory child. The infants, when first introduced to these abodes of torture, are put at stripping the full spools from the spinning jennies and replacing them with empty spools. They are put to work in a long room where there are about twenty machines. Each child is furnished with a little stool on which to sit. There will be from eight to ten children on each side of the machine. They begin at one end of the room and strip the full spool off, then from there to the next machine, and so on until they get to the other end of the room. When they get there the machine at which they started will be full again. The spindles are apportioned to each child, and woe be to the child who shall be behind in doing its allotted work. The machine will be started and the poor child's fingers will be bruised and skinned with the revolving spools. While the children try to catch up to their comrades by doing their work with the speed of the machine running, the brutal overlooker will frequently beat them unmercifully, and I have frequently seen them strike the children, knocking them off their stools and sending them spinning several feet on the greasy floor. Hell, or the Spanish inquisition, never witnessed more heartless barbarity than is practised upon these poor innocents. It is a pitiful sight to see these children, as they rush from one machine to another trying to recover their lost ground, the tears streaming down their cheeks and sobbing as though their little hearts would break; a sight one would think that would melt the heart of a savage; and all that these children have done to merit this is to be born poor. Such is the penalty of poverty in Lancashire.

I toiled at this work enduring all its horrors and barbarities for about two years. About that time, being about 10 years of age, I was out to tending the elevator, my work being to take the spools that came up from the carding room to the machines on the floor on which I worked, and to take the full spools, after they had undergone the process of being spun into a condition for the warpers to take them and make the warps of them for the weavers, and load them onto the elevator car and send them up to the warpers. This was heavy work for a boy, but as I was thought a stout boy I was put to this, and, notwithstanding that it was heavier work, I liked it better, and I worked at it till I was 18 years of age, when I became, according to law, a full-timer. The children under that age at that time not being allowed to work had a half a day at the mill and were compelled to go to school the other half. The factory act of England compels each employer of half-timers to keep a school for them to go to the other half day; they are very strict about this; so much so that no child could stay away from school a half-day without being compelled to lose a half-day in the mill also. This, when you take in consideration the importance that the child's wages are to the family, is practically compulsory education. For this work we used to get from one shilling and six pence (36 cents) to two shillings and six pence (60 cents) a week.

If I remember rightly, when I first became a full-timer, I received six shillings ($1.50) per week. At this time I was given work in the warehouse or filling-room, where the weavers received their filling. I worked here two years, when I went to learn to weave. I learned to weave under my father. I worked at this branch of factory-work until I became 20 years of age, when I went to work as a beamer. That is, I wound warps onto beams, and at this I continued until I came to the United States, at the age of 21, in 1868.

Soon after I left the half-time school and had become a fulltime worker in the mill, I was called upon to testify in a celebrated trial, between two of the residents of town which was tried at Liverpool. The case grew out of the intense religious partisanship which existed in the neighborhood, and was between the Unitarians[82] and the Methodists. About this time the religious feeling had been running unusually high, though it never ran very low; but at this time it was at fever-heat. I believe the immediate cause of the trouble was some lectures which had been delivered by a fiery advocate of the mysterious doctrines of the trinity. I remember trying to get into the hall to hear the fun, but could only get within some distance of the door; however I saw through the door, when it opened, the flaming countenance of the orthodox gladiator. I thought the gentleman was in the last stage of apoplexy. However, the upshot of the affair was that a methodist grocer, named Ainley, charged the unitarian teacher of the factory school which I had attended, with taking advantage of his position to inculcate unitarian heresies into the minds of the children of orthodox parents. This made the teacher, Mr. Harrison, mad, and he thought that his reputation had been injured at least 500 pounds worth. Since recent decisions of law have come under my observation, I think this was very foolish; he ought to have had Dr. Brindley arrested and held accountable, since he had set causes at work which had resulted in his being charged with this heinous offense.

But this only shows how slow and dull people are under the effete monarchies of Europe. If he could only have found out who had set Dr. Brindley at work, and prosecuted him, he would have been still nearer the actual criminal, and if he had been conscientious enough in his determination to find out who was the first person to set causes at work which had resulted so disastrously to his reputation, he would undoubtedly have summoned Martin Luther, the members of the councils of Trent and Nice, Jesus Christ and God Almighty. It was true that the schoolmaster had introduced the bible into the school and had taught us some things that were not orthodox. I, who had received my theological training in a methodist Sunday school up to this time, was somewhat impressed one day when, after reading a lesson in the new testament, the schoolmaster in explaining it to the scholars, said that we were not to believe everything that was in the bible to be absolutely true. This so impressed me that when my father came home that night I called his attention to the heresy of the schoolmaster.

My father mentioned this to some of his associates, upon which a discussion had arisen, and through this I was brought to the attention of the lawyers of Mr. Ainsley. A lawyer came to the house and took down my statement, and told me that I should have to go to Liverpool to testify in the case. He left a sovereign for me to get some things to take with me, and in about a week I was informed that I must go in a day or two, telling me the day. Now if there was one place above another that I would have wished to see that place was Liverpool. I had read much of it in the newspapers, and I knew that the sea was there, and that ships from every point of the world were to be seen there. I had read much of adventures by sea; shipwrecks and hair-breadth escapes of sailors, and in my imagination a sailor was the man above all to be envied, and his occupation the most pleasant, and, to my mind, romantic. About this time I had been mastering a plan of running away from home and going to sea, and strange as it may appear, I do not remember a single factory lad of my acquaintance who was not thinking of doing the same. It makes me shudder now to think of the horrible conspiracies we used to enter into, and what a good thing it was for the North American Indians' peace of mind that they did not know of the plans that these factory lads were laying for their destruction, for, coupled with the romance of going to sea was the romance of the trapper and hunter and backwoods settlers, for the dime novel had appeared, and I had devoured all the contents of half a dozen of them.

I remember that I even thought of sneaking away from the party when I should get to Liverpool, and letting the schoolmaster and the grocer go on with their quarrel about the bible without my assistance. Well, the eventful day arrived for my departure for the legal-theological duel. I had never ridden on a railroad before, but the novelty of a railroad ride was soon lost in the anxiety to arrive at my destination, and I worried the elderly gentleman, as indeed we all did, for there were about a dozen of the graduates of Mr. Harrison, of both sexes in the party, with questions at every mile that we traveled, as to how far we had to go yet, and how long it would take us before we could see the masts of the ships? At last the wished-for destination was reached, and as soon as we had our dinner we insisted on going down to the docks and seeing the ships and those gallant and romantic heroes—the sailors.

Well, I was shocked and indignant at seeing these heroes as I found them. Instead of finding Mercantile Jack, as Dickens calls him, with a dark blue cap, with ribbons hanging down behind, upon his head, and the dark blue blouse, with wide collar, around his body, and white pants, very wide below the knees; instead of this kind of being I saw him as he was, with a battered old hat, or a souwester (such as I had seen the canal men use at home), an old patched shirt of almost any and every color, a pair of greasy and well-tarred pants—indeed he resembled what we would call a roustabout; this was Jack stripped of his romance and as he appeared to me, though I have no doubt that in this greasy, tarred form there beats as brave a heart as ever romance could conjure or imagination could depict. But if Jack was not all that I had expected, the ships made up for it, for I was never tired of admiring them. I wandered through all the docks and took notice of all the names and destinations or the ports from which they hailed, and in this way I imagined that I caught a glimpse of strange lands and strange people.

We stayed in Liverpool about a week waiting for the trial to commence, and in the meantime seeing the sights of the far-famed city. On the Sunday that we were there we went on an excursion to the famous Menai bridge in Wales;[83] I believe at that time the longest suspension bridge in the world—this was in 1860. The day of trial at length arrived, and we went to court and there I was not only astonished but positively alarmed; there sat the judge with his gown on, and on his head an enormous gray wig with flounces of curls hanging down over his shoulders, and in front of him were, I should think, as I remember, some thirty or forty gentlemen wearing the same ridiculous and awe-inspiring headgear. When I was called upon the stand to testify, and felt that the small eyes of these strange animals were turned upon me, I was, in the language of American slang, perfectly paralyzed. I could not find my tongue when the learned counsel began to question me, but looked imploringly to the monster upon the bench for protection. I was afraid, when I saw that he noticed me, that he would demolish me altogether. Judge my surprise when the judge repeated the kindest voice that I ever remember to have heard, the question of the learned counsel. I found my voice, and immediately felt as though I was recovering. After this there was no difficulty, and I escaped with my life, but I have hardly ever looked at a court house since that time without the feeling of thankfulness taking possession of me at the thought of the narrow escape I had on this occasion.

But as everything must come to an end, so the celebrated case of Harrison V. Ainley did the same, the result being that instead of Mr. Harrison getting £500, the judge gave him 1 farthing (½ cent) and ordered both parties to pay their own expenses. The case created a great deal of interest in Todmorden, and the people had kept track of it, so that when we arrived home on the next day the streets around the station were packed with people. This may seem strange, but to a people to whom every day of their lives was one continual animal existance, sensations did not occur often, and when there was an excuse for the making of one, they did not allow the opportunity to slip by without being improved, and so out of this little affair we who had figured in the case were the lions of the hour. To Mr. Ainley, the defendant in the case, it was a dear trial. He was ruined, and soon after left the town a sadder if not a wiser man. As to Harrison, no doubt the rich Fielden Bros., whose factory school teacher he was, paid his legal expenses, as they were the main support of the unitarian church in the town. Soon after this a charge was made against him of indecent behavior toward some of the older female scholars. Opinions were divided as to his guilt, and the fact that one of the children who made the charge was the grandchild of the prominent methodist local preacher went a little way to support the claim that it was blackmail and persecution, which many of the people believed. Be this as it may, I never believed the charge, and though I have suffered many a thrashing at his hands, I always thought of him with a feeling of compassion. He was a very strict master but I believed that he was a good scholar and thoroughly devoted to his profession, and I always believed that the scholars learned a great deal more under him than under his predecessors.

For some years before this time of which I now write there had appeared in my native town at different times, several colored lecturers who spoke on the slavery question in America. I went frequently to hear them describe the inhumanity of that horrible system, sometimes with my father, and at other times with my sister. One of these gentlemen called himself Henry Box Brown;[84] this gentlemen brought with him a panorama, by means of which he described places and incidents in his slave life, and also the means of his escape. He used to march through the streets in front of a brass band, clad in a highly-colored and fantastic garb, with an immense drawn sword in his hand. He claimed that he had been boxed up in a large box in which were stowed an amount of provisions, the box having holes bored in the top for air, and marked, "this side up with care." Thus he was shipped to Philadelphia via the underground railroad, to friends there, and this was why he called himself Henry Box Brown. He was a very good speaker and his entertainment was very interesting.

Another one of these gentlemen was called, if I remember right, Henry Green; he was a very fiery orator. I heard him very often. These lectures had a very great effect on my mind, and I could hardly divest myself of their impressions, and I used to frequently find myself among my playmates dilating much upon the horrors of slavery. I read much of the system from the books of travelers. I remember to have read at a very early age the travels of Harriet Martineau.[85] I also read "Uncle Tom's Cabin."[86] When the American civil war broke out I was an enthusiastic champion among my fellows of the cause of the north, and, in fact, so were all the family, my sister not being undone by any of us. During all that terrible struggle intense interest was manifested by the people of Lancashire, and all during the summer months every night in the week there would be seen groups of men collected in the streets, and at the prominent corners, discussing the latest news and forecasting the next, and in these groups there was always to be heard the advocates and champions of both sides. I used to listen to these orators with a great deal of interest.

I remember that on one occasion I had the effrontery of challenging something that was said; whether it was that I had said something that was worth refuting, or whether the gentleman was so enthusiastic in the cause of the south that he could not stop to consider me as being too young for his steel, I do not know; all that I know is that, at the age of 15 years I was soon in the midst of a heated argument with a man old enough to be my father. Now, it so happened that my father was taking a stroll in the cool of the evening, looking, I suppose, as he used to say about this time when he would go out at night, to see if he could find any slave-drivers, and in his stroll he meandered towards the group that I was trying to enlighten on the horrors of slavery and the hopelessness of the cause of the slave-drivers. He came up to the crowd without my seeing him, but he no sooner saw me than he got me by the scruff of the neck and, in a tone of thunder, demanded what I meant to be talking to people older than myself. He ignominiously dragged me out and sent me home, while the crowd laughed and shouted, "Oh! he's a chip off the old block!" I don't think that he was as angry as he tried to look; anyway, for some reason I did not feel as much afraid of meeting him in the morning as I had often before when I knew he had found me doing something wrong.

But the struggle continued, and its effect upon the people became more and more apparent. Mills began to run short time, then no time at all. Then when they could get a little Surat cotton from India, they would run a few days a week. This Surat cotton was terrible stuff to weave; it was full of little chips, and the threads were always breaking, so that the weavers were compelled to have all their looms stopped at once, until they could get time to go from one loom to the other to tie up the threads. How the people prayed for the "war to cease." Famine, gaunt and fierce, stalked abroad in the land, and in many cases brought death to end the sufferings of the wretched Lancashire operative. The finances of the relief system was exhausted, private charity was taxed until it could expend no more. Tramps filled the streets and highways, young women went from town to town, and when they would come to some town they would walk slowly over the streets, holding each other by the hand, and singing some song, which it was hoped would bring some gift of succor to appease their hunger and preserve their weary lives. Many in their desperation were compelled to barter their honor for their lives. Such is the penalty of poverty.

During the panic, as we called it, the mill in which I, my father, sister and brother worked, shut down entirely several times. I went to work assisting to drain some land on which one of my employers has since built a magnificent castle, which is called Dobroyd castle. I was put to work carrying tiles to the men who laid them; it was in the winter time, and I had to pick the tiles up out of the ice and water. One day I became chilled to the marrow; I began to grow dizzy, then it grew dark and I fell to the ground insensible. I was carried home and thawed out, and the next day I had to go out to the same work again.

My elder brother had for some time been working as undergardener for one of our employers. He was a young man of more than ordinary intelligence, and much of the information which I was enabled to pick up I gleaned from his books. He was also quite radical in his views, and therefore it was a constant torment to him to have to debase himself before his master as lackeys were compelled to do in England. Now one of these means of debasement was being compelled to put his hand to his cap, in fact, to bow down to Gesler. He endured this as long as he could bear it, when one day he met his master in the town accompanied by his brother. My brother walked past him, pretending not to see him, and therefore did not pay his obedience to his master. The next day, as he was working in the garden, his master came to him and asked him if he had met him the night before on the street and why he had not made his manners to him. My brother told him that he did not think of it. His highness then fixed his eye upon him and replied, "I thought of it, and so did others," meaning his brother, and added, "you must be a boor." This was too much; and my brother telling me about it after we had retired at night, said he would never humble himself before him again, as it would be harder than ever to do it after what had occurred. He soon after left Mr. Fielden's employment. Thus must the proletariat bow the knee to the bourgeoisie or starve, and some people call this liberty of contract. There was no work to be had in the town, and he was compelled to go on a tramp.

Having heard that there were fine gardens about Edinburgh, Scotland, he tried to work his way thither, walking all the way and trying to get work on the road; sometimes he would get a little to do; sometimes he had to ask for bread; sometimes he had to apply to the town authorities for lodging, for which he had to break stone on the turnpike to pay for it. Arriving at Edinburgh he found it impossible to get work there; off again he pursued his fruitless search, until one morning he found himself within forty miles of home. He felt that he must make home that day or die. He therefore with the resolution of despair set out at night. He came into the house emaciated, hungry and sick, a mere shadow of himself. After eating his supper he tried to make his way to bed, but his legs refused to carry him.

The next morning a violent fever had taken possession of him; for weeks he lay between life and death, and this was the penalty of refusing to bow the knee to Gesler.

All these horrors we suffered, as did thousands of others, and be it remembered the Lancashire operatives never passed a resolution to recognize the south as a belligerent, never dreamed of interfering in any way, morally or otherwise, though they were the only sufferers, and those who did in England were those who were placed above the possibility of being affected by the war.[87] But the war at last came to a close, and New Orleans cotton arrived. It was a time of thanksgiving, and remarkable scenes were witnessed in some of the Lancashire towns when the first installment of cotton arrived. The operatives gathered about the depots, brass bands were in readiness, and men with patched clothes and thin features, and women with haggard looks and draggled garments, holding their children in their arms or leading them by the hand, according to their size, crowded around. Eyes that seemed but a short time before had lost their luster, now beamed with a light which had seemed to have left them forever but a short time before; forms whose every motion had seemed for months to speak of despair, were now animated by elasticity and eager hope had come again to the despairing, and work would now be had; and this was the open sesame to heaven and earth. At last the gates of the yards are thrown open and large ing* draught horses are seen moving slowly toward the gates, while piled high into the air behind is seen that which to those poor starving people meant the staff of life—cotton, American cotton.

A shout goes up which is almost enough to shake the bales from their foundations; men shake each other's

---

* The word is illegible; it may be "lumbering."

hands; the tears of gladness are seen in the eyes of the women; such hilarity, such congratulation, such quaint jokes are thrown around when amidst the confusion the band strikes up an air which had become as familiar in England as in America—"John Brown's body lies mouldering in the grave, but his soul goes marching on."[88] The men joined in, the women joined in, and the children joined in, while the players tried in vain to make themselves heard except at intervals. And thus they marched in front of the great loads of cotton to the mills. Work immediately became more plentiful, and as nothing prospers when workingmen are poor, so everybody soon became happy and comparatively prosperous.

About this time, 1865, I joined the methodist (Wesleyan) church.[89] I had not been a member long before I began to speak in the prayer and experience meetings, and indeed it became such a usual thing for me to talk in these meetings that on one occasion, when it seems that the spirit did not move me and I really did not feel as though I wished to speak, the minister remarked that it was getting late, but there was one person who he wished to hear from before he adjourned. Everybody knew who was meant and I had to speak. I think I may say that I became somewhat popular in these meetings. I was most thoroughly in earnest and nothing that I could do did I leave undone to further the cause I had espoused. I had not been a member of the church long before I and three others formed what we called the Methodist exhorters, and we used to go around and hold meetings in houses and outside meeting-places. Almost every night in the week I was out to some meeting of some kind.

Around the town there were several small villages within a distance of three or four miles. These were composed of from twenty to fifty houses, in the neighborhood of which there was a cotton mill, and here, for the convenience of the people who lived here, there were small chapels or meeting-houses. These were included in what was called the Todmorden circuit, the central church being situated in the town of Todmorden. There were two regular ministers appointed by the general Methodist conference of Great Britain and to this circuit there were also a number of what we called local preachers, who were taken from members of the churches in the circuit. They were composed of men from all walks of life, and among them were men who had hard work to provide the wherewith to feed their familes, and yet there were men of this class who were better preachers and speakers than the regular ordained ministers. I call to mind men who earned their bread at the loom, at the spindles and in the quarries, whose eloquence would have graced the grandest cathedral in the land. I have always thought that the strength and the power of the Methodist church was more due to these intelligent, earnest, talented and self-sacrificing men, than to any other merit that it possessed. I saw this disinterestedness. I came in contact with them. I was moved by their rude eloquence. I could not conceive of anything more worthy of imitation than they were, and I accompanied them to their appointments. I assisted them by leading out the hymns; sometimes by making the opening prayer. I thus became imbued with their devotion and sincerity. I tried to imitate them, for, to my young mind, there was not anything more worthy of imitation than these grand men.

It is true that I was ignorant and inexperienced, but though I have lived nearly twenty years of a somewhat varied life since that time, and though I now think that these men's ideas were wrong, yet never, until my hand has dropped nerveless by my side, until my eyes shall have closed in the eternal sleep and my tongue shall have become incapable of doing good or ill by its utterance of my thought, and until my heart shall have fluttered its last feeble pulsation—never till then will I refrain from saying the thanks of a grateful soul that I became imbued with the sterling honesty of these men by my coming in contact with their noble and generous lives in my youth.

Through my constant attendance at the different places of worship I became enabled to understand the technicality of the theology of the Methodist church, and consequently I became enabled to defend and advocate the doctrines of the church. I became one of the superintendents of one of these village Sunday schools. I became prominent at the revival meetings, and many a night have I wandered through the snow to meetings miles away from my home.

Thus my life was spent from the time between the ages of 18 to 21. In the spring of 1868 I was placed on the plan on trial as a local preacher, and in the same spring, the Halifax (Yorkshire) *Courier* contained the notice that the chapel anniversary sermons of the Blackshawhead Wesleyan chapel had been preached by John Greenwood and Samuel Fielden.

I continued to follow this life until July, 1868, when I left home for the United States. I had frequently talked to my father of my desire to come to America. My father had tried to dissuade me from doing so, but seeing that I was determined to go, he told me that when I became of age, that is 21 years of age, he would have no more control over me, but until then he refused to give me consent to leave the parental roof. I accordingly remained until the month of July, 1868. On the morning of my departure there were present quite a number of those who had known me and had been associated with me in my religious work. During my trial here, a letter was written and published in the

Chicago *Tribune*, by some person signing himself J.H. of New York, in which the writer states that he knew me in England and was a member of the same church. He states that I was well-known there, and from his acquaintance with me says that at that time I gave promise of becoming what he, the writer, calls himself an intelligent man, saying that I was a good debater. He refers to my departure from my home as being something remarkable for a young man, who had spent all his life in a Lancashire factory; numbers of my friends flocked around me to bid me God speed. I arrived in New York in the latter part of July, 1868, with £3 in my pocket. I immediately procured work in Prentice's hat factory, Brooklyn. I only worked there two days when I left, as the wages were very low and the work not very agreeable.

I next went to Providence, and procured work in Chapin & Downs' Riverside mills, working at the washing machine at first. I seemed to gain favor with the foreman, and he soon gave me a better job in the warehouse at packing the cloth in cases for shipment. My wages had been $7.50 a week, and I received $8 at my new work. I worked at this for some time, when I was offered $8.50 a week at the adjoining delaine mills, owned by the Sprague Bros. I gave notice to the superintendent, who was a brother of Mr. Downes, and with whom for the time I had been in his employ, I had become quite intimate and friendly. He asked me where I wanted to go, and I told him. I did not know that I was getting any one into trouble, but I was. There was an understanding between the two mills that neither one was to entice the help of the other away from them. When I went home a few days after this I was met by the foreman who had offered me the job in the other mills, who informed me that Mr. Downes had reported him for trying to entice his best help, and that I could not get the job, as it had become known and was against mutual understanding between the two mills. Now as I taught another man to do my work because I did intend leaving the following Saturday, I thought that I was in a pickle, as it looked as if I was thrown out of both mills. Immediately there and then I posted off to Mr. Downes' house in a very angry frame of mind. I found him in, and I immediately charged him with being guilty of a very mean act in thus heading me off from improving my prospects. To my surprise he took it very coolly, and finally told me that if I would stay with him he would give me in a short time a better job than I should have had at the delaine mills. I finally begged pardon for my hastiness, and we were both of us good friends afterwards. He was as good as his word. In a few weeks he gave me a light job by the piece at which I could make from two to two and a half dollars a day. I worked there all that fall and winter, but in the later part of the following March I lost some time through the non-arrival of material to work upon. I therefore determined that I would take this opportunity of leaving, and put into effect my determination of going west. I therefore drew what was due me and left. It was the more easy to do this as the superintendent was away at that time.

I had been a constant reader of the New York *Tribune,* and I had become infatuated with the idea of farming and the glorious opportunities held out by the philosopher of the *Tribune,* to the young man in the West.[90] I therefore took his advice and started for the west. During my stay in Olneyville, North Providence, I had attended the Baptist church in that place, as there was no Methodist church there. I had however, attended the Methodist church in Providence where a somewhat well-known divine named Rev. Mark Trafton, was the pastor. On my way west, I stopped at Niagara Falls to view that world-renowned phenomena. From there I went to Cleveland. I had no well-defined idea of where I was going up to my arrival in Cleveland, but as I had saved a little money, I thought I would make an excursion into the country to see if I should find any place to suit me. I went to the lake shore depot, and I looked over a railroad map and I thought that Berea would be a good thing to try, as it was only about 15 miles out, and I thought it would ruin me anyway, so I went there.

I arrived there in the afternoon, and took the first road I saw that seemed to lead into the country. I was soon outside the town, and after traveling for about a mile through the sticky clay roads which were churned to the consistency of butter, I came to a farm house and at the risk of being eaten up by two of the most villainous dogs that I ever saw, I climbed through the fence and approached the house. I found that the inhabitants were of that race which are to be found in every place and country on the face of the globe. They were Irish. I found that the lord of the manor was not at home, but the wife asked me to come in, with true Irish hospitality. After I had told her what I was after, which was work on a farm, she made me partake of some milk and bread and butter, to which I did simple justice. She then directed me to a Mr. Adams, whom she thought I might hire out to. I started out across the wet fields and reached Mr. Adams' house just before dark. I succeeded in inducing him to try me, and the following day I was set to work at the wood-pile. Now, this was new work for me, and before I had been at it an hour I began to think that my back was broke, especially as the woodshed was attached to the kitchen, and I was afraid that if I stopped for a moment he would think I was lazy. I managed to live, however, and I successfully passed the period of probation.

Mr. Adams was a deacon of the Methodist church in the town of Olmstead Falls, and I, of course, joined the church. I stopped with Mr. Adams until the following August, during which time I preached several times in the Methodist church there. Mr. Adams advised me to stop with him, promising me that during the following winter he would board me for the chores I could do nights and mornings, while he would lend me a horse to ride to and from the Methodist college at Berea, and thus I could find myself for the ministry. I, however, declined, and in the month of August I arrived in Chicago, and, strange as it may appear, the first house that I entered was the frame house adjoining the brick building on the northwest corner of Randolph and Desplaines street and directly opposite to me when I addressed the Haymarket meeting on the 4th of last May. A plumber named Mr. Still lived there at the time. He was born in the same town that I was born in England, as well as his brother John, and also their brother-in-law John Mills, who occupied a plumbing store on the south side of Crane's alley, in the rear of Bryan's saloon. I was acquainted with their relatives in England.

The first work I did in the state of Illinois was on the farm of John Wentworth at Summit station. I worked there during the fall, and following spring worked for the Fox & Howard Co. on the Illinois and Michigan canal. During that winter, however, I had overhauled my religious opinions, and having found some cobwebs therein I brushed them away and became a freethinker. I visited Farwell hall, where I heard the since world renown Dwight L. Moody.[91] On reaching home I indicted a letter to Mr. Moody, and in a few days I received an answer, in which he informed me that he would like to see me. On the following Sunday evening I went again to Farwell hall and heard Mr. Moody refer to the letter he had received during the week.

After the service was over, and as Mr. Moody was going down below to gather in the spiritually wounded, I tapped him on the shoulder and informed him that I was the guilty wretch that had written the letter to him. He tried to get me to go down stairs with him, but I declined, and he informed me that he would talk with me at Illinois street mission the next night. Well, I went there, and soon after my arrival an honest looking fellow got upon the floor, and during his remarks referred to the rascality of the methods of business, concluding by expressing the opinion that no businessman could be a Christian. A young stripling, evidently of the genus counter-jumper, then rose to his feet and informed the audience that he was a Christian and a businessman, and went on to dilate upon the virtues of businessmen and their piety until I was thoroughly convinced that all a man needed to do in this world in order to make his calling and election sure in the next was to sell for a dollar what only cost fifteen cents. This little speech seemed to relieve the audience greatly, which had undoubtedly been much discomposed by the speech of the common and ordinary-looking man who had preceded him. At last the meeting came to a close, and I moved up toward the stove and presented myself to Mr. Moody. We sat down and we had quite a good and at times animated conversation for perhaps an hour and a half, when I thought that it was about time for my opponent to be convinced, and Mr. Moody thought the same about me, so that we each moved out to meet the starlight. I think Mr. Moody will remember this occurrence, and I will say that there was nothing said on either side that would or did hurt the feelings of the other. We parted at the door with the best feeling toward each other. I am only sorry to say that my opponent has persisted in following the wrong path to this day. I am truly sorry for him. I only wish that we both turn to the right before it is everlastingly too late.

I worked as I stated, on the Illinois and Michigan canal. In the next fall I went south, having heard much of the opportunities there were to make money there in the winter. I embarked as a deck passenger on a steamboat, with two others who accompanied me from Chicago, for Vicksburg, Miss. After nearly a week we arrived at our destination. As we rounded the bend above the city I saw the national cemetery where lay all that remained of those who had left their homes in the full flower of their youth and health, filled with enthusiasm, to battle and to die for their country. I had no sooner landed than I proposed to visit this cemetery at once, which we did. As we walked up the narrow street toward the outskirts of the city I overheard a Negro, who was detailing to another some everyday occurrence, and I heard him say: "I told Mr. Johnson if he would give me $2 for the job I would do it, but I would not do it for $1.50." This made quite an impression upon me and I remarked to my companions: "There speaks the man and not the slave. The man could say no; the slave had to do as he was bid. The man could resist; the slave must submit." And what a difference there is in this man's condition, from what it had been but a few years ago; that he could say I won't unless you give me what I want or ask, and as I wandered through the cemetery and looked at the little pieces of board which marked the resting place of the brave men who had died in the mighty struggle, the American civil war, I thought these men have died that that Negro might be able to say, "No, if you give me $2 I'll work for you, if you don't I won't." This was the light in which I saw these conditions then, but I saw these things in a different light before I came north; in a light that made me feel as though the inhabitants of the silent graves in the cemetery had almost, if not entirely, given their lives for nothing as far as any advantage accruing to the Negro was concerned.

I worked before my return to north in the states of Louisiana, Mississippi and Arkansas, and I took every opportunity I could get to learn about the condition of the Negro, and I learned that in many cases he was as much a bondsman as ever he was, and in many cases worse. I inquired particularly into the share system which took the place of the much dreamed of ten acres and a mule, which Sambo had so confidently looked forward to possessing after his emancipation. I found that this system was nothing more or less than a species of robbery, and that by its means the Negro was held in as absolute bondage as he was before the war.

The share system operated in this wise: It is well known that the result of the rebellion left the southern planter generally stripped of everything in the shape of property but his land. That property which he had held in human beings had been taken from him by a strong arm of force. It also left the Negro without a master, and the first thing Sambo had to do was find a master, and the first thing the former slave owner had to do was to turn the only means in his possession to some account, and he might possibly have thought that it was worth the considering how he should get possession of the property which had been taken away from him, and the brilliant idea may have entered his head that the remaining property might be utilized for that purpose. Be that as it may, if he did not think of this then it certainly occurred to him afterward and he did not fail to take advantage of it in the near future, but at the present the old master or his residuary legatees had the land, but had no slaves to work it whereby it might be made to support its owner in idleness, the southern slave-holder having constitutionally as much of an objection to work as Harry L. Gilmer has of the truth. Sambo had the necessary qualification, that is a willingness to work, but he had nothing to work with or upon. Thus it came that the old master said to Sambo, how would you like to rent ten acres of land from me and raise a crop of cotton for yourself? Sam thought he saw visions of a condition beside which the ten acres and a mule faded into insignificance.

Arrangements were at once entered into, and Sambo being furnished with a mule, and having agreed that half of the crop of cotton should pay for the use of the land, and that he should have a certain amount of rations advanced for his support and the mule's, and that out of his share of the proceeds of the experiment he should reimburse the landlord for the advance of rations to himself, family and mule, a careful account of which should be kept by his benefactor, the landlord.[92] These things having all been satisfactorily arranged, especially to the satisfaction of the landlord, Sambo started the mule and started on the road to fortune and glory. All through the hot summer he worked with a light heart and visions of future greatness before him, on into the fall when the bolls of cotton plant burst open, and before the eyes of the delighted Sambo is exposed the realization of all his dreams. The cotton is picked and baled, and to the nearest market or landing is the cotton hauled, in many cases Sambo taking all the family in his enthusiasm. The cotton is weighed, and Sam's share is told of. Sam is delighted when he is told that his share amounts to $150 or $200. He immediately begins to think about buying the old master out, but he whistles on the other side of his mouth when the little bill which the master presents for advanced rations and the loan of the mule is brought forward, and which amounts to more than his share of the crop.

There is a terrible disappointment but there is no getting over it. The master having pocketed all the share of the same, and having realized as he had foreseen that it has been a profitable arrangement, has another scheme ready for this emergency. He has a large tract of timber land, which, if he can get cut up into cord wood, will furnish him with fuel and also bring in some money at the adjacent landing, and seeing the despondent attitude of Sambo, he magnanimously comes forward with a proposition to allow him the privilege of paying his indebtedness to his kind benefactor by clearing this land.

This scheme and others of a similar character have been played very successfully upon the so-called freedmen of the south. In cases where the unfortunate victim has tried to escape this form of slavery by attempting to leave the country, he has been arrested and imprisoned, and sometimes as a prisoner of the county he has been hired out to planters or contractors. Thus did the latter kind of slavery becomes worse than the former. I have received in every state that I visited in the south incontrovertible proof that this prevailed, not only from the statements of the victims themselves, but I have heard the perpetrators boast of it, and this was the chief cause of the exodus of the Negro from the south to the west and north.[93] The south has been blessed by nature with a soil that is calculated to support a vaster population than would or could settle in it for the next hundred years if it were not for the blighting curse of human avarice which there, as everywhere else, makes the bounteous gifts of nature to her children to produce, instead of happiness and comfort, which they are naturally calculated to produce, in their stead misery, want, degradation and crime.

In the fall of 1870 I first went into the south, in the month of October. I stayed there until the following May, when

I returned to Chicago. During my sojourn there I visited every principal city on the Mississippi river from St. Louis to and including New Orleans. I lived among the roughest class of men on the face of the earth. I worked with this class of men on railroads and upon levees. I tramped hundreds of miles in search of work. I lived in levee camps and rail camps. I slept in calico tents and on the bare wet ground. I slept in lodging houses in towns, which were always associated with the inevitable saloon, and where was sold the most wretched liquor that ever went down a fool's throat. The keepers of these places seemed to look upon the levee laborers with something like the same interest that Dickens has described the grog-shop keepers and others of Liverpool as having for mercantile Jack, that is, as their legitimate prey. The whisky was poor, the food was poor, the sleeping arrangements were horrible, and the charges were damnable.

As illustrating this, I heard a conversation as I lay in bed in a den of this kind in a small river town in Louisiana between two evidently disgruntled Irishmen, who occupied another bed in the same room. After grumbling for a while, one of them asked what was the name of the woman who kept the place we were staying in; the other one replied that he thought it was Mrs. Killpatrick. After a short pause the other one replied, "Faith, if it is not her name, it ought to be, for she'd kill the devil, let alone Patrick." I thought the remark did not do Mrs. Killpatrick any injustice, considering the supper I had and the bed I was vainly trying to sleep on and the prices I had to pay for such miserable accommodations.

After my return to Chicago in May I worked upon the dredge I had worked upon the year before, and which was finishing up the deepening of the canal at Sagbridge. I worked there until the work was all finished. Soon after that three west parks were commenced, Douglas, Central and Humboldt parks. I was one of the first men who turned a sod in Douglas park. I worked in this park until about three weeks before the great Chicago fire, which occurred this same year (1871). At the time of the fire I was living in the town of Lyons, and was working in Mud Lake. Mr. Nickerson, I believe, was doing the work, which was about two miles north of where Mud Lake joins the Desplaines river. I came into Chicago on Tuesday following, and walked through the streets of smouldering ruins. The following year I worked in Chicago, and since that time I have lived and worked mostly, in fact almost entirely, in Chicago. I have worked at street scraping all over the prairie between Ashland avenue and Lawndale. I lived a little west of Lawndale when there was but one house there; but this was before the fire.

I pass over the next few years as containing but little that would be of interest to the average reader. During those years I worked almost entirely in stone yards up to 1879. I worked at all kinds of work in these yards, including driving team. During those years I was somewhat studious in my habits. I spent a considerable part of my spare time in the reading room of the public library. I attended quite a number of lectures, hearing Mr. Bradlaugh, the English reformer and freethinker, Tilton, Bayard Taylor, Robert Collier, James Freeman Clarke, Joaquin Miller, Robert Ingersoll, James Parton,[94] and many others. I attended regularly the 10 cent lecture held at McCormick's hall. I forget the year now, but I think it was in 1876. I took books from the public library almost all the time from its inauguration until the present.

In the fall of 1879 I paid a visit to England. I had intended for years to visit my native home, but financial embarrassments had interposed insurmountable obstacles.

My principal reason for going was to fulfill a matrimonial engagement which I had entered into eleven years before. Another was to see my aged father once more. I also thought that I might be able to find something which would offer at least as favorable inducements to stay there as any that I had found on this side of the Atlantic; but I found that while there had been a period of very great prosperity during my absence, at the time of the visit, the condition of industry was very disheartening. I fulfilled the engagement referred to above and returned to the United States in February, 1880. The fruit of my marriage has been two children, one a girl of 2½ years age, the other a boy who has been born since my imprisonment.

On my return I invested what money I had in a team of horses, so that I became what Chicago *Tribune* calls a capitalist. I have earned my living by this means, that is, hauling stone, from that time to the time of my arrest. In the summer 1880 I was informed that there was being attempted to formation of the teamsters' union. I learned of the place, and went to listen to what it was intended to do; on my second visit to this embryo union, I took some part in the proceedings. A temporary organization was effected, with a temporary president, vice-president, secretary and treasurer. A Mr. Oberndorf was elected president; he being a German, suggested to some persons present that the vice-president ought to be an Irishman; this was approved, and your humble servant was elected. The organization did not prove a success, and it finally died. I believe there is a teamsters' union in the city, but I believe that it is confined to the brick-hauling branch of that industry.

About this time, in the fall of 1880, I was informed of the calling of a meeting for the reorganization of the liberal league, the principal object of which organization was the total separation of church and state. I attended the meeting at 54 West Lake Street, and after listening to the preceedings and the statement of the objects of the proposed society, I joined the society then and there. A hall was rented at the corner of Halsted and Madison streets, and the society entered upon its mission. Lectures and discussions were the feature of the exercises. Theology, science, philosophy, of every quantity and quality; political economy, social economy, domestic economy, and, in fact, every kind of economy, and perhaps a little extravagance thrown in once in a while as a condiment, the diet being of a rather heavy character. However, I became acquainted with a very intelligent, as well, I believe, as a very conscientious class of people. I took part in the discussions and became more or less prominent in the society, being elected financial secretary, vice-president and delegate to the national congress held at Milwaukee in the fall of 1884, which I attended, taking part in the proceedings and supporting the adoption of a labor plank in the platform or constitution of the society.

During the year 1883 labor meetings were held on the lake front and I was invited to speak there. I hesitated and asked what was the object. The person who asked me replied, "You are not afraid to speak in the cause of labor, are you?" I replied "No!" and I accordingly spoke there several times that fall, as well as at other parts of the city in the open air. I had not at that time any preference for any labor organization but thought the subject of labor offered a broad enough field for agitation. I spoke on the general question of the wrongs of labor. I continued my connection with the liberal league.

In the following summer, having become a socialist by conviction, through listening to and taking part in the discussions at the Labor league, I became connected with the International Working People's Association. As a member of that organization I have spoken all over the city of Chicago, in the open air on the lake front and in halls in other parts of the city. I have also addressed meetings in St. Louis and Cincinnati. At the latter place I was speaking to a large mass meeting in front of the custom house, and would you suppose one of the truthful reporters of the Chicago *Times* swore on my trial that I was urging an audience to sack Marshall Field's store at a meeting held the same day and same hour on market square in this city. I have also spoken in Pittsburgh, Pa., Canton, Ohio, and other smaller places, as well as at meetings in the suburbs of this city.

I was a member of the American group, which held meetings in different halls in the city for the discussion of social and industrial economy. For the purposes of attending one of these meetings I went to Grief's hall on the evening of Sunday, May 2, 1886. I had to speak that night at Zepf's hall at Brewers' union, but thought I could speak to the brewers and then attend the American group meeting before it adjourned. I therefore went into Grief's hall in order to tell any one of the American group that I might see that I would try to come there after leaving the Brewers' union. I met a member of the American group and told him, and as I was leaving the saloon a gentleman who is a member of the International Cigarmakers' union called me to sit down a minute until he could inform me of what had transpired at the Trade and Labor assembly that afternoon, at which meeting he had been present. While this gentleman was detailing the proceedings of the Trade and Labor assembly a young German came to me and asked me to speak the following night at the same place, 54 West Lake Street, to the wagonmakers. I promised him I would. Another middle-aged German, whom I knew to be associated with the Central Labor union; asked me if I could address a meeting at 358 West Twelfth street on the following Tuesday night which would be May 4. After thinking a little and finding that I had no other engagement I promised to do so, and after hearing what my friends had to relate about the T. and L. assembly, I went to Zepf's hall, and read to the English-speaking brewers the proposition of the employers to them. After I was through I left them to discuss it between themselves, leaving the copy of the proposition with them and I went to the American group at Grief's hall, which was then drawing to a close. I afterwards went back to Zepf's hall to see what they had done about the terms of the employers.

I found two or three of them sitting at a table, and in response to my question, they said they had not decided. I had a glass of beer with them and then went home. On the following day I worked three-quarters of a day and at night I went to the wagon-makers' meeting, which I addressed afterwards leaving the hall and entering into a conversation with some of the men on the sidewalk in front of the saloon. After talking with them for some time I went inside with them, and after a short talk there I went home, leaving the hall with Mr. Brown.

I worked all the next day, which was the 4th of May, taking a load of stone to Waldheim cemetery, which is a day's work. I returned home, getting to the stable about half-past 5 in the evening, when I took care of my horses and went home to my supper, intending to go to the meeting at 368 West Twelfth street. Just before going into the house I brought an *Evening News,* and looking over the announcement column, I saw that there was a call there for the American group to meet at 107 Fifth avenue. I hardly knew what to do. I knew that I ought to attend the American group, as I was treasurer of the group, and it was the period for election of officers, and I also knew that if it was a meeting that would require any money I ought to be there. I finally concluded to go there.

I left home about 7:20, taking a Twelfth street car. I stood on the front platform, as I was smoking. When a car reached the Van Buren street viaduct the bridge swung and we were bridged. We were held there quite a while; the light on the board of trade was visible, and a conversation sprung up between a fireman and the driver as to the time by the board of trade clock. They, afterwards, began to talk about the horses that were attached to the cars in which I joined and spoke about driving street cars myself ten years ago. At last the bridge swung back to its place and the cars started. I left the car at the corner of Washington, as did also the fireman. I think the fireman walked east on Washington. He was a tall, spare man, with a moustache, and possibly a goatee, but not a beard, as I remember now.

If he should see this statement he will doubtless bear testimony that I speak the truth when I say that it was close to 8 o'clock when he left the car at the corner of Washington and Fifth avenue on the evening of the 4th of last May, and yet at that time I did not know that there was going to be, or had been, a meeting called at the Haymarket that night. We had both got off the car on the north side of Washington, and as 107 is a few doors south of Washington, I walked back across Washington to 107 and went up stairs. I found a number of persons in the front room of the first floor in the business office and there and not till then at that hour, 8 o'clock, did I know that there was to be a meeting at the Haymarket. I found out after entering the room that the meeting had been called for the purpose of considering whether the American group should attempt the organization of the sewing girls of the city, whose wages were pitilessly low. Mr. and Mrs.

Parsons had anticipated that the group would vote in the affirmative and had taken the responsibility of having a number of hand-bills printed, which hand-bills were present at the meeting, or some of them. On asking what the meeting was called for, I was shown one of these bills, and was told that was what the meeting was called for. I tried to tell the jury this, but was told that that was not the law, although I had been sworn to tell the whole truth. Is it not a queer thing, law? When I entered the room I had seen and spoken to Mr. Rau, and he had asked me to go over to the Haymarket.

I told him that I had come in response to the advertisement in the *Evening News,* and knew nothing about the meeting at the Haymarket; that if it had not been for the announcement I would have been speaking at Twelfth street, where I had an engagement to speak that night. I therefore sat down and waited until Mr. and Mrs. Parsons should come. After waiting some time they came, and we decided to try to organize the sewing girls of the city. Mr. Parsons made a motion that the treasurer should pay over to the ladies the sum of $5, which should pay for the bills which had been printed, $4, and the other dollar should go for the car-fare and incidental expenses in looking around for halls, etc. This was agreed to. I paid the money and received a receipt for the same; in the meantime Mr. Schwab had come in and a telephone dispatch had been received asking for speakers at Deering, where there had been a meeting called. The young man, Louis Brandt, attended to the telephone. Mr. Schwab went out, and I did not see him any more that evening.

About this time Mr. Rau came in and said that he had been over to the Haymarket and there was a large crowd over there and no one to address them but Mr. Spies, and that he wanted Mr. Parsons and I to go over there and assist him. We went over there, and Mr. Spies, who was speaking, stopped in a short time after we arrived and introduced Mr. Parsons. Mr. Parsons spoke at considerable length, as has been reported.

When I was introduced by Mr. Spies, the audience was getting smaller and I had told Mr. Spies that it was hardly worth while for me to speak. He said I might make a short speech. I spoke for about fifteen to twenty minutes, when, without the slightest intimation or thought of such a thing, on turning my face to the south, I saw the police approaching. They were, in fact, very close to me when I first saw them. I stopped talking and was undecided what to do. The meeting had been more than ordinarily peaceable one, and had been getting smaller and more quiet up to that time, so that there were not more than two or three hundred at the most, in my opinion, when the police arrived. A few minutes before this the weather had become somewhat threatening; a very large black cloud had rolled up from the north, causing quite a stampede. On this account Mr. Parsons called out from the crowd that the meeting had better adjourn to Zepf's hall on the next corner. Some one replied that this hall was occupied, and then I said to the audience that I would be through in a minute or two and we would all go home. I then began to draw my remarks to a close. Before I could do this, however, the meeting was invaded by the police, and Capt. Ward, in a very loud voice cried out: "In the name of the people of the state of Illinois I command this meeting to peaceably disperse."

Whatever had been my doubts at the intention of the police, they were at once removed and I at once thought that I would try to prevent any trouble between the meeting and the police. This was my object in staying on the wagon after I saw the police on the ground, and as Capt.

Ward uttered the above expression I stepped down toward him and replied: "Why captain, this is a peaceable meeting." I did this for the purpose, more than anything else, of trying to allay the excitement and nervousness under which he was laboring, and thus, by this conciliatory manner, showing to him that we were not disposed to be quarrelsome. Had the captain at the time met me in the same manner, even though he had still insisted on the dispersal of the meeting, I myself would have dispersed it, and believe all would have been well, but the captain, in a very violent manner, altogether ignoring my pacific attitude, turned to the police, saying as near as I can remember: "I command this meeting to disperse, and I call on you to disperse it now." This is what I thought he said at the time. He said, "I call upon you to assist in dispersing it now." As this is a true and dispassionate recital of the events transpiring at the Haymarket meeting on the night of May 4, 1886, I will not dispute with him about this; he may tell the truth about this, and I may be mistaken.[95]

I say this may be possible, because, as the captain began to give the second command, I stepped from the wagon, leaping down at the south end of the wagon. As soon as I reached the ground I said: "All right, we'll go," or "Well then; we'll go," and walked towards the sidewalk. I think I had just stepped on the sidewalk when I saw the flash in the middle of the street and heard the explosion of the bomb. Almost if not entirely simultaneously with this explosion the police began to fire into the crowd. The crowd ran in every direction. I happened to have my face turned to the south at the time of the explosion, and I ran in that direction. Immediately after the explosion, I was struck in the knee by a bullet, which after striking the bone, traveled upward and slightly across, and then came out making two holes. I felt the blow, but did not know what it was.

I continued to the corner of Randolph and Desplaines streets, running as fast as I could, for the crowd who were falling down and crawling on the sidewalk, and calling: "O, God! O, God! Save us," while volley after volley of bullets were poured into the wildly flying and unresisting mass. I finally reached the corner and ran east. As soon as I felt myself safe I felt of my knee and found that my knee was wet. I knew that I was wounded. After going over to the south side to look for some of my companions of the evening, being anxious to discover what had become of them, I went and had my knee dressed.

The next morning I was arrested. On the afternoon of the same day, 5th of May, without having had an opportunity of seeing a friend or a lawyer, I, with A. Parsons, A. Spies, and Mr. Schwab, was railroaded through a coroner's jury, at which jury the assistant state's attorney stood between the coroner and the several witnesses and, in whispers, prompted them what to say.

How different this coroner's jury from the jury that inquired into the death of poor Bealey at the stock yards, and where the Pinkerton murderers were allowed to have able lawyers who bull-dozed the coroner and all the witnesses, and which was adjourned from time to time until the jury got ready to let the suspects go, and where the obliging coroner and attorneys of the suspects retired into the ante-room from time to time in the most fraternal manner! From that time until the present I have been confined in the county jail of Cook county, Illinois. I had forgotten to state that I was arrested at my home, where I waited to give myself up to the authorities if they should want me. Of my subsequent trial and conviction the public are aware.

This is a truthful narrative of my life and my connection with the Haymarket affair, for which I am held as accessory to the act of a person with whom I have no connection or knowledge, and with whom no witness had ever during the whole of this trial, stated that I knew of his existence, and, as far as this record goes, who is as much a stranger to me as he is to Judge Gary or the state's attorney.

Hoping the reader of this will calmly and dispassionately consider those facts, and feeling sure that whoever does so will feel that if any person can be connected and convicted as accessory to the act of some person unknown to the accused, the innocence of a crime is no shield or security to any member of society. If this conviction is just, then whenever any crime is committed all that is necessary for the authorities to do is to find some persons obnoxious to them, present them to the jury and tell the jury that though they may not have committed the crime they are charged with, yet it is the opinion of the prosecution that it will be a good thing to get rid of them anyway, and this is the handy way of doing it. Patient reader, I remain faithfully yours,

S. Fielden.

9

Autobiography of Oscar Neebe

I was born on the 12th day of July, 1850, in the city of New York. My parents went to Germany to give us children a good education. My childhood and school days I spent in Hesse Cassel. I returned to New York when I was 14 years old, and happy to be back again in the Land of the Free; then no more slavery existed, the bloody war was just over. I saw the sun-burned soldiers in their torn garments returning from the south, where they fought for freedom and liberty, and broke down the slavery of the black race to enter the slavery of the white.

From that period dates the time when a free citizen of the United States can work or starve in this glorious free country. After consulting my oldest brother it was decided that I should learn the gold and silver beating trade, and I entered a shop in Houston street, New York, and commenced with $2 a week. I worked quite a while and had to give it up on account of pains in my chest (lungs). I noticed that this branch of business is very low. The older hands do not like to learn the younger ones. I don't know if it is that way in all shops of that trade. I only worked in one.

Horace Greeley said: "Young man, go west," and I, the 16-year-old boy went to the Garden City, Chicago, but could not find work. After I had sold all my clothing and trinkets to pay my board during the time I was looking for work, and when I had nothing more than the suit I had on, the friendly (?) boarding-house keeper showed me the door and said I should look for another boarding-house, and I left. Hungry, I went to seek work, and when night came I went to a pile of lumber near the lighthouse and slept in open air. The next morning I went to the lake, washed my face, and drank out of my hand the water. I had 40 cents yet, and brought a loaf of bread and a newspaper.

Through an advertisement in the paper I had bought I got a situation as a waiter in the Lake house saloon, kept by Martin Keller, and later on I was promoted to bartender. I was treated by these kind people, Mr. and Mrs. Keller, as their son, and I never worked for better people. Here I had a chance to see and study the life of the working people. Mostly workmen from the McCormick Machine works stopped there, and many of them made good wages. I saw and heard how it was made; I saw that foremen received commission and royalty from the poorer workmen; saw how sneaks and spies watched every word the workman said, to report the same to the foreman, and saw good workmen sent away. Of course they were men, and no cowards, sneaks and spies, like a great many who work for McCormick today under those conditions, and are the first ones to stay like dogs, on the side of McCormick and others.

I saw the eight-hour movement in 1866–7: saw how bosses made contracts with the workingman, to break those contracts or promises with the aid of the police, and what profit did the workman have from it—none—more than now. Then they were talking of fighting about certain persons, of how high the wages should be, and the bosses knew their weakness and profited by it; the rich got richer, and the poor poorer; that is the tactics of harmony between capital and labor. McCormick's workmen know it the best; he gathered millions, is a millionaire, and his workmen got to be paupers and tramps, who worked and made the millions. Was it you workmen or was it McCormick? As it is with him the same way it is with many other manufacturers.

I stayed with Martin Keller until 1868, when I went on a vessel of the lake as cook and stayed there and traveled the lakes during the summer. In the fall of 1868 our ship landed at Cleveland. I was tired of this life and left the ship and the west and went back to New York with the intention to learn a trade. I was fortunate to be an apprentice in a tinsmith shop. The owner was an excellent man and a good workman, and I learned the trade as tinsmith and cornicemaker to perfection in all its branches. Here I had the best chance to see in the tenement houses the life of the poor workingman, packed like herring in a few rooms. Many jobs I have done where it was impossible for me to take any money for work done, as I could plainly see that they needed the few cents for bread to keep the wolf, hunger, from the door. I knew what it was to be hungry myself, and when the poor wife and mother thanked me with tears in their eyes I was repaid enough.

One day my boss told me: "Oscar, I have a good situation for you where they manufacture milk cans. You can make more there than what I can pay you for work you can do. I can get along with a boy and I cannot pay you what you are worth. You can commence Monday." On his recommendation I started to work the next Monday. It was a new place. A new patent milk can. In a short time the business increased and there were fourteen workmen. We could make each from 25 to 30 cans a week, but some of the workmen were too greedy; that was not enough. They worked harder and made from 35 to 40 cans a week, and that was too much to pay a week, $35 to $40, to a workman by the company who worked said patent can, the price was reduced to 75 cents apiece, but the selling price was increased from $6 to $7 apiece. Now the workmen worked to their utmost strength, so as to make the same wages as before, and I told them they would, by doing so, reduce the price of wages furthermore. A short time after that the price was reduced to 65 cents apiece. A friend of mine, Barny Collins and I were appointed a committee to consult the company and let them know that the workmen would not make a can for that price. Collins and I went to Mr. Sheppard and laid the resolution of the workmen before him. He laughed, and offered to bet that the others would work for 65 cents. We told him no. He offered us two, as we were his oldest and best hands, to give us 75 cents. We told him we and our comrades would not do so, would rather stop than to make those cans less than 75 cents; he went to one of the workmen and asked if he would rather stop than to make the cans for 65 cents. He said Yes, if the others would, he would, of course. Through their cowardice and breaking their word, Collins and I left. It was the first time I saw skilled workmen, who were wanted and needed, back down. It was in 1871. I heard later that the price was reduced to 45 cents. Mr. Sheppard got to be a wealthy man and his workmen poorer and poorer through the cowardice of the workmen.

I commenced work in another factory where they made oil cans and tea-caddies. That was the first place where I saw children from 8 to 12 years old work like slaves, working on machines; most every day it happened that a finger or hand was cut off, but what did it matter, they were paid off and sent home, and others would take their places. I believed that children working in factories has for the last twenty years made more cripples than the war with the south, and the cut off fingers and mangled bodies brought gold to the monopolies and manufacturers. How often has the sweat of a poor man or child paid for the silk dress of a kept woman of these men, whose only desire is "to have lots of fun and a good time."

I want to say a few words concerning the curse of piece work. I have seen certain workmen get four or five boys to teach each one a certain part, and paid them $3 to $5 per week, and they themselves made $60 to $70 per week. The ever hungry manufacturers found out and engaged children themselves, direct, and such workmen would receive only a certain piece or part to make, and where they formerly, in their greediness, made from $60 to $70 per week they earned only $8 to $15, and now they are regular machines, work like a machine, and have hardly ten minutes to spare and rest, or they could not turn out a certain amount of work. That is the curse of piece work. Look at the workmen who work in the tin factories. They all look thin and consumptive, but it is the fault of the workmen themselves, as they do not keep together. How long will it be before you will not find a good skilled tinsmith? Women and children take their places, and what becomes of the men? Paupers, tramps and jailbirds, they will fill the prisons, and by their prison labor will reduce the wages of the unfortunate women and children, and that is the curse of the modern times.

My brother Louis had removed to Philadelphia (to the City of Brotherly Love), where he was born. I followed him, thinking to better my condition. Here I made the acquaintance of a young girl, my wife, whom I married in 1873. We returned to New York, but as my wife did not like it we went back to Philadelphia, where I received work. Philadelphia is a beautiful city (if you have lots of money to live with), but for the workmen I think it is the poorest and meanest in the United States. There the workmen are more in slavery than our colored brothers in the South were and they are afraid to belong to a labor organization, as they might be discharged, and put on the so-called black list; but they must belong to a building association of which are many at Philadelphia. The ambition to have their own home makes them join them and by their wages, where they hardly have enough to keep hunger from the door, they starve to keep up the weekly payments; but you see it is so nice to have your own house before you die of consumption, or after paying for a few years to have the sheriff take hold of it and some rich man buy it for almost nothing, and as I have said before, making the rich richer and the poor poorer.

I have seen in 1876 that over 12,000 buildings of these unfortunate workmen were sold that way. I say the building associations are another curse and it will come here in Chicago the same way as in Philadelphia. Go and ask the stockholders and they will tell you how long they have to wait for their money, so that the building association can be paid; some of the workmen I presume will not believe me, but wait, you will find the truth of what I say. In 1876–1877 times were hard like now, and when the workman does not consume you cannot produce. I only warn you, workmen, it will not be long and the crisis which destroyed thousands of happy homes will be felt here.

In February, 1877, I went back to Chicago and got work at Adams' Westlake Manufacturing company and was paid good wages until July 1, when I was discharged because I stood up for the right of the workmen and afterwards could not receive any work at my trade. I managed to live through the hard years, 1877–1879, and many times my family had no bread. I often felt discouraged, but the help and assistance and cheerful ways of my dear wife, kept me up.

In 1879 I got a situation as a salesman for the Riverdale Distilling Company, selling compressed yeast, and worked for them until 1881. Then I commenced with my brother Henry, Peter J. Leng, and Rudolph Bohn, the Acme Yeast Company. Since I am in prison, these three have managed to put me out of the firm and sell yeast under the name of Riedeburg & Co. I had my route on the southwest side, and I had an opportunity to learn how poor the workman here is in Chicago. In the neighborhood of the poor nothing but poor material for the food is sold. That part would be a good field for our health officers. These storekeepers buy up the poorest and oldest stuff and sell it at high prices, and the poor also get cheated by short weight and measure, but they cannot complain or the storekeeper will sell them nothing on trust in books as they have no steady cash, as they do not get paid regular weekly in cash by their bosses. I saw mothers cry, as they had to send their little ones (who by right belonged in school) to the factories or stores so they could live. I saw a little girl who had worked at Lehmann's Fair for $3 per week who had frozen both legs, as the poor parents had no money to buy good, warm shoes and clothing; they needed the money for bread. How many thousands of these little girls are in the same way working in the South side for these human beings? You expect to raise children and citizens for this glorious free country. Idiots and prisoners you will raise, and their system will be punished in the coming third or fourth generation.

I am a great friend of reading, and have been reading since I was a little boy, and have studied the history of all nations and the world in general. I have read of the war of the peasants, the religious wars, etc., and have seen in the history of the world the judgment of the world's doings. I have read Thomas Paine and Jefferson and works of other great men. I was educated in the protestant religion and was taught to hate those who believed in another form or way concerning a God; my religion I was told was the only, the best.

As I read of the many wars and slaughters in the name of God, the thought came to me, what kind of a God that could be, who should not be kind and good and also almighty. As a boy, already many contradicting thoughts came over me. I read Thomas Paine[96] and I made up my mind that a God who was almighty and who would allow so many cruel and terrible acts to be performed in his name, could not be a just and a good one, and became a free thinker, but although a free thinker, I went to church, and when I heard the preacher describe how beautiful heaven was, I thought why not have heaven now here on earth. Hell we had already. I saw the sparkling eyes of the devoted, and how many poor, deluded workmen would think by the description of heaven which is for the poor; how his oppressor and slavedriver would be punished in hell and roasted, and all that for ever and ever. This delusion of the workman and promising of the glories of heaven is performed so that the poor workman should not think for himself, think that he might have heaven on earth, if he only wanted. Here you would be certain but what is behind the clouds is a fable. Here it could be set aside for a while if the pleasure would be too great to bear. In my 20th year I had cut myself off from all religious sects.

Then came the years 1870 and 1871; the war between French and Germans, and the murder of the workmen of Paris.[97] The communists of New York arranged a solemn death celebration in open air, but it was prohibited by the police, of course it was on a Sunday, the committee rented a hall and held the meeting. Here it was that I heard the first communistic speech and that all men are equal. I tried in my union to have a speaker, but the president said, we are no communists, we don't want to divide. I told them I had heard the speech and not a word of dividing had been said. I was overruled and the union went on its old way and went to the dogs, through their more valuable employment of drinking beer and running one another down. The members all had fair wages and so they needed no union and no more meeting to discuss the labor question. I visited the meetings of the communists and joined them here in Chicago in 1877, from which time I took an active part in it until 1880. I have nothing to say about that as Parsons has said all I could have said.

The managers of the *Arbeiter Zeitung* reported in 1880 that if there was no money raised the paper could not be published, that if they were to publish it as a private business that they could borrow $15,000 that way. The Socialistic Publishing society refused to do that and selected a new lot of managers, of which I was one. The business of the Socialistic Publishing society was almost bankrupt when August Spies was elected the business manager, and his doings and his work helped to build up the paper. The old managers and their friends done all in their power to destroy us. Many business men and working men will remember the time how certain parties (names I will not mention) worked against the new management and its doings. After the congress in Pittsburgh the *Arbeiter Zeitung*, *Vorbote* and *Fackel*, kept their work and designs within the sense and limits of the Pittsburgh programme and was selected as the organ of the International Workingmen's association. Often the remark has been made "we were working against the interest *(gewerkschaften)* of the Knights of Labor," but that was not so, we were not against them, only against the way these organizations were made and kept. Did not hundreds of our speakers speak to the workingmen to organize themselves, no matter in what form (as gewerkschaften) as unions or Knights of Labor, that in organization lay their strength? I have done my utmost to organize the Central Labor union and increase its membership and today it is the best labor organization in Chicago, with over 10,000 members. That is all I have to say about my life as a workman.

In May, 1886, I was arrested and accused of murder and sentenced to fifteen years in the penitentiary, but for what I have not been able to find out up to the present time.

The man Grinnell, who wanted to make a new history of the world, told me personally a few days after my arrest that a few prominent Germans had told him I was a very dangerous man, and I can understand out of his remarks that these prominent Germans were a few German democratic beer brewers of Chicago, and to please them I received fifteen years in the penitentiary for daring to organize their employees. These brewers cannot forget that they have to pay their workmen $15 more wages per month for only ten hours work, and should I have to be at penitentiary fifteen years I can still have the good thought that I have done my share to improve the condition of the poor workman and I am convinced that during these long fifteen years my three little children (two girls and one boy) will be taken care of by you. Doubly orphaned now that my poor wife was so suddenly taken from me—stricken down by the weight of anguish and trouble weighing on her tender heart—I call on all workingmen or working women of all nationalities and all countries to unite and down with your oppressors.

Your friend,

Oscar Neebe.

10

Autobiography of Louis Lingg

I beheld the light of this world on the 9th day of September, 1864, in Mannheim, Grand Duchy of Baden. In the middle ages Mannheim was a fortress, but she cast off her protective garments on the occasion of the third conquest by the French in 1678. At the present time Mannheim is, because of her prominent location as a centre of navigation and railway traffic, a flourishing city, with a population of about 65,000. The Rhine connects Mannheim with the North Sea, while the famous St. Gothard tunnel, which perforates the Alps, places here in direct railway conjunction with Switzerland and Italy.

My father, Friedrich Lingg, toiled in a lumber yard, and my mother kept a laundry, and thus they were enabled to provide for their modest wants, and the education of their children, myself and six-years' younger sister. At the age of five years I visited school, first—the so-called city or elementary school—and, later, after the general reorganization of the school system, at the time of the reunion of

Germany, following the French-German war,[98] the mixed public school, so-called because children of all confessions are being admitted. Being cared for sufficiently by my parents, my earliest youth was a happy one indeed, until a fatal accident which befell my father brought about such a change in our situation, that not very seldom want and hunger were questions in our family, and only the untiring efforts of my mother prevented their visits from becoming daily ones.

In his efforts to contribute to the wealth of his employer, a dealer, my father undertook a task which all of his fellow-slaves refused to do, to wit: he endeavored to replace a heavy log of oak which had slipped from the banks upon the frozen surface of the river Neckar, to the shore. In his zeal to accomplish the task, the treacherous icy crust gave way, and father disappeared below the ice in the waters of the river, and could be saved only after the most strenuous efforts and diligent search. This event destroyed his robust nature to such a degree that his working capacity was reduced by it very much. In consequence thereof, his noble employer saw the necessity of reducing the salary of the wage-slave, who had worked for him for twelve long years and whose health had been ruined in his zeal to further the interests of his master, and after a little while my father was discharged altogether from the employ of the lumber dealer, with the flimsy excuse that business had decreased, and that some of the hands were, therefore, superfluous. It is true, after a space of time father secured work suitable to his broken health, as a laborer in the employ of the municipal government, but the compensation for these services was so small that it sufficed hardly to satisfy his own personal living expenses.

Three years after the above described sad experience, since which period he had been in a state of stupidity, my father died. At the request of mother, the remains of father were dissected, and the physicians gave their opinion that the stupidity (or stupefaction) which had befell him had its origin in said fatal accident.

This was in the year of 1877. At this time I was thirteen and my sister seven years old, and at this age I received my first impressions of the prevailing unjust social institutions, i.e., the exploitation of men by men. The main circumstances which caused this reflection in my youthful mind were the experiences of our own family. It did not escape my observation that the former employer of my father grew continually richer, despite the extravagant life he and his family were leading, whilst, on the other hand, my father, who had performed his respective part in creating the wealth his employer possessed, and who had sacrificed his all, which was his health, in his effort to serve his master, was cast aside like a worn-out tool which had fulfilled its mission and could now be spared.

Shortly, all the incidents which I have narrated before, implanted into my mind the seed of bitter hatred against the existing society, which feeling grew still more intense with my entrance into the industrial arena, and which has inspired me in my late agitation against capitalistic society with its barbarous and inhuman effects. The life which was allotted to us after my father's death, was only a further source to inflame my embitterment and hatred and we were, to a great extent, subjected to the freaks of our rich customers who were living in grand style, by creating debt everywhere. Sometimes, when were in need of money, my mother would send me on a tour of collections to our different customers, but I returned with empty hands and aching heart, very often with the message that Mrs. A. or B. had company, and therefore could not see me. Under such conditions I did not dare to tell mother that I was in want of clothing, and even school books which latter were conscientiously procured by her, but very often at the sacrifice of the last penny. But, in another respect, my mother would punish me severely whenever I committed the slightest offences, especially when followed by a material damage.

The natural consequence was that, instead of being possessed of genuine childlike love toward mother, I dreaded her in a certain degree, although or perhaps just because I was her confidential companion in all her griefs and sorrows, in the same ratio in which my mind became embittered toward, and probably repulsive to, all persons with whom I came in contact. This circumstance exercised also a disadvantageous influence upon my perfection, when I was given in tri-annual apprenticeship to a carpenter boss; and, as it is the custom in Germany that apprentices receive no compensation for their work during the time they spend in learning the trade, but have to be supported by their parents, I was very much grieved that I could not aid in the support of mother, but, on the contrary, was still a burden to her. Very often mother reproached me because I had chosen the carpenter trade for the occupation of my life; she had hoped that I might secure a situation as copyist in some office, which would have had the advantage of enabling me to earn a little money from the beginning. But I stuck to my choice for various reasons. I deemed the knowledge of a distinct trade the best for me, because I was opposed to being dependent on one master, and especially because I had desire to travel, and see the world. So my mother, at last, renounced her objections, and yielded to my desire with the words: "A man's will is his heaven." After I had served my apprenticeship, which lasted from 1869 until 1882, and during which time my master had endeavored rather to make capital out of me than to interest himself in my thorough accomplishment, I took up the wanderer's staff in order that I might see the world, and to perfect the knowledge of my trade among other surroundings and deal with other people.

I first worked a short time in Strasbourg, province Alsace, and then in Fribourg, Baden, at which place I joined the working men's educational society, which organization was the remnants of the German National Working Men's Union, founded by the noted socialistic agitator Lassalle, in the year of 1863. Some branches of this organization are yet in existence, but almost exclusively in South Germany. In these clubs I received the first real information about the doctrines of socialism and communism—that is, so far as this was possible on account of this despicable exceptional laws against socialism which were enacted in 1878. At these places I profited, also, by practical communism, although it consisted only in the form of societies of consumption, or rather eating-associations. Certainly the fact that we were wage slaves, prejudiced our communistic experiment very much.

In the spring of 1883, I directed my steps to Switzerland, the splendid reputation of which country, with regard to its beautiful landscapes and to its free institutions, had attracted my attention, and had aroused my admiration. I traveled through the major part and most beautiful portions of Switzerland on foot, and had therefore ample occasion, not only to enjoy the wondrous sceneries, but to study the life, peculiarities and customs of the people. Briefly described, I made the following traveling tours: From Basel I made my way to Bern. The road between these two points distinguishes itself only in the beginning, along the shores of the Rhine, from which region the wanderer has an aspect of the Black Forest of Baden. Leaving Bern in the rear, I traveled through those parts of the little republic, which, when beheld from the vicinity of Bern, leaves the impression upon the tourists of being even more wonderful than we can picture paradise to ourselves. The beauty of nature in this corner of the world is simply indescribable. The next village I came to was Fribourg. This village is located between a group of hills, and is cut through by the river Aar, whose waters wend their way through perhaps 120 feet high, and 200 feet wide, clefts in rocks. Romantic chain bridges allow the people to cross over the yawning abysses, with their rushing waters, from rock to rock. Next I admired the fascinating location of Lausanne, on the shores of the Geneva Lake.

From Lausanne one can overlook the city of Geneva on the beautiful lake, and also view Mont Blanc, whose top seems to reach as high as heaven. As I could obtain no work at any of these villages, I pursued my journey in a left backward direction and surmounted the Black Hills. The weather was bright, and had not been for the shady descent I would have suffered the heat very much. Having made my way over the mountains, I arrived at Thun, and thence, crossing the Thuner Lake, at Interlaken. This village lies at the foot of the Alps, with their everlasting snow, at intermissions changing with thriving meadows. This is the Eldorado of European tourists. From the top of the Brunig I enjoyed once more the whole view over the romantic upper country of Bern, and then I descended, and crossing the Vierwaldstadter Lake, went to Luzern. Next I worked my way to the mountains Pilatus and Rigi. To ascend, one is subjected to much disagreeableness, but once on the top the pleasure of a most extraordinary view presents itself to a weary tourist, and is a more than generous compensation for his trouble. For the convenience of travelers a cog-wheel road leads up to the Rigi but as the use of this road is connected with considerable expense (the fare amounting to nine francs, or $1.80), and as the benefits of the acquisitions of science in general mostly serve the wealthy people only, the son of the proletariat is bound to depend upon his legs in making the descent. Beyond Luzern, along the Vierwaldstadter Lake, extends the Axen road, which, in describing many curves and windings, offers various interesting sceneries. For instance, the famous Tell Plate, and vis-a-vis can be seen the Rutli, the historical nightly plotting places of the patriots of the Canton Uri Schwys and Unterwalden, who were fighting against the tyranny of Gessler.[99] In my opinion this landscape is one of the most beautiful in Switzerland, if not in whole Europe.

Zurich was the next place I visited. This city and its suburbs are also charming, being located on the shores of Lake Zurich; but as I had had occasion to admire more attractive displayments of nature in Switzerland, this section did not impress me in an extraordinary manner. The same can be said of the village Winterthur and Frauenfeld. Near Aargau I ascended the flanks of the limestone containing Jura Mountains, from which point of view the half-decayed ancient castle of the Hapsburg dynasty is visible. The history of this castle aroused the thought within me that the victory in the contests between liberty-loving and for liberty-fighting people and tyrants must always ultimately be on the side of the oppressed people, as this has been the case in the struggle of the mountaineers of Switzerland against the Emperor Maximilian of Austria in the middle of the only silent deponent of ancient tyranny.

On my journey via Olten, Solothurn and Biel to Neufchatel and La Chaux-de-Fond I inspected nearly a score of ruins which were the remnants of the castle tyranny and serfdom that kept the people in slavery in past centuries. Some of these relics of barbarism rest peaceably amid fertile vineyards, to whose grapes I helped myself whenever I longed for them, without paying tribute to the modern robbing knights, the capitalists or the vassals, the second hand "business men." Not being able to secure employment at the last mentioned place in the little republic, I returned from La Chaux-de-Fond to Bern, and at this place I enjoyed the hospitalities of several with whom I had been in personal connection and steady correspondence for some time. By this time my military duty in Germany (I ought to have reported for inspection in the "fatherland" before this) rendered my sojourn in Switzerland, according to a treaty between the two countries, illegal, and as I was too well known in Bern my stay in this place was but a brief one. I trusted my luck now for the second time, and with more success, in Zurich. After having worked here for nearly a year, I quitted this place, and worked a couple of weeks in Aargau. This was the terminating point of my career in Switzerland.

The picture which I have drawn in the foregoing account of my sojourn in Switzerland were only the bright sides of my experience. But, dear reader, you must not think that because Switzerland is a romantic and beautiful country it is also a land where grievances and miseries are unknown.

The unfavorable sides which were impressed upon me consisted of my disappointments and experiences with regard to freedom, political as well as economical. The first city where I succeeded in obtaining work was Bern. Here I joined the "General Working Men's Society," an organization which has a socialistic tendency, and has branches throughout Switzerland. Soon after my arrival in Bern, this organization split into two factions, one social democratic, and the other anarchistic, and, as at this time I was not familiar with the doctrines of socialism in such a degree as I am now, I did not know which course to take, and therefore, my participation in the labor movement was but humble.

In Luzern, the second town which furnished me with work, things were a little different. Feuds between the anarchistic and social democratic factions were on the calendar here also, and at first I was inclined neither to one nor the other. But then I took occasion to study the matter of dispute with more zeal, and became more pronounced in my principles. The consideration of the circumstances that in Germany (the real battle ground of the German socialists being in Switzerland) the there existing exceptional laws against the socialistic movement prevented a peaceful, that is, lawful, agitation; and, secondly, that in Switzerland (toward its citizens the politically freest cultured state in the world) a peaceful social development is rendered impossible by its economical conditions, and, further, to a certain degree, also, by the illusion of a great many native born, that they are free (as in the United States) I became a social revolutionist, and shared the tactics of the anarchists. I approved of the propaganda of the deed, which was carried on very vigorously at this time, by, among others, Tellmacher and Kammerer whom I knew personally as honest and true working men—at Vienna, Frankfort, Strasbourg, etc. As the final aim of the socialistic movement at this time, I still possessed the idea of a socialistic-communistic State.

In the meantime, in the spring of 1884, the period had arrived when my stay in Switzerland was no longer possible, on account of my military duty. I had no desire to spend three of the best years of my youth in military service for the defence of throne, altar and money-bag, or even to satisfy the caprices of some crowned idiot in causing wholesale murders, commonly called wars. As the much-praised freedom of Switzerland had sunk so low that its government does not allow a German, who has evaded military service to remain within its borders, I was first expelled from the Canton Lucerne. This could by no means induce me to return to Germany, or, what would be the same thing, to walk into the barracks, and so I tried to make my living without the permission of the police, by visiting, incognito, cities like Bern, Biel, Neufchatel, La Chaux-de-Fond, Zurich, Aargau, Winterthur, St. Gallen, Frauenfeld and others, but in each instance my stay in those places lasted only so long as the police (by means of an existing law which compels all employers and boarding house keepers to report all new comers to the authorities) discovered my identity, and hunted me out of town. This procedure did not give me much chance to participate in the labor movement to such a degree as I wished, or to the further study of the social questions; but on the other hand, it served only to strengthen my hatred against the capitalistic society, republican or monarchical in form. In Zurich, though, I succeeded, after a great deal of rambling, to keep my ground for nearly a year, this being attributable to the circumstance that this is a comparatively large town, and further, that I was as careful as possible.

In this period of party life, experiences led me to the conclusion that in a centralistic organization, with a representative system, all power and activity is concentrated in the hands of the few, thus inducing them to corruption and imperiousness, whilst the great masses are inclined to become indifferent and stupid.

In the spring of 1885 I was obliged to vacate the room which I had occupied hitherto, and by chance the police discovered that my house-boss had not reported me. I was ordered to leave the country, and, as this was the second general notice which was served upon me, the police hinted, not to be very slow about it, either, if I would prefer not to be transported over the frontier by gendarmes. Fortunately, a short time previous to this, I had received a letter from my mother, in which she informed me that she had induced my step-father (in 1885 my mother had married again) to advance to me the funds necessary to carry me to America, and, in order to forward the money to me, she requested a safe address, so I would be sure to get it. Now I intended to go unobserved to Basel on the German Swiss frontier, where I would await the money, thereby stopping on the road at Aargau for the purpose of bidding farewell to my friends, with whose assistance I had founded a socialistic section at that place. I did stop at Aargau, but, at the suggestion of my friends, did not go to Basel, but agreed to await the money from my step-father here and work in the meantime, although this was a dangerous proceeding on account of my being banished from Switzerland. At last the money arrived; however, it was just enough to pay the fare for the voyage. In Germany and Switzerland a carpenter-boss furnishes the tools for his working men, while I learned from friends who had been in America that on the other side of the ocean the working men themselves were bound to keep their own tools. What I wanted, therefore, was enough means to buy tools on my arrival in America. I communicated my wish to my step-father and urged him to advance to me a sufficient sum of money for the purpose, but before an understanding could be reached the police detected my unlawful sojourn in Aargau, and without much ado, I started on my way to America, via Havre, France.

On a beautiful morning in the middle of July, 1885, I landed in New York, and from there came directly to Chicago. In order to procure employment I visited the buildings being constructed, and sought a position as carpenter, and immediately joined the "International Carpenters' and Joiners' Union."[100] When I put in my appearance at the place of action next morning my employer was quite astonished because I had no tools. Nevertheless, I started to work, the boss offering to furnish the necessary tools on condition that he should abstract 75 cents every day from my wages. Although this seemed to be a very big price for the use of an axe and saw, which were the only tools I needed for my work, I was bound to accept these terms, and when after some time my job was finished and I discharged, I was allowed to keep these two articles. How generous! Certainly my "noble boss" must have made an enormous profit on this bargain. After I had made some necessary additions to my tools, I was lucky enough to obtain employment as carpenter in a factory, which lasted till Thanksgiving Day of the same year. On this day myself and another member of the union were discharged because we had refused to fill the places of outside workers, who struck for, and later obtained, higher wages. In the meantime I had become very well known among the members of our union, and made many friends, among whom Seliger, (the false witness in the trial against anarchism),[101] who secured work for me in the same factory in which he was employed, and who persuaded me to room and board with him. But this job did not last very long, either, and I had ample time during the winter to form an idea as to the "free institutions of this glorious country," which compel the working men to go idle and enjoy the "free air" until some "boss" is in need of their services again.

My union had elected me as delegate to the "Central Labor Union" by this time, and being tired of my involuntary idleness, I devoted my leisure time in agitation for that body. It had long since been my opinion that in the present state of society the working classes could make no gain in the direction of improving their condition by means and ways of Trade Union, but, nevertheless, I participated in the organization of the latter, because I knew that the working men from their past and coming experiences and disappointments would soon become revolutionists. It was for the same reason that I accepted the office of organizer of the "International Carpenters and Joiners Union;" and I am proud to say that this union possesses more strength now—in spite of the general reaction of the trades union movement—than was the case at the time of its entrance into the eight-hour movement;[102] which circumstance is the result of the recognition by the members that trades-unionism is only the means to further the design and not the object of its endeavor. The part I took in the organization of working men, and the fact that I held the opinion that the forces by which the workers are kept in subjugation must be retaliated by force, was sufficient for the guardians of this system of exploitation—Gary, Grinnell & Co.—to deem me a dangerous enemy to society, and one that ought to hang.

At present I am imprisoned behind iron bars, and can for pastime reflect on this "land of the free and home of the brave." Fortunately, those who still believe this land to be "free" are either fools or knaves. It is my conviction that every intelligent and upright man will admit that the United States of America are nowadays simply and purely the land of capitalistic tyranny and the home of the most brutal police despotism.

To waste words as regards our trial would be to carry water to the sea, so manifest were the machinations and hatred against us. As regards my alleged "moral guilt," which Judge Gary proclaimed in obedience to the wishes of the money aristocracy,[103] I will here ask the reader two questions: If the police had not unlawfully attacked the people at the Haymarket, would the bomb have been thrown! If the police were not justified in violating the right of free assemblage, then would the unknown have had less desire and less right to throw the missile had I never existed!

Two factors in my history may be missing here; that relating to my boy love, and that which might shed light on my religious or non-religious views. Those who know best of my career in beautiful Switzerland have often guessed the motive of my frequent visits from Zurich to Bern. No doubt they were right in concluding that a daughter of the fabled Eve was in question.

There are many perhaps who may be curious to learn something of my non-religious convictions. Well, the population of my native city was to a great extent liberal. Not only this, but liberalism was, during the period of my school-years, nursed by the government, because of the "Kulturkampf."[104] So I can thank luck that our school teachers inculcated substantial knowledge instead of beliefs in something about which nobody knew anything and united learning could explain nothing. Accordingly, though used to deplore the fact, that taxes on labor prevailed, I rejoiced in the conviction that penalties and taxes on thought had ceased. I availed myself of the situation and was naturally a freethinker, a domain in which greater men than I have trod, and still greater than they will continue to walk.

11

Notes to autobiographies

1. Sir William Hamilton (1788–1856) was a Scottish philosopher and authority on Germany philosophy and Presbyterian church affairs.

2. This is a quotation from the Declaration of Independence, but there is an error in the sentence as published in the *Knights of Labor.* The entire sentence reads: "Prudence, indeed, will dictate that governments long established should not be changed for light and transient causes; and accordingly all experience hath shown that mankind are more disposed to suffer while evils are sufferable, than to right themselves by abolishing the forms to which they are accustomed."

3. Friedrich Schiller (1759–1805) German poet and dramatist, noted for his opposition to the existing social order and his hatred of despotism.

4. James Russell Lowell (1819–1891), American poet, and author, among other writings, of *A Fable of Critics* (1848) and *The Bigelow Papers* (1848). In the latter work he used the vernacular to denounce the Mexican War. Later in life he was United States Minister in Spain and to Great Britain. From 1857–1861, he was editor of the *Atlantic Monthly.* The quoted poem, here given exactly, dates from 1865 and is in Lowell's *Poetical Works* (Boston, 1888), IV, 18–19.

5. A "powder monkey" was a boy who carried or had charge of powder. It originally applied to a powder boy on board a war vessel.

6. The Red River Expedition was designed to establish Union control in one point in Texas, mainly as a counter to the movements of the French in Mexico. It began in the spring of 1864, under the command of General Nathaniel P. Banks, heading a force of 27,000 men. On April 9, a battle was fought at Pleasant Hill in which both parties claimed the victory. Banks, due largely to lack of ammunition and supplies, was forced to fall back, and, on May 13, evacuated Alexandria. The expedition proved to be a disaster for the Union forces.

7. General James Longstreet (1825–1904) was one of the most distinguished officers in the Confederate Army. After the Civil War he supported the Reconstruction measures of the Republican Congress and joined the Republican Party in New Orleans.

8. Slavery was legally ended by the thirteenth amendment to the Constitution, adopted in 1865. The fourteenth amendment, adopted in 1868, made the Negro a citizen, and the fifteenth amendment, adopted in 1870, provided that a citizen's right to vote should not be denied by a state or by the national government because of race or color.

The Reconstruction measures were first adopted by Congress under the leadership of the Radical Republicans in March, 1867. They placed the South under military rule, permitted military tribunals in peacetime, disqualified from voting former leaders of the Confederacy, and gave the vote to former male slaves.

9. The Ku Klux Klan was a secret organization established in the South during the Reconstruction period. It aimed, through terror and violence, to re-subjugate Negroes and to prevent the development of a democratic South. It was responsible for the murders of hundreds of black and white people.

10. Albert R. Parsons married Lucy Eldine Gonzalez.

11. Ulysses S. Grant (1822–1885) was President of the United States from 1868 to 1872. Although personally honest, his administrations became notorious for corruption and poor organization.

12. The great Chicago fire started on October 8, 1871 in the barn of Catherine O'Leary, and before the flames had burned themselves out, nearly 100,000 persons were made homeless and 73 miles of street and 17,500 buildings of all kinds destroyed. Relief societies were immediately established in Chicago.

13. As a result of the Paris Commune the name "communists" became a popular epithet in the United States in the 1870's.

14. "Forty acres and a mule" was the slogan popularized among the freedmen during and after the Civil War. It aroused their hope that they

would obtain land and a mule from the federal government so as not to be at the mercy of the white planters.

15. The Workingmen's Party of the United States was organized at a convention in Philadelphia in July, 1876, not at Pittsburgh. At the convention, nineteen American sections of the International Workingmen's Association (the First International) dissolved the I.W.A., and a few days later, they organized the Workingmen's Party of the United States. The Social-Democratic Party of North America, founded in 1874 by followers of Ferdinand Lassalle, merged with the W.P. of U.S. A year later the new party changed its name to the Socialist Labor Party of North America.

16. The great Railroad strike of 1877 started after the Pennsylvania Railroad announced in mid-May, 1877 a new 10 per cent wage cut to become effective on June 1. (This came on top of previous wage cuts during the depression which began in 1873.) Other eastern roads announced wage cuts to become effective on July 1st, and also began to intensify the discharge and blacklisting of members of the three conservative railroad brotherhoods—locomotive engineers, firemen, and conductors. A planned strike to begin on June 27, organized by a secret "trainmen's union," under the leadership of Robert H. Ammon, never took place. But on July 16, a strike began on the Baltimore and Ohio line at Camden Junction, Maryland, and spread the next day on the same line at Martinsburg, West Virginia. State militia proving ineffective to break the strike, federal troops were asked for, and with their arrival, the strike was smashed. But, in the meantime, the strike had spread westward into Cumberland, Maryland and into Kentucky and Ohio. It also spread to other lines, and bitter battles between strikers and police and militiamen occurred at Philadelphia, Harrisburg, Scranton, Reading and other points along the route of the Erie and New York Central in New York. Railway workers also quit work at Columbus, Cincinnati, Chicago, and St. Louis. The strikes were broken by police, vigilantes, militia and Federal troops, and by August 2 railway service had been restored.

The strike was the largest in number of persons involved of any in the nineteenth century. It was not confined to railroad workers; it was joined by miners, millhands and unemployed workers.

17. This was the second rally the Workingmen's Party of the United States held in Chicago during the great strike. The mass meeting took place on July 23, 1877 at Market and Madison streets. Parson's statement that 30,000 workingmen attended the meeting is an exaggeration. Probably no more than 6,000 were present.

18. Joseph Medill (1823–1899) bought an interest in the Chicago *Tribune* in 1855 and used the paper to support the newly-organized Republican Party. In 1874 Medill bought a majority of the stock of the *Tribune* company, and during the remainder of his life, controlled the paper's policy. Medill was elected mayor of Chicago in 1871 after the great fire which swept the city.

19. For a vivid description of the battle of the 16th street viaduct, *see* Robert V. Bruce, *1877: Year of Violence,* (Indianapolis, 1959), pp. 248–50.

20. The Noble Order of Knights of Labor was formed in 1869 in Philadelphia. The Order grew slowly, but during the Railroad Strike of 1877, in which the Knights did not participate officially, its membership rapidly increased. The Order's great growth, however, occurred in the years 1883–1886. In 1883 it had about 42,000 members, in July, 1885, 104,000 members, and in 1886, it boasted 703,000 members. It never reached the figure of one million members as Parsons states.

21. Richard F. Trevellick (1830–1895) was president of the International Union of Ship Carpenters and Caulkers in 1865; president of the Detroit Trades' Assembly, and president of the National Labor Union in 1869, 1871 and 1872. He helped form the Greenback Party and was active in movements for currency reform as well as for the eight-hour day.

Charles H. Lichtman (1849–1902) was National Secretary of the Knights of St. Crispin and General Secretary of the Knights of Labor for fourteen years. He was an active lobbyist at Washington, often at his own expense, for eight-hour legislation.

Dyer D. Lum (1840–1893) dedicated much of his life to the cause of the labor movement after service in the Civil War. In 1876 he was a candidate for Lieutenant Governor in Massachusetts, and later served as secretary to a congressional committee. A firm revolutionist, he contributed frequently to the anarchist press.

Nothing was accomplished by the lobbying activities of the National Eight-Hour Association.

22. The quotation is from *The Communist Manifesto* by Marx and Engels. The *Manifesto* was prepared by Marx and Engels in 1848 at the invitation a year before of the Congress of the Communist League in London.

23. At its 1884 convention, the Federation of Organized Trades and Labor Unions of the United States and Canada, the original name of the American Federation of Labor, adopted a resolution asserting that eight hours should constitute "a legal day's labor from and after May 1,

1886," and calling upon labor organizations to "so direct their laws as to conform to this resolution by the time named."

24. Mrs. Sarah E. Ames had also been arrested in the original police round-up following the Haymarket Affair, but had been released.

25. The editorial appeared on page 9 in the *New York Times* of April 25, 1886 under the heading, "The Financial World." The words "short" and "easy" in the first paragraph are not italicized in the original. The second paragraph quoted by Parsons reads as follows in the original: "Another way suggested is to pick out the leaders, and make such examples of them as to scare the others into immediate submission." Parsons, however, omitted the next sentence which reads: "It is not, however, a sure thing that even this would be entirely successful; and it is confessed among the more thoughtful men of the Street that the labor problem as now presented is a serious one, and that the solution will be worked out slowly."

26. Parsons exaggerates in stating that the Haymarket Affair caused the eight-hour strike to be broken and the movement to fall to pieces. Actually, the eight-hour movement was not a total failure and it did result in some shortening of working hours.

27. The thirty years war began in 1618 with an open rebellion of the Bohemian nobles, in answer to the forced acceptance by the Bohemian Diet of the Catholic Duke Ferdinand of Styria as future king of Bohemia. As the war progressed, it involved almost every state in Europe. It ended with the Peace of Westphalia in 1648 which marked the end of the Holy Roman Empire of the German nation as a political power. Germany was devastated by the war and pestilence which accompanied it. It has been estimated that the density of the population of Germany as a whole decreased by nearly two thirds.

28. The Pinkertons was an organization founded by Allan Pinkerton which became notorious for anti-union and anti-labor activities. In many strikes of this period, workers had to combat "Pinkerton strikebreakers."

29. Martin Luther (1483–1546), leader of the German Reformation, stayed at the Wartburg, in disguise, for almost a full year after he was condemned as a heretic in the "Edict of Worms," May 8, 1521. It was while he was in the Wartburg that Luther translated the New Testament from Greek into German.

30. Thomas Muenzer (c. 1490–1525) was a priest who became the revolutionary and religious leader of the masses during the Reformation. He was an adherent of the Reformation, but, influenced by the Hussite

and Taborite ideas, called for a more basic attack on traditional Christianity as well as for a popular revolution against the feudal ruling class. He was a leader of the Peasants' War of 1524–1525, and attempted to link the uprisings of the peasants to the revolutionary movements of urban workers and miners. Muenzer denounced Luther for his relations with the evangelical princes and landowners, and was, in turn, denounced by Luther for his radical program. After the defeat of his forces in the battle of Frankinhausen, Muenzer was put to death. His ideas, however, continued to influence German social and radical movements.

During the Peasants' War, Luther sided with the German Princes and advised the lords to drown the revolt in blood.

31. Oliver Cromwell (1599–1658) was lord protector of the Commonwealth of England, Scotland and Ireland from 1653 to 1658. He was one of the leaders of the Puritan Revolution against King Charles I.

Armand-Jean Du Plessis de Richelieu (1585–1642) was the famous French Cardinal and statesman who set out to make King Louis XIII of France actual master of the entire realm and assure him supremacy in Europe.

32. Honore Gabriel Riquetti Comte de Mirabeau (1749–1791) was the leader of the French National Assembly (1789–1791) and is regarded by some as the author of the Declaration of the Rights of Man. He was a champion of complete religious and intellectual freedom.

33. Only nine states established unqualified age limits below which child labor was prohibited, the highest being thirteen years and the lowest ten. In these and at least eleven other states, the age limits for child laborers were based upon school attendance or ability to read or write. But the means of escaping the restrictions were numerous and the penalties for violation so mild that the legislation did not prevent the employment of young children in industry.

34. Aristotle (384–322 B.C.) was the great Greek teacher and philosopher, psychologist, logician, political thinker and father of literary criticism.

35. The quotation is from Karl Marx's *Capital: A Critique of Political Economy* (Volume I, New York, 1967, p. 408). The name of the Greek poet who lived at the time of Cicero was Antipatros.

36. Johann Wolfgang Goethe (1749–1805) was Germany's greatest creative personality. His masterpiece was the *Faust* drama which he completed a year before his death.

37. Henry Thomas Buckle (1821–1862), English historian, was the author of *History of Civilization in England* (2 volumes), published in

1857–1861. It was translated in all European languages, and is considered one of the most important works in the history of social sciences.

Lewis Henry Morgan (1818–1881), American ethnologist, published his masterpiece, *Ancient Society or Researches in the Lines of Human Progress,* in 1877.

The first edition of *Das Kapital* by Karl Marx (1818–1883) was published in Germany in 1867.

38. E.S. Dreyer was a banker who served as foreman of the grand jury which indicted the anarchists. Later, he joined in the movement to persuade Governor Altgeld to pardon Neebe, whom he thought entirely innocent, and Fielden and Schwab, who although in his opinion were guilty to some extent, had suffered enough.

39. The Turner Bund was a social organization of German-Americans.

40. From the beginning the Knights of Labor surrounded itself with ritualism and required its members never to reveal the name of the Order or the names of its members. In 1881 the Knights made the name of the Order and its activities public. Members, however, were still forbidden to reveal "to any employer or other person the name . . . of any . . . member of the Order without the permission of the member."

41. In 1884 the miners in the Hocking Valley, Illinois refused to accept a wage cut proposed by the Columbus and Hocking Valley Coal and Iron Company. When the miners decided to strike, the company discharged all strikers. The strike, which lasted from July, 1884 until March, 1885, involved 4,000 miners, and caused much suffering among the strikers and their families. In the end the miners were forced to accept the operators' terms.

42. Spies was the first of the condemned men to address the court. He protested his innocence, charged that it was not murder for which he was being tried, but for his belief in Anarchism. While he did not deny that he and his comrades advocated the use of dynamite, he justified this in the fact that the ruling class employed force to prevent all reform and progress. He denied, however, that he and his comrades deliberately planned the violent destruction of the existing social order on a specific date. He closed his lengthy speech to the court with the statement that he and his comrades were ready to follow in the path of Socrates, Christ, Giordano Bruno, Huss, and Galileo.

43. The Hanseatic League was a co-operative association of German cities for the protection of mutual commercial interests. The League comprised the most important cities of northern Germany; its mem-

bership at one time was close to one hundred cities. The League held a monopoly of the Baltic trade and controlled the important herring and cod industries; it reached its greatest prosperity in the second half of the fourteenth century.

44. The Franco-Prussian War began in August, 1870 and ended with the signing of the final peace treaty at Frankfurt on May 10, 1871. The French were quickly defeated, and, in the same peace treaty, without consulting the wishes of their populations, the provinces of Alsace and part of Lorraine were annexed by Germany and incorporated into the Prussian system of administration. In addition to these territorial losses, France had to agree to German occupation of her key fortresses, until the war indemnity of five billion francs (about one billion dollars) was paid in full.

45. Red Cloud (1822–1909) was an American Indian chief of the Oglala tribe and of the Sioux and Cheyenne Indians, who opposed the westward movement of the white man. He signed a treaty with the government of the United States in 1868, and thereafter advocated peace. He died in the Pine Indian Reservation in South Dakota to which his tribe had been removed.

46. The doctrine of individual Anarchism, as propounded by Pierre Joseph Proudhon (1809–1865), with its demand for complete individual liberty and opposition to the State and all other coercive and restrictive social institutions, appealed to the working-class in France but primarily to intellectuals in the United States. It was the teaching of Anarchist-communism, carried over to the United States by Johann Most, that attracted the revolutionaries who had broken away from the Socialist Labor Party.

47. Dr. Edward Aveling was the husband of Eleanor Marx Aveling, the daughter of Karl Marx. He and his wife visited the United States in 1886, and while they defended the Haymarket defendants, they also indicated that they, as Socialists, did not approve of Anarchism. It is doubtful that Aveling would have denied that he was a State-socialist, meaning a socialist who believed in the use of political methods, since he made it clear in the book, *The Working-Class Movement in America,* written with his wife and published in 1887, that he supported the Socialist Labor Party.

48. During the Civil War, President Lincoln promoted compensated emancipation as a solution for slavery, particularly in the border states. But his proposals met with no favorable response from the slaveowners. Compensated emancipation, however, was adopted in the Act of

Congress abolishing slavery in the District of Columbia. One million dollars was appropriated to pay loyal masters of slaves.

49. At East St. Louis in 1885 a railroad corporation imported thugs from other states to help break the strike of switchmen. The strike-breakers were made deputy sheriffs. Without provocation they fired upon a crowd of strikers and citizen sympathizers, killing several and wounding many. The thugs were arrested as a result of public outcry, but the courts and grand jury of St. Clair county refused to try them.

In 1885 the quarry workers at Lemont, a Chicago suburb, staged a walkout against a pay reduction. The militia shot and killed two strikers before it was over.

50. During a street-car strike in Chicago in 1885 not only were strikers clubbed right and left by the police, regardless of whether they engaged in violence, but non-striking workers and even businessmen who happened to be in the strike zone were similarly treated.

51. John Waller was the leader of the social-revolutionaries in Chicago, and spoke frequently at their meetings. It was disclosed that Waller had been promised immunity by the police if he testified properly during the trial, threatened with death if he did not, and that parts of Waller's testimony injurious to the Haymarket defendants were dictated to him by police.

52. In his testimony during the trial, Mayor Carter H. Harrison stated: "There was no suggestion made by either of the speakers looking toward calling for the immediate use of force or violence towards any person that night; if there had been, I should have dispersed them at once. . . . When I went to the station during Parson's speech, I stated to Captain Bonfield that I thought the speeches were about over; that nothing had occurred yet, or looked likely to occur, to require interference, and that he had better issue orders to his reserves at the other stations to go home. . . ."

53. Harry L. Gilmer testified that he had seen Rudolph Schnaubelt, a young German radical who had been twice arrested, released and then disappeared, throw the bomb and that Spies had supplied the match with which the fuse was lit. He also testified that Schnaubelt was five feet, ten inches in height (not five feet, eight as Fischer states). It was made clear during the trial that Spies did not leave the wagon when the police came on the scene and could not have provided the match as Gilmer testified. Actually, Gilmer contradicted himself throughout his testimony.

54. The two Elbe duchies of Schleswig-Holstein were united with

Denmark in 1460, but trouble arose because the language spoken in Holstein and southern Schleswig was German and the sympathies of the population were with Germany. In 1848 the two duchies rose in revolt against Denmark's repeated attempts to deprive them of their independence. Although the war ended with a Danish victory, the Treaty of London (1852) decreed that Schleswig-Holstein should retain its semiautonomous political organization in continued personal union with the King of Denmark. The Treaty was signed by all the great European powers, including both Prussia and Austria.

In 1863 King Christian IX of Denmark published a new Constitution for all Danish territories, including the duchies, and this was considered a breach of the London agreement. At the same time, Duke Frederick of Augustenburg received the claims of his line for succession to Schleswig-Holstein and was supported by the German Confederation.

Bismarck, determined to incorporate Schleswig-Holstein into the Prussian state, used this situation to achieve an agreement with Austria to settle the question by force of arms. In 1864 Prussian and Austrian troops invaded Schleswig. When Denmark, in negotiations during the truce refused to accept Bismarck's proposal that Schleswig-Holstein receive political autonomy with a continued personal union with the Danish crown, hostilities were resumed. In the Peace of Vienna, Denmark agreed to cede the duchies of Schleswig-Holstein unconditionally to Prussia and Austria. The Danish campaign had lasted from February to October, 1864.

55. The reference is the "Seven Weeks' War" between Prussia and Austria caused by a renewed dispute over the Schleswig-Holstein question. Austria was decisively defeated, and in the forced Peace of Prague (August 23, 1866) was compelled to consent to the reorganization of Germany under Prussian leadership. Schleswig-Holstein was annexed by Prussia.

56. In 1878 two attempts were made on the life of William I, in the second of which the emperor was severely wounded. Although the perpetrators were radicals without Socialist party affiliations, these incidents gave Bismarck the excuse to introduce his anti-socialist bill. When it appeared that a parliamentary majority would not go along with the repressive legislation, Bismarck had the Reichstag dissolved. The newly-elected representatives adopted the bill which was renewed in 1880, 1884, and 1886.

The passage of the German "exceptional laws," placing heavy penalties on active socialists, led to an emigration of many of them to the United States.

57. The majority of the Socialist Labor Party favored fusion with the Greenbackers and the S.L.P. participated as a party in the Greenback convention which nominated James B. Weaver for president. But a number of the German members and many English-speaking socialists in Chicago bolted, and nominated their own local ticket.

58. Harmodius and Aristogiton were Greek patriots who slew the Athenian tyrant Hipparchus in 514 B.C.

Lucius Junius Brutus was the traditional founder of the Roman republic in 509 B.C. Marcus Brutus (85?–42 B.C.) was the Roman senator who was a leader of the conspirators who assassinated Julius Caesar on the Ides of March 44 B.C.

59. Peisistratus (c. 600–528 B.C.) was the "tyrant" of Athens who seized power in 561–560 B.C., lost and regained it twice, and died after a long rule. He left the state to his sons Hyppias and Hipparchus.

Julius Caesar (100–44 B.C.) was the Roman general, statesman, and dictator of Rome, assassinated on the Ides—the fifteenth—of March, 44 B.C.

60. On September 2, 1870, six weeks after the start of the Franco-Prussian war, a French army of 86,000 men, with Emperor Napoleon III in their midst, was forced to surrender at Sedan. Two days later the Second Empire of France collapsed and a republican provisional government of National Defense, headed by the French lawyer Gambetta, was proclaimed in Paris.

61. Among the Germans who protested the war was August Bebel, the socialist, who was sent to prison in 1870–1871 for opposing the war.

62. Ferdinand August Bebel (1840–1913) was a wood turner who became a founder and leader of the German Social-Democratic Party.

Adolph Hepner (1846–1923) was a German Socialist who became a member of the First International; he emigrated to the United States in the 1880's and returned to Germany in 1908.

Wilhelm Liebknecht (1826–1900) was the founder of the German Social-Democratic Party and editor of the party paper, *Vorwarts.*

Bebel and Liebknecht were found guilty of "high treason" and were in prison from 1873–1875.

63. Ferdinand Lassalle (1825–1864) was a German lawyer and labor leader who founded the German Workers' Union in 1863 and continued to play a leading role in the German Labor and Socialist movement. Among his published works were *Die Wissenschaft und die Arbeiter*

and *Die Agitation fur den Allgemeinen deutschen Arbeiterverein Das Jahr 1863, Polemik.* His proposed "productive associations" of workers under the protection of the state was rejected by Marxists as a reform brand of Socialism.

64. Alexander von Humboldt (1769–1859) was a famous German scientific geographer who collected a tremendous wealth of material on his many travels to foreign lands and continents, especially during his trip to the Spanish colonies of South America. He was the brother of Wilhelm von Humboldt (1767–1835), noted German educational reformer.

65. Between 1877 and 1887 the Social-Democrats had increased their vote from 500,000 to 763,000. But they were not yet the strongest party in Germany. It was in the election of 1912 that they obtained 110 seats (out of 397) and thus became the strongest party in the Reichstag.

66. The fusion of the Social-Democratic Workers' Party of Germany, led by Liebknecht and Bebel, with the General Association of German Workers (the Lassalleans) took place at the Gotha Unity Congress, May 22–27, 1875.

67. The poem by Heinrich Heine (1797–1856) is entitled "The Silesian Weavers."

68. About thee is the story told.

69. George Bancroft (1800–1891) was the author of the ten volume *History of the United States,* the first volume of which was published in 1834 and the final volume in 1874. The work ends with the peace between the United States and Great Britain in 1783.

70. The truck system provided for payment of wages in goods instead of cash. In the mines particularly, where the company store system prevailed, wages were often paid in company scrip, redeemable in the company's store. When taken in trade in other than the company's store, it was discounted at fifty percent. If exchanged in national currency, it was worth only forty cents on the dollar. Since the prices in company stores were invariably higher than in ordinary retail shops, the scrip represented a wage cut even at par value.

71. Paul Grottkau was a leading figure in the Chicago social-revolutionary movement.

72. The Latin should read: "Dies irae, dies illa solvet solum in favilla." "The day of wrath, that day will dissolve the earth in ashes."

73. Joaquin Miller, the West Coast poet, wrote a poem entitled "In Memory of Sophie Peroffsky," the Russian nihilist. (Her name is variously spelled.) She had assassinated Czar Alexander II in March, 1881,

and was executed. The poem, published in *Truth* (San Francisco), December 6, 1882, contained the lines:

The Czar is dead, the woman dead,
  About her neck a cord,
In God's house rests his royal head—
  Hers in a place abhorred;
Yet I had rather have her bed
  Than thine most royal lord.

Yea, rather be that woman dead,
  Than this new living Czar,
To hide in dread, with both hands red,
  Behind great bolt and bar—
While, like the dead, still endless tread
  Sand exiles tow'rd the star.

74. Labor solidarity was the accepted and official policy of the Knights of Labor and was symbolized by the slogan, "An Injury to One is the Concern of All." For the first time in American labor history, the Knights of Labor united skilled and unskilled, men and women, Negro and white, native-American and foreign-born workers, of all religious and political opinion. Negro workers were recruited in large numbers; Negro organizers were appointed by the Knights and Negroes played important roles in the organization. John W. Hayes, secretary of the Order, estimated that the Knights of Labor had 60,000 Negro members in 1886, many of them in the South, and other estimates ran even higher.

75. The ten-hour agitation led to the introduction of a bill in Parliament by John Fielden in 1846 limiting the hours of work in factories to ten hours a day. The bill passed the House of Commons on May 3, 1847.

76. The Chartist movement of 1837–1848 derived its name from the People's Charter, the program drawn up by six members of the Working Men's Association and six radical members of Parliament. It was published on May 8, 1838, and demanded six changes in the existing system: universal manhood suffrage, the ballot, payment of members of Parliament, abolition of the property qualifications for members of Parliament, equal constituencies, and annual elections. The Chartists presented a huge petition to Parliament in 1839, signed by a million and a quarter names, but it was rejected. In 1848 another petition, said to be

signed by over five and a half million people, was once more presented to Parliament, but was again rejected. Following this defeat, Chartism declined until its death in 1855. But it was an important educational movement for organizing the British working class.

77. Fergus O'Connor was a leader of the Chartist movement. After his election to Parliament was invalidated in 1835 because he did not fulfill the pecuniary qualifications prescribed by law, O'Connor moved to the north of England where he organized the Radical Association. In late 1837 he founded his paper the *Northern Star* in Leeds through which he conducted a vigorous campaign for universal suffrage.

78. The cooperative movement in England became strong after the collapse of Chartism. Generally the co-operative societies were based on the ideas of the Rochdale Pioneers. Organized in 1844 at Rochdale, England, by twenty-eight persons, the "Rochdale Plan" involved the purchase by members of shares of stock, which brought interest. Goods were sold for cash, and at the end of stipulated periods, the profits were divided among the members according to a prepared system.

79. The movement to disestablish the Anglican Church in Ireland, which though ministering to no more than an eighth of the population, enjoyed wealthy endowments, was a major issue in British politics in the 1840s.

80. The movement for universal suffrage in England revived in the 1860s and led to the passage of a law in 1867 providing for limited concessions in the right to vote to non-propertyholders.

81. William Cowper (1731–1800) was an English poet whose hatred of oppression is expressed in his denunciation of slavery in *The Task* and in a series of other poems.

82. Unitarianism was a social and religious viewpoint which challenged the concept of the Trinity, conceiving of God as one.

83. The suspension bridge crossed the Menai strait, a channel of the Irish sea, separating Anglesey from Abermenai.

84. Henry Brown, a slave in Richmond, Virginia, ordered a specially designed and equipped box to be built in which he could be shipped to freedom. Three feet long and two feet wide, containing food and water, it was carefully marked so that Brown would be traveling with his head up. It was shipped to Abolitionist headquarters in Philadelphia by a white shoe dealer in Richmond, named Smith. The box reached Philadelphia, via Adams Express, after twenty-six hours en route. When the box was delivered, the four men who were awaiting its arrival, pried off the lid. Then, according to William Still, one of the four men, "the marvellous

resurrection of Brown ensued. Rising up on his box, he reached out his hand, saying, 'How do you do, gentlemen?'"

85. Harriet Martineau's *Society in America,* with its frequent denunciation of slavery, was published in 1837.

86. *Uncle Tom's Cabin* by Harriet Beecher Stowe was published in 1852. The novel sold more than 300,000 copies in the first year of its publication and was soon dramatized in theatres throughout the North. It was read widely in England.

87. For a description of the suffering of the English working class during the Civil War and their refusal to support the South, see Philip S. Foner, *History of the Labor Movement in the United States,* (New York, 1947), I, pp. 312–17. For a reevaluation of this subject, see Royden Harrison, "British Labour and the Confederacy," *International Review of Social History,* II, 1957, pp. 79–86 and Joseph M. Hernon, Jr., "British Sympathies in the American Civil War: A Reconsideration," *Journal of Southern History,* XXXIII, August, 1967, pp. 356–67.

88. During the Civil War, Union soldiers took up the song "John Brown's Body."

89. The Methodist (Wesleyan) Church was founded by John Wesley (1703–1791). It had a great following among the poor and working classes to whom Wesley sent many of his preachers.

90. The reference is to Horace Greeley (1811–1872), editor of the New York *Tribune* and an advocate of many reforms.

91. Dwight Lyman Moody (1837–1899), the famous evangelist, was especially well-known and popular in Chicago.

92. The sharecropping system emerged during Reconstruction in the South. Under the system, the sharecropper, or tenant farmer, was subject to the control of the owner. The landlord took one third of the harvest for the use of the land, one third for feed, tools, provisions and other necessities, and the sharecropper received what was left; and the plantation owner kept the accounts.

Fielden's use of the name "Sambo" for the Negro no doubt was resented by many readers of the *Knights of Labor,* white as well as Negro.

93. After the close of Reconstruction in 1876, emigration movements arose in many southern states as Negroes sought to escape the conditions they were forced to live under. By 1879, thousands of Negroes, especially in Mississippi, had joined in a great trek to Kansas, Missouri, and Indiana.

94. Charles Bradlaugh (1833–1891), English free-thinker and radi-

cal was prominent during the second half of the nineteenth century for his championship of individual liberty. He was involved in a long struggle to gain his parliamentary seat from which he finally emerged victorious.

Theodore Tilton (1835–1907) was a distinguished editor and reformer until his career was disrupted by the great Beecher scandal involving his wife's alleged intimate relations with the pastor of Plymouth Church.

Bayard Taylor (1825–1878) traveler, translator, and man of letters, frequently lectured on German literature, especially on Goethe, whose *Faust* he had translated into English.

Fielden must mean Robert Collyer (1823–1912) the clergyman born in England who emigrated to the United States in 1850 and became an active abolitionist. He became a Unitarian minister in Chicago in 1859 and played an important role in the city until he moved to New York to become pastor of the Church of the Messiah.

James Freeman Clarke (1810–1888), Unitarian clergyman, active in behalf of temperance, anti-slavery and woman suffrage. He was a prolific writer and lecturer.

Joaquin Miller (1839–1913) was the pen name of Cincinnatus Hiner Miller. He took the name Joaquin after his defense of a Mexican bandit, Joaquin Murietta. He was born in Indiana, but became famous as a poet in San Francisco.

Robert G. Ingersoll (1833–1899), lawyer and defender of free speech and free press. He was most widely known as "the great Agnostic," and lectured frequently on the theme that the Bible was a compilation of falsehoods. Ingersoll spoke out against the verdict in the Haymarket cases, declaring that the "men were tried during a period of great excitement" when a fair trial was an impossibility.

James Parton (1822–1891) was biographer of Burr, Jackson, Franklin, Jefferson, and Voltaire.

95. Captain Ward's actual words were variously reported in the press the next day. Most reporters agreed that he said: "In the name of the people of the State of Illinois, I command this meeting immediately and peaceably to disperse." After waiting a minute, he repeated the order, and added: "And I call upon you and you (here he turned and pointed to bystanders) to assist."

96. The work of Thomas Paine (1737–1809) which influenced Neebe was undoubtedly *The Age of Reason,* in which Paine affirmed his belief in God but maintained that the Bible was not infallible and Christianity merely "mythology."

97. The reference is to the crushing of the Paris Commune of 1871 by the French government. Many Parisian workers lost their lives in the repression. It is estimated that between twenty and thirty thousand citizens of Paris were executed.

98. The new German Empire was proclaimed in the Hall of Mirrors in Versailles on January 18, 1871, the anniversary of the creation of the Kingdom of Prussia 170 years before. As later constituted the Empire comprised twenty-five sovereign States, besides the imperial province of Alsace-Lorraine.

99. Like most Germans, Lingg knew of the struggle of the Swiss people against Gessler's tyranny through Schiller's last completed play, *Wilhelm Tell,* published in 1804, with the whole Swiss people as its hero.

100. The United Brotherhood of Carpenters and Joiners, the official name of the union, was organized in 1881 by Peter J. McGuire, a former Lassallean Socialist who became a leader in the organization of trade unions. McGuire is also known as the father of Labor Day.

101. William Seliger had been indicted for murder together with those on trial. He became a witness for the state and testified that Lingg, who occupied a room in the house in which Seliger resided, had been engaged in manufacturing dynamite bombs. However, no evidence was produced that one of Lingg's bombs was thrown at Haymarket Square on the fourth of May, 1886.

102. In 1890 the United Brotherhood of Carpenters and Joiners led the way for a new mass labor struggle for the eight-hour day. The union gained the eight-hour day for many of its members and recruited new workers to its ranks.

103. In his lengthy address to the prisoners before pronouncing sentence, Judge Gary accused them of being "morally guilty" because they sought to change the existing order of society by terror and dynamite.

104. The "Kulturkampf" refers primarily to the conflict between Bismarck and the Catholic Church which got under way in 1870. Bismarck sought to establish his powerful state without interference from the Church and he took steps to put down its power. He decreed that marriages could be performed in civil ceremonies and that clergymen must not speak out about politics. While progressive, Bismarck's reforms were basically aimed at consolidating his power. What he did not foresee was that the "Kulturkampf" would have a tremendous influence on German workers. It stimulated the emphasis of a "Paradise on Earth rather than in Heaven," and fostered the growth of free thinking movements among workers and other sections of the population.

12

Bibliography

Aveling, Edward & Eleanor Marx, *The Working-Class Movement in America,* Second Edition, London, 1891.

Barnard, Harry, *"Eagle Forgotten": The Life of John Peter Altgeld,* Indianapolis, 1938.

Beckner, Earl H., *A History of Labor Legislation in Illinois,* Chicago, 1929.

Cahill, Marion Cotter, *Shorter Hours: A Study of the Movement Since the Civil War,* New York, 1932.

The Chicago Anarchists and the Haymarket Massacre. Complete History of the Growth of Anarchism in Chicago—The Great Dynamite Conspiracy—The Bomb-Throwing—Official Police Report of Casualties—The Trial, Evidence, Conviction and Sentence of the Accused, Speeches of Counsel and Defendants, Chicago, 1887.

The Chicago Martyrs. The Famous Speeches of the Eight Anarchists in Judge Gary's Court, October 7, 1886, and Reasons for Pardoning Fielden, Neebe and Schwab, by John P. Altgeld, San Francisco, 1899.

David, Henry, *The History of the Haymarket Affair,* revised edition, New York, 1963.

Foner, Philip S., *History of the Labor Movement in the United States,* vol. II, New York, 1955.

Gompers, Samuel, *Seventy Years and Life and Labor,* 2 vols., New York, 1925.

Hillquit, Morris, *History of Socialism in the United States,* New York, 1903.

Johnson, Michael R., "Albert R. Parsons: An American Architect of Syndicalism," *Midwest Quarterly,* Winter, 1968, pp. 195–206.

Kogan, B.R., ed., *The Chicago Haymarket Riot: Anarchy on Trial,* Boston, 1959.

Life of Albert R. Parsons with Brief History of the Labor Movement in America. Also Sketches of the Lives of A. Spies, Geo. Engel, A. Fischer and Louis Lingg, Second Edition, Chicago, 1903.

Trumbull, M.M., *Was It a Fair Trial? An Appeal to the Governor of Illinois.* Chicago, 1887.

Wish, Harvey, "The Haymarket Affair," *Journal of the Illinois Historical Society,* December, 1938, pp. 200–14. Indianapolis, 1938.

INDEX

RELATED READING

Revolutionary Continuity

Marxist Leadership in the U.S.

The Early Years, 1848–1917
Birth of the Communist Movement, 1918–1922

FARRELL DOBBS

"Successive generations of proletarian revolutionists have participated in the movements of the working class and its allies. . . . Marxists today owe them not only homage for their deeds. We also have a duty to learn what they did wrong as well as right so their errors are not repeated." —*Farrell Dobbs*
Two volumes, $17 each.

"It's the Poor Who Face the Savagery of the US 'Justice' System"

The Cuban Five Talk About Their Lives Within the US Working Class

How US cops, courts, and prisons work as "an enormous machine for grinding people up." Five Cuban revolutionaries framed up and held in US jails for 16 years explain the human devastation of capitalist "justice"—and how socialist Cuba is different. $10. Also in Spanish, Farsi, Greek.

The Great Labor Uprising of 1877

PHILIP S. FONER

In 1877 a battle by West Virginia rail workers against wage cuts effectively shut down the US rail system and turned into the country's first nationwide general strike. Welcomed by Karl Marx as the "first eruption against the oligarchy of associated capital" since the US Civil War, the uprising coincided with the bourgeoisie's betrayal of Radical Reconstruction in the South and the first steps in the rise of US imperialism and its counterrevolutionary course worldwide. $17

DEFENDING CONSTITUTIONAL FREEDOMS

Under the constitution "the power of censorship rests with the people over the government, not the government over the people."
—James Madison, *1794*

50 Years of Covert Operations in the US

Washington's Political Police
and the American Working Class

LARRY SEIGLE, FARRELL DOBBS
STEVE CLARK

How class-conscious workers have defended constitutional freedoms and fought the capitalists' drive to build the "national security" state essential to maintaining their rule. $10. Also in Spanish and Farsi.

Socialism on Trial

Testimony at Minneapolis Sedition Trial

JAMES P. CANNON

The revolutionary program of the working class presented in federal court in 1941 on the eve of US entry into World War II. The frame-up charges of "seditious conspiracy" targeted leaders of the Socialist Workers Party. $15. Also in Spanish, French, Farsi.

FBI on Trial

The Victory in the Socialist Workers Party Suit Against Government Spying

MARGARET JAYKO

The record of a historic victory in the fight for political rights, including the 1986 federal court ruling against government spying and excerpts from trial testimony by SWP leaders Farrell Dobbs and Jack Barnes. $17

CAPITALIST CRISIS AND THE FIGHT FOR WORKERS POWER

The Low Point of Labor Resistance Is Behind Us

The Socialist Workers Party Looks Forward

JACK BARNES
MARY-ALICE WATERS
STEVE CLARK

The global order imposed by Washington is shattering. A long retreat by the working class and unions has come to an end. The bosses and their government are stepping up attacks on our wages, conditions, and constitutional rights. This book highlights opportunities for building a mass proletarian party able to lead the struggle to end capitalist rule, opening a socialist future for humanity. $10. Also in Spanish, French, Greek.

Is Socialist Revolution in the US Possible?

A Necessary Debate Among Working People

MARY-ALICE WATERS

Fighting for a society only working people can create, it is our own capacities we will discover. And we will answer the question posed here with a resounding "Yes." Revolution is possible but not inevitable. That depends on us. $7. Also in Spanish, French, Farsi.

The Clintons' Anti-Working-Class Record

Why Washington Fears Working People

JACK BARNES

What working people need to know about the profit-driven course of Democrats and Republicans alike over the last three decades. And the political awakening of workers seeking to understand and resist the capitalist rulers' assaults. $10. Also in Spanish, French, Farsi, Greek.

Malcolm X, Black Liberation, and the Road to Workers Power

JACK BARNES

"The conquest of state power by a class-conscious vanguard of the working class is the mightiest weapon possible in the fight against Black oppression, the subjugation of women, Jew-hatred, and every form of human degradation inherited from class society." $20. Also in Spanish, French, Farsi, Arabic, Greek.

Capitalism's World Disorder

Working-Class Politics at the Millennium

JACK BARNES

The social devastation and financial panic, coarsening of politics, cop brutality, and imperialist aggression—all are products not of something gone wrong with capitalism but of its lawful workings. Yet the future can be changed by the united struggle of workers and farmers increasingly conscious of their capacity to wage revolutionary struggles for state power and to transform the world. $20. Also in Spanish and French.

Are They Rich Because They're Smart?

Class, Privilege, and Learning Under Capitalism

JACK BARNES

Exposes growing class inequalities in the US and the self-serving rationalizations of well-paid professionals who think their "brilliance" equips them to "regulate" working people, who don't know what's in our own best interest. $10. Also in Spanish, French, Farsi, Arabic, Greek.

PATHFINDERPRESS.COM

New International

A MAGAZINE OF MARXIST POLITICS AND THEORY

NEW INTERNATIONAL NO. 7

Opening Guns of World War III: Washington's Assault on Iraq

JACK BARNES

The murderous assault on Iraq in 1990–91 heralded increasingly sharp conflicts among imperialist powers, growing instability of capitalism, and more wars. Also includes:

1945: When US Troops Said 'No!'
by Mary-Alice Waters
Lessons from the Iran-Iraq War
by Samad Sharif

$14. Also in Spanish, French, Farsi.

NEW INTERNATIONAL NO. 11

U.S. Imperialism Has Lost the Cold War

JACK BARNES

The collapse of regimes across Eastern Europe and the USSR claiming to be communist did not mean workers and farmers there had been crushed. In today's sharpening class conflicts and wars, these toilers are joining working people the world over in the class struggle against capitalist exploitation. $14. Also in Spanish, French, Farsi, Greek.

NEW INTERNATIONAL NO. 12

Capitalism's Long Hot Winter Has Begun

JACK BARNES

Today's global capitalist crisis is but the opening stage of decades of economic, financial, and social convulsions and class battles. Class-conscious workers confront this historic turning point for imperialism with confidence, Jack Barnes writes, drawing satisfaction from being "in their face" as we chart a revolutionary course to take power. $14. Also in Spanish, French, Farsi, Arabic, Greek.

THE WORKING CLASS AND THE FIGHT AGAINST JEW-HATRED

The Fight Against Jew-Hatred and Pogroms in the Imperialist Epoch

Stakes for the International Working Class

V.I. LENIN, LEON TROTSKY
FARRELL DOBBS, JAMES P. CANNON
JACK BARNES, DAVE PRINCE

Jew-hatred and pogroms—such as Hamas carried out on October 7, 2023—are part of the social convulsions and wars of the imperialist epoch. The authors explain why fighting Jew-hatred is decisive to the working class and oppressed nations of the world—and *what is to be done to end it*. $10. Also in Spanish, French, Greek.

Imperialism's March Toward Fascism and War

JACK BARNES

"There will be new Hitlers, new Mussolinis. That is inevitable. What is not inevitable is that they will triumph. The working-class vanguard will organize our class to fight back against the devastating toll we are made to pay for the capitalist crisis. The future of humanity will be decided in the contest between these contending class forces." In *New International* no. 10. $14. Also in Spanish, French, Farsi, Greek.

The Jewish Question

A Marxist Interpretation

ABRAM LEON

The battle against reactionary forces aiming to exterminate the Jews remains central to world politics, as shown by the genocidal October 2023 pogrom in Israel. Why is Jew-hatred still raising its ugly head? What are its class roots? Why, as Abram Leon explains, is there no solution "independent of the world proletarian revolution"? Revised translation, new introduction, 40 pages of illustrations and maps. $17. Also in Spanish, French, Greek.

PATHFINDERPRESS.COM

CUBA'S SOCIALIST REVOLUTION

New!

Revolution and the Road to Peace in Colombia

The Example of the Cuban Revolution

FIDEL CASTRO

"No crime can be committed in the name of revolution," Fidel Castro declares, drawing from the example set by working people of Cuba as they took state power out of the hands of its capitalist rulers. In 2008, as part of efforts to end six decades of armed conflict in Colombia, he shared the exemplary record of Cuba's revolutionary struggle with the Revolutionary Armed Forces of Colombia (FARC) and the world. $10. Also in Spanish and French.

Cuba and the Coming American Revolution

JACK BARNES

This is a book about the example set by the Cuban people that socialist revolution is not only necessary—it can be made. A book about the struggles of workers and other exploited producers in the imperialist heartland, and the youth attracted to them. About the class struggle in the US, where the revolutionary capacities of working people are as utterly discounted by the ruling powers as were those of the Cuban toilers. $10. Also in Spanish, French, Farsi.

The First and Second Declarations of Havana

Nowhere are the questions of revolutionary strategy that today confront men and women on the front lines of struggles in the Americas addressed with greater truthfulness and clarity than in these uncompromising indictments of imperialist plunder and "the exploitation of man by man." Adopted by million-strong assemblies of the Cuban people in 1960 and 1962. $10. Also in Spanish, French, Farsi, Arabic, Greek.

New!

Cuba and the Independence War in Guinea-Bissau and Cape Verde

The Fall of the Last Colonial Empire in Africa

VÍCTOR DREKE

In 1974–75 the people of two West African countries, Guinea-Bissau and Cape Verde, put an end to 500 years of Portuguese colonial exploitation. Led by a popular movement forged by Amílcar Cabral, their struggle triggered the collapse of Portugal's entire colonial empire and brought down the 40-year fascist dictatorship in Portugal itself. Víctor Dreke's firsthand account brings to life this decisive victory. $12. Also in Spanish and French.

Women in Cuba: The Making of a Revolution Within the Revolution

VILMA ESPÍN, ASELA DE LOS SANTOS
YOLANDA FERRER

The integration of women in the ranks and leadership of the Cuban Revolution was intertwined with the proletarian course led by Fidel Castro from the start. This is the story of that revolution and how it transformed the women and men who made it. $17. Also in Spanish, Farsi, Greek.

Playa Girón/Bay of Pigs

Washington's First Military Defeat in the Americas

FIDEL CASTRO, JOSÉ RAMÓN FERNÁNDEZ

In less than 72 hours of combat in April 1961, Cuba's revolutionary armed forces defeated a US-organized invasion by 1,500 mercenaries. The Cuban people set an example for workers, farmers, and youth the world over that with political consciousness, class solidarity, courage, and revolutionary leadership, we can stand up to seemingly insurmountable odds—*and win*. $17. Also in Spanish.

BUILDING A PROLETARIAN PARTY

In Defense of Marxism

Against the Petty-Bourgeois Opposition in the Socialist Workers Party

LEON TROTSKY

A reply to those in the revolutionary workers movement in the late 1930s who buckled to bourgeois patriotism during Washington's buildup to enter World War II. Trotsky explains why only a party fighting to bring workers into its ranks and leadership can steer a communist course. In the process, he defends the materialist and dialectical foundations of Marxism. $17. Also in Spanish, French, Farsi.

The Struggle for a Proletarian Party

JAMES P. CANNON

"The workers of America have power enough to topple the structure of capitalism at home and to lift the whole world with them when they rise," Cannon asserts. On the eve of World War II, a founder of the communist movement in the US and a leader of the Communist International in Lenin's time defends the program and party-building norms of Bolshevism. $20. Also in Spanish and Farsi.

What Is to Be Done?

V.I. LENIN

The stakes in creating a disciplined organization of working-class revolutionaries capable of acting as a "tribune of the people, able to react to every manifestation of tyranny and oppression, no matter where it appears, to clarify for all and everyone the world-historic significance of the struggle for the emancipation of the proletariat." Written in 1902. $20. Also in Spanish.

THE RUSSIAN REVOLUTION'S WORLD EXAMPLE

Lenin's Final Fight

Speeches and Writings, 1922–23

V.I. LENIN

In 1922 and 1923, V.I. Lenin, central leader of the world's first socialist revolution, waged what was to be his last political battle—one that was lost after his death. At stake was whether that revolutionary government and the world communist movement it led would remain on the revolutionary proletarian course that brought workers and peasants to power in Russia in 1917. $17. Also in Spanish, Farsi, Greek.

The Revolution Betrayed

What Is the Soviet Union and Where Is It Going?

LEON TROTSKY

In 1917 workers and peasants of Russia were the motor force of one of the deepest revolutions in history. Yet within ten years a political counterrevolution by a privileged social layer, whose chief spokesperson was Joseph Stalin, was being consolidated. The classic study of the Soviet workers state and its degeneration. $17. Also in Spanish, Farsi, Greek.

The History of the Russian Revolution

LEON TROTSKY

How, under Lenin's leadership, the Bolshevik Party led millions of workers and farmers to overthrow the state power of the landlords and capitalists in 1917 and bring to power a government that advanced their class interests at home and worldwide. Unabridged, 3 vols. in one. Written by one of the central leaders of that socialist revolution. $30. Also in French and Russian.

MARXIST LEADERSHIP IN THE UNITED STATES

The Teamster Series

FARRELL DOBBS

Four books on the 1930s strikes, organizing drives, and political campaigns that transformed the Teamsters into a militant industrial union movement. Written by the organizer of these battles and leader of the Socialist Workers Party. A tool for workers seeking to use union power and advance the fight for a party of labor. $16 each, series $50. Also in Spanish. *Teamster Rebellion* is also available in French, Farsi, Greek.

The Turn to Industry

Forging a Proletarian Party

JACK BARNES

A book about the working-class program, composition, and course of the only kind of party in the imperialist epoch worthy of the name "revolutionary." A party that can recognize the most revolutionary fact of this epoch—the worth of working people, and our capacity to change society when we organize and act to win power from the capitalist class. $15. Also in Spanish, French, Farsi, Greek.

America's Revolutionary Heritage

Marxist Essays

GEORGE NOVACK

A materialist explanation of the American Revolution, Civil War and Radical Reconstruction, genocide against the Indians, rise of American imperialism, first wave of the fight for women's rights, and more. $23

THE LONG VIEW OF HISTORY

Labor, Nature, and the Evolution of Humanity

The Long View of History

FREDERICK ENGELS, KARL MARX
GEORGE NOVACK
MARY-ALICE WATERS

Without understanding that social labor, transforming nature, has driven humanity's evolution for millions of years, working people are unable to see beyond the capitalist epoch of class exploitation that warps all human relations, ideas, and values. $12. Also in Spanish and French.

The Communist Manifesto

KARL MARX AND FREDERICK ENGELS

Communism, say the founding leaders of the revolutionary workers movement, is not a set of ideas or preconceived "principles" but workers' line of march to power. It springs from a "movement going on under our very eyes." $5. Also in Spanish, French, Farsi, Arabic.

Woman's Evolution

From Matriarchal Clan to Patriarchal Family

EVELYN REED

An expedition from prehistory to class society that reveals women's contributions to civilization and pinpoints the historical factors that led to the subordination of women as a sex. Reed offers new insights on the struggle against women's oppression and for the liberation of humanity. $25. Also in Spanish, Farsi, Indonesian.

PATHFINDERPRESS.COM

To Speak the Truth

Why Washington's 'Cold War' Against Cuba Doesn't End

FIDEL CASTRO, CHE GUEVARA

In historic speeches before the United Nations and UN bodies, Guevara and Castro address the peoples of the world, explaining why the US government so fears the example set by the socialist revolution in Cuba. $15. Also in Greek.

Malcolm X Talks to Young People

"The young generation of whites, Blacks, browns, whatever else—you're living at a time of revolution," said Malcolm in 1964. "And I for one will join with anyone, I don't care what color you are, as long as you want to change this miserable condition that exists on this earth." Four talks and an interview in the last months of Malcolm's life. $12. Also in Spanish, French, Farsi, Arabic, Greek.

Pathfinder Press **accessible e-books** for the blind, those with low vision, or other challenges reading print books

For a list of current accessible titles, go to: pathfinderpress.com/collections/books-for-the-blind.

Visit bookshare.org for information on how to sign up.

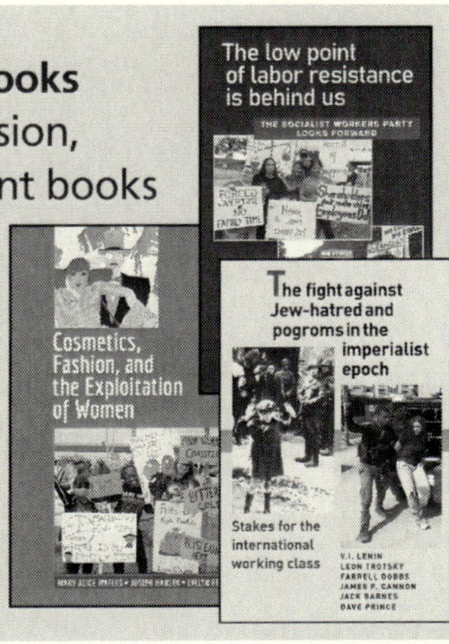

PATHFINDERPRESS.COM